T0100477

# ARTIFICIAL INTELLIGENCE FOR THE INTERNET OF EVERYTHING

# ARTIFICIAL INTELLIGENCE FOR THE INTERNET OF EVERYTHING

Edited by

**WILLIAM LAWLESS**

**RANJEEV MITTU**

**DONALD SOFGE**

**IRA S. MOSKOWITZ**

**STEPHEN RUSSELL**

ACADEMIC PRESS

An imprint of Elsevier

Academic Press is an imprint of Elsevier
125 London Wall, London EC2Y 5AS, United Kingdom
525 B Street, Suite 1650, San Diego, CA 92101, United States
50 Hampshire Street, 5th Floor, Cambridge, MA 02139, United States
The Boulevard, Langford Lane, Kidlington, Oxford OX5 1GB, United Kingdom

**Notices**
Knowledge and best practice in this field are constantly changing. As new research and
experience broaden our understanding, changes in research methods, professional practices,
or medical treatment may become necessary.

Practitioners and researchers must always rely on their own experience and knowledge in
evaluating and using any information, methods, compounds, or experiments described
herein. In using such information or methods they should be mindful of their own safety and
the safety of others, including parties for whom they have a professional responsibility.

To the fullest extent of the law, neither the Publisher nor the authors, contributors, or editors,
assume any liability for any injury and/or damage to persons or property as a matter of
products liability, negligence or otherwise, or from any use or operation of any methods,
products, instructions, or ideas contained in the material herein.

**Library of Congress Cataloging-in-Publication Data**
A catalog record for this book is available from the Library of Congress

**British Library Cataloguing-in-Publication Data**
A catalogue record for this book is available from the British Library

ISBN 978-0-12-817636-8

For information on all Academic Press publications
visit our website at https://www.elsevier.com/books-and-journals

Working together
to grow libraries in
developing countries

www.elsevier.com • www.bookaid.org

*Publisher:* Mara Conner
*Acquisition Editor:* Mara Conner
*Editorial Project Manager:* Peter Adamson
*Production Project Manager:* Vijay Bharath
*Cover Designer:* Mark Rogers

Typeset by SPi Global, India

# CONTENTS

# CONTRIBUTORS

**Spencer Breiner**
Information Technology Lab, National Institute of Standards and Technology, Gaithersburg, MD, United States

**Shu-Heng Chen**
AI-ECON Research Center, Department of Economics, National Chengchi University, Taipei, Taiwan

**Hesham Fouad**
Information Technology Division, Information Management & Decision Architectures Branch, CODE 5580, Naval Research Laboratory, Washington, DC, United States

**Adam Fouse**
Aptima Inc., Woburn, MA, United States

**Boris Galitsky**
Oracle Corporation, Redwood Shores, CA, United States

**Barry M. Horowitz**
Systems and Information Engineering, University of Virginia, Charlottesville, VA, United States

**Brian Jalaian**
Battlefield Information Processing Branch, US Army Research Laboratory, Adelphi, MD, United States

**Alexander Kott**
U.S. Army Research Laboratory, Adelphi, MD, United States

**W.F. Lawless**
Departments of Math & Psychology, Paine College, Augusta, GA, United States

**Georgiy Levchuk**
Aptima Inc., Woburn, MA, United States

**Joseph B. Lyons**
Air Force Research Laboratory, Dayton, OH, United States

**Sean Mahoney**
Air Force Research Laboratory, Dayton, OH, United States

**Robert McCormack**
Aptima Inc., Woburn, MA, United States

**John McDonald**
ClearObject, Fishers, IN, United States

**Ranjeev Mittu**
Information Technology Division, Information Management & Decision Architectures Branch, CODE 5580, Naval Research Laboratory, Washington, DC, United States

**Ira S. Moskowitz**
Information Technology Division, Information Management & Decision Architectures Branch, CODE 5580, Naval Research Laboratory, Washington, DC, United States

**Michael Mylrea**
Cyber Security & Energy Technology, Pacific Northwest National Laboratory, Richland, WA, United States

**Anna Parnis**
Department of Biology, Technion-Israel Institute of Technology, Haifa, Israel

**Krishna Pattipati**
Aptima Inc., Woburn, MA, United States

**Mark A. Roebke**
Air Force Institute of Technology, Dayton, OH, United States

**Stephen Russell**
Battlefield Information Processing Branch, US Army Research Laboratory, Adelphi, MD, United States

**Daniel Serfaty**
Aptima Inc., Woburn, MA, United States

**Alec Shuldiner**
Autodesk, Inc, San Francisco, CA, United States

**Donald A. Sofge**
Distributed Autonomous Systems Group, Code 5514, Navy Center for Applied Research in Artificial Intelligence, U.S. Naval Research Laboratory, Washington, DC, United States

**Ram D. Sriram**
Information Technology Lab, National Institute of Standards and Technology, Gaithersburg, MD, United States

**Ethan Stump**
U.S. Army Research Laboratory, Adelphi, MD, United States

**Eswaran Subrahmanian**
Information Technology Lab, National Institute of Standards and Technology, Gaithersburg, MD; Institute for Complex Engineered Systems, Carnegie Mellon University, Engineering and Public Policy, Pittsburgh, PA, United States

**Niranjan Suri**
Battlefield Information Processing Branch, US Army Research Laboratory, Adelphi, MD, United States

**Michael Wollowski**
Rose-Hulman Institute of Technology, Terre Haute, IN, United States

**Kevin T. Wynne**
University of Baltimore, Baltimore, MD, United States

# CHAPTER 1

# Introduction

## W.F. Lawless*, Ranjeev Mittu†, Donald A. Sofge‡, Ira S. Moskowitz†, Stephen Russell§

*Departments of Math & Psychology, Paine College, Augusta, GA, United States
†Information Management & Decision Architectures Branch (CODE 5580), Information Technology Division, U.S. Naval Research Laboratory, Washington, DC, United States
‡Distributed Autonomous Systems Group, Code 5514, Navy Center for Applied Research in Artificial Intelligence, U.S. Naval Research Laboratory, Washington, DC, United States
§Battlefield Information Processing Branch, Computational Information Sciences Directorate, Army Research Laboratory, Adelphi, MD, United States

## 1.1 INTRODUCTION: IOE: IOT, IOBT, AND IOIT—BACKGROUND AND OVERVIEW

The Internet of Everything (IoE) generalizes machine-to-machine (M2M) communications for the Internet of Things (IoT) to form an even more complex system that also encompasses people, robots, and machines. From Chambers (2014), IoE connects:

> people, data, process and things. It is revolutionizing the way we do business, transforming communication, job creation, education and healthcare across the globe. … by 2020, more than 5 billion people will be connected, not to mention 50 billion things. … [With IoE] [p]eople get better access to education, healthcare and other opportunities to improve their lives and have better experiences. Governments can improve how they serve their citizens and businesses can use the information they get from all these new connections to make better decisions, be more productive and innovate faster.

From a recent view of IoE, IoT is "all about connecting objects to the network and enabling them to collect and share data" (Munro, 2017). With the approach of IoT in everyday life (Gasior & Yang, 2013), on battlefields—Internet of Battlefield Things (IoBT), in the medical arena—Internet of Medical Things (IoMT), distributed with sensory networks and cyber-physical systems, and even with device-level intelligence—Internet of Intelligent Things (IoIT) comes a number of issues identified by Moskowitz (2017), which are the explosion of data (e.g., cross-compatible systems; storage locations); security challenges (e.g., adversarial resilience, data exfiltration, covert channels; enterprise protection; privacy); and self-* and autonomic behaviors, and the risks to users, teams, enterprises, and institutions.

*Artificial Intelligence for the Internet of Everything*
https://doi.org/10.1016/B978-0-12-817636-8.00001-6

As presently conceived, "Humans will often be the integral parts of the IoT system" (Stankovic, 2014, p. 4). For IoE, IoT, IoBT, IoMT, IoIT, and so on, and so on, will manifest as heterogeneous and potentially self-organizing complex-systems that define human processes, requiring interoperability, just-in-time (JIT) human interactions, and the orchestration of local-adaptation functionalities as these "things" attempt to achieve human objectives and goals (Suri et al., 2016). IoE is already impacting industry, too: the Industrial Internet of Things (IIoT).[2]

Presently, there are numerous practical considerations: whatever the systems used for the benefits afforded, each one must be robust to interruption and failure, and resilient to every possible perturbation from wear and tear in daily use. For system-wide failures, a system must have manual control backups; user-friendly methods for joining and leaving networks; autonomous updates and backups; and autonomous hardware updates (e.g., the list is similar to re-ordering inventory or goods automatically after a sale event or in anticipation of scheduled events by a large retailer like Amazon, Wal-Mart, or Target). A system must also provide forensic evidence in the event of mishaps, not only with onboard backups, but also with automatic backups to the cloud.

For new and future systems, there are several other questions that must be addressed: Will systems communicate with each other or be independent actors? Will humans always need to be in the loop? Will systems communicate only with human users, or also with robot and machine users?

For future systems, we are also interested in what may happen when these "things" begin to "think." Foreseeing something like the arrival of the IoE, Gershenfeld (1999, pp. 8, 10), the former Director of the MIT Media Lab,[3] predicted that when a digital system:

> has an identity, knowing something about our environment, and being able to communicate ... [we will need] components that can work together and change ... [to produce a] digital evolution so that the digital world merges with the physical world.

Gershenfeld helped us to link our AAAI symposium with our past symposia on using artificial intelligence (AI) to reduce human errors.[4] Intelligence is

---

[2] For example, from General Electric on IIot, see https://www.ge.com/digital/blog/everything-you-need-know-about-industrial-internet-things.

[3] Gershenfeld is presently the Director, The Center for Bits and Atoms, MIT, Cambridge, MA; gersh@cba.mit.edu.

[4] For example, see our AAAI Symposium at Stanford in 2016 at http://www.aaai.org/Library/Symposia/Spring/ss16-01.php.

perceived to be a critical factor in overcoming barriers in order to direct maximum entropy production (MEP) to solve difficult problems (Martyushev, 2013; Wissner-Gross & Freer, 2013). But intelligence may also save lives. For example, a fighter plane can already take control and save itself if its fighter pilot loses consciousness during a high-g maneuver. We had proposed in 2016 that with existing technology, the passengers aboard Germanwings Flight 9525 might have been saved had the airliner safely secured itself by isolating the copilot who committed murder and suicide to kill all aboard (Lawless, 2016). Similarly, when the Amtrak train derailed in 2015 from the loss of awareness of its head engineer loss of life could have been avoided had the train taken control until it or its central authority could affect a safe termination (NTSB, 2016); similarly for the memory lapse experienced by the well-trained and experienced engineer who simply failed to heed the speed limit approaching a curve, killing three and injuring multiple others (NTSB, 2018).

Gershenfeld's evolution may arrive when intelligent "things" and humans team together as part of a "collective intelligence" to solve problems and to save lives (Goldberg, 2017). But autonomy is turning out to be more difficult than expected based strictly on engineering principles alone (e.g., for driverless cars, see Niedermeyer, 2018). Researchers involved with the IoE must not only advance the present state of these "things," but also address how they think that the science of "collective intelligence" may afford the next evolution of society.

## 1.2 INTRODUCTIONS TO THE TECHNICAL CHAPTERS

The first research chapter, Chapter 2, titled "Uncertainty Quantification in the Internet of Battlefield Things," was authored by Brian Jalaian[5] and Stephen Russell. The authors are scientists at the U.S. Army Research Laboratory in Adelphi, MD. Their focus in this chapter is on mixed technologies that must be fully integrated for maximum military effect in the field (i.e., technologies built by different businesses at different times for different purposes must somehow become integrated to work seamlessly; e.g., recently the Army was successful in integrating multiple technologies for National Defense (Freedberg, 2018)). They begin their chapter by reviewing a wide range of advances in recent technologies for IoT, not only for

---

[5] Corresponding author: brian.a.jalaian.civ@mail.mil.

commercial applications, but also their present and future use in military applications that are now evolving into IoBT. From their perspective, the authors believe that IoBT must be capable of not only working with mixed commercial and military technologies, but also leveraging them for maximum effect and advantage against opponents in the field. These applications in the field present several operational challenges in tactical environments, which the authors review along with the proposed solutions that they offer. Unlike commercial applications, the IoBT challenges for the army include limitations on bandwidth and interruptions in network connectivity, intermittent or specialized functionality, and network geographies that vary considerably over space and time. In contrast to IoT devices' common use in commercial and industrial systems, army operational constraints make the use of the cloud impractical for IoBT systems today. However, while cloud use in the field is impractical now, the army's significant success with an integrated mission command network (e.g., NOC, 2018) is an encouraging sign and motivation for the research proposed by Jalaian and his coauthor. The authors also discuss how machine learning and AI are intrinsic and essential to IoBT for the decision-making problems that arise in underlying control, communication, and networking functions within the IoBT infrastructure, as well as higher-order IoBT applications such as surveillance and tracking. In this chapter they highlight the research challenges on the path towards providing quantitative intelligence services in IoBT networked infrastructures. Specifically, they focus on uncertainty quantification for machine learning and AI within IoBT, which is critically essential to provide accurate predictive output errors and precise solutions. They conclude that uncertainty quantification in IoBT workflows enables risk-aware decision making and control for subsequent intelligent systems and/or humans within the information–analytical pipeline. The authors propose potential solutions to address these challenges (e.g., machine learning, statistical learning, stochastic optimization, generalized linear models, inference, etc.); what they hope is fertile ground to encourage more research for themselves and by others in the mathematical underpinnings of quantitative intelligence for IoBT in resource-constrained tactical networks. The authors provide an excellent technical introduction to the IoT and its evolution into the IoBT for field use by the US army. The authors are working at the cutting edge of technological applications for use in the field under circumstances that combine uncertainty with widely varying conditions, and in a highly dynamic application space.

Chapter 3, titled "Intelligent Autonomous Things on the Battlefield," was written by Alexander Kott[6] and Ethan Stump, both with the U.S. Army Research Laboratory in Adelphi, MD. Kott is the Chief Scientist in ARL's laboratory and Stump is a robotics scientist at ARL. In their chapter they propose that it is very likely that numerous, artificially intelligent, networked things will soon populate future battlefields. These autonomous agents and humans will work together in teams coordinating their activities to enable better cooperation with human warfighters, but these environments will be highly adversarial. Exploiting AI, these systems are likely to be faster and much more efficient than the predecessor systems used in the past (e.g., McHale, 2018). The authors point out that AI will make the complexity of events increase dramatically. The authors explore the characteristics, capabilities, and intelligence required for a network of intelligent things and humans, forming IoBT. IoBT will involve unique challenges not yet sufficiently addressed by the current AI systems, including machine-learning systems. The authors describe the battlefields of the future as places where a great diversity of systems will attack each other with physical cyber systems and electromagnetic weapons. In this complex environment, learning with be a challenge as will the ever-present need for real-time situational assessments of enemy forces, placing a premium on sensible decision making. This complexity motivates a series of new needs that the authors discuss, including the need for reliable systems under difficult field conditions (e.g., sources of power in the field); the need to be able to model systems and events ahead of time in preparation for battle, and in real time as events unfold; the need to be able to discover emergent behaviors and to control them when they do occur; and, among others, the need for autonomous systems to be able to explain themselves to humans. The description of future battlefields by the authors provides significant motivation to address the problems that need to be confronted soon and in the future to be able to deploy IoBT for the US army. The sketch of the problems described by the authors does not, nor can it, offer complete solutions today. But it is helpful to have this vision of how sophisticated researchers and users must become to master and to survive in this new environment.

Chapter 4, titled "Active Inference in Multiagent Systems: Context-driven Collaboration and Decentralized Purpose-driven Team Adaptation," was written by Georgiy Levchuk,[7] Krishna Pattipati, Daniel Serfaty,

---

[6] Corresponding author: alexander.kott1.civ@mail.mil.
[7] Corresponding author: georgiy@aptima.com.

Adam Fouse, and Robert McCormack. Levchuk is a Senior Principal Research Scientist and Corporate Fellow at Aptima Inc. in Woburn, MA, and is an expert in relational data mining, distributed inference, and reasoning under uncertainty. Professor Pattipati is a Board of Trustees Distinguished Professor and a UTC Professor in Systems Engineering in the Department of Electrical and Computer Engineering at the University of Connecticut; Serfaty is the Chief Executive Officer, Principal Founder, and Chairman of the Board of Directors of Aptima; Fouse is the Director of the Performance Augmentation Systems Division and Senior Research Engineer with Aptima; and McCormack is the Principal Mathematician and Lead of Team and Organizational Performance at Aptima. From the perspective of the authors, for modern civilization, IoT, ranging from health care to the control of home systems, is already integral in day-to-day life. The authors expect these technologies to become smarter, to autonomously reason, to act, and to communicate with other intelligent systems in the environment to achieve shared goals. The authors believe that sharing the goals and tasks among IoT devices requires modeling and controlling these entities as "teams of agents." To realize the full potential of these systems, the authors argue that scientists need to better understand the mechanisms that allow teams of agents to operate effectively in a complex, ever-changing, but also uncertain future. After defining the terms they use in their chapter, the authors construct the framework of an energy perspective for a team from which they postulate that optimal multiagent systems can best achieve adaptive behaviors by minimizing a team's free energy, where energy minimization consists of incremental observation, perception, and control phases. Then the authors craft a mechanism with their model for the distribution of decisions jointly made by a team, providing the associated mathematical abstractions and computational mechanisms. Afterwards, they test their ideas experimentally to conclude that energy-based agent teams outperform utility-based teams. They discuss different means for adaptation and scales, explain agent interdependencies produced by energy-based modeling, and look at the role of learning in the adaptation process. The authors hypothesize that to operate efficiently in uncertain and changing environments, IoT devices must not only be sufficiently intelligent to perceive and act locally, but also possess team-level adaptation skills. They propose that these skills must embody energy-minimizing mechanisms that can be locally defined without the need for agents to know all global team-level objectives or constraints. Their approach includes a decomposition of distributed decisions. The authors introduce the concept of free energy for teams and the interdependence among the members of a team, predicting that optimal decisions made by a team are reflected in its actions by seeking its lowest level of free energy. They test their idea with a mathematical model of a team and have provided one of the first manuscripts to tackle the challenges associated with the rational management of teams.

Written by Barry M. Horowitz, a former Cybersecurity Commissioner for the Commonwealth of Virginia, Chapter 5 is titled "Policy Issues Regarding Implementations of Cyber Attack. Resilience Solutions for Cyber-physical Systems." Horowitz is presently the Munster Professor of Systems and Information Engineering at the University of Virginia in Charlottesville, VA.[8] He is primarily interested in the policy implications of cyber security; in building cyber-security prototype and standards focused on achieving cyber-attack resilience; and in the education of future cybersecurity engineers. From his perspective, IoT is dramatically increasing complexity in cities, with commerce, and in homes across the country. This complexity is increasing vulnerability to cyber threats (e.g., see Zakrzewski's, 2017, interview of John Carlin, the chairman of the global risk and crisis management group at Morrison & Foerster LLP and a former assistant attorney general in the national security division of the U.S. Justice Department). To reduce these risks, resilient cyber-physical systems must be able to respond to different types of disturbances (errors; cyber attacks). He has written that risks to organization, system, and infrastructure security systems challenge existing policies, indicating that new ones must be crafted that reduce cyber risks instead of focusing on reaction to the damage caused by a cyber attack. The author argues that these new policies require responses that anticipate attacks yet are able to distinguish anomalies caused by human error from those driven by the malicious cyber attackers who intend to cause significant damage to infrastructure and even to human health and life, or hope to control systems to achieve these or other malevolent purposes (e.g., Stuxnet). He concludes that anticipatory resilience solutions for cyber-physical systems will require teams of government and commercial organizations to work together to address the consequences of cyber attacks, to detect them, and to defend against them. The author offers a long-term view of cyber-security policies, operational standards, and the education of cyber-security professionals, especially engineers. The overview of cyber security provided by this chapter lets the reader know how much more work needs to be done to make cyber security a profession with standards.

---

[8] Corresponding author: bh8e@virginia.edu.

Chapter 6 provides a psychological approach to the study of human-machine interaction; it is titled "Trust and Human-Machine Teaming: A Qualitative Study," and it was written by Joseph B. Lyons,[9] Kevin T. Wynne, Sean Mahoney, and Mark A. Roebke. Lyons is a recognized subject-matter expert in human-machine trust research at the Air Force Research Laboratory; Wynne is a Professor of Management, Department of Management and International Business at the University of Baltimore; Mahoney is a Program Manager at AFRL; and Roebke is a Course Director and Instructor for the Air Force Institute of Technology's School of Systems and Logistics at Wright-Patterson Air Force Base, OH. Their chapter discusses concepts for human-machine trust in human-machine teams. They present data from their qualitative study regarding the factors that precede trust for the elements of human-machine teaming. The authors reviewed the construct of human-machine trust and the dimensions of teammate-likeness from a human-robot interaction perspective. They derived the antecedents of trust from the open literature to develop the reasons why individuals might have reported trust of a new technology, such as a machine. The dimensions of human-machine teaming were taken from a recent conceptual model of teammate-likeness, forming the basis of the coding scheme that they used to analyze their qualitative data. US workers were asked to: (1) identify an intelligent technology that they used on a regular basis; (2) classify interactions with that technology as either a teammate or a tool; (3) report their reasons why they trusted or distrusted the technology in question; and (4) report why they might have viewed the relationship with the machine as a teammate or as a tool; also, if they reported viewing the technology as a tool, they were asked what in their view would it take for the machine to be viewed as a teammate. Their results, especially for reliability and predictability, were consistent with the published literature. Their results regarding human-machine teaming were also mostly consistent with an emerging model of teammate-likeness as discussed in the recent literature. But they found that most subjects reported the technology as a tool rather than as a teammate for human-machine teaming. Based on their research and its conclusions, the authors believe that the future offers many more research opportunities for this complex topic. The authors include the value of interdependence and its social impact on human members of teams. They studied synchrony and they reported on the value of transparency in building trust for complex human-machine teammates. They authors

[9] Corresponding author: joseph.lyons.6@us.af.mil.

distinguished between whether an autonomous machine is a teammate (partner) or a tool. Further research on this question appears to offer an important research direction.

Chapter 7 was written by Michael Wollowski[10] and John McDonald. Wollowski is an Associate Professor of Computer Science and Software Engineering at the Rose-Hulman Institute of Technology in Terre Haute, IN; and McDonald is the Chief Executive Officer of ClearObject in Fishers, IN. Their chapter is titled, "The Web of Smart Entities–Aspects of a Theory of the Next Generation of the Internet of Things." The authors illustrate their ideas about the accelerating growth of the IoT by using a future scenario with IoT and health care for human patrons. They provide this scenario to develop their theory of a broad web of smart software entities that are able to manage and regulate the routine and complex health-care behavior of their human participants (e.g., the timing and coordination of exercise, diet, healthy eating habits, etc.). In their view, the web of smart entities is informed by the collection of data, whether the data collected is from sensors, data manually entered, or data gathered from other smart entities. Based on this trove of data, which has to be curated, in turn, smart entities build models that capture routine (health) behavior to enable them, when authorized, to automatically act based on the results from the analyses of the data collected (e.g., monitoring a diabetic; in Gia et al., 2017). Although IoT is bringing about rapid change, much remains to be done, not only for the analytics associated with the data collected, but also with the privacy concerns raised both by these data and by their analyses (e.g., Datta, Aphorpe, & Feamster, 2018). The authors describe the likely effects of the as yet–unforeseen hyper-automation, but when it comes, they provide a description of several ways in which humans and machines can interact to control the resulting automation. The authors have provided a useful model with illustrations of IoT that allows them and the reader to be able to better view the fullest range of operations with IoT from automatic to fully autonomous. The authors provide a broad sketch of a fully connected IoT that will dramatically change life in ways not only already anticipated, but also not yet expected or foreseen.

Chapter 8, "Parenting AI," was written by Alec Shuldiner,[11] an IoT researcher working in the San Francisco Bay Area at Autodesk, Inc. In Shuldiner's view, AI systems are rapidly growing more sophisticated, largely

[10] Corresponding author: wollowski@rose-hulman.edu.
[11] Corresponding author: alec.shuldiner@autodesk.com.

by increasing in size and complexity. Shuldiner writes that while nature is often complex beyond our fullest understanding, and while the things that humans make are often more understandable, this is not always the case; for example, the parts that presently comprise the IoT form a whole that is often too complex even for experts (King, 2017). The author writes that, in contrast to nature, there is a clear direction between what humans intend to build and what they hope to achieve. Of course, he writes, there are exceptions. But still we humans associate this belief closely with our expectations for new technologies. In his view AI is being used to do the tasks that humans cannot easily perform (e.g., we humans can operate business spreadsheets by hand with pencil and paper, but neither as fast nor as reliably as can software; VisiCalc, for example, the first spreadsheet software demonstrated the power of personal computing; in Babcock, 2006). The author writes that as AI helps humans to achieve their intentions; it helps us to better understand nature, our cultures, societies, and economies, including many of the complexities that we humans face or have faced in the past. However, the point the author wants to make is that as we use AI more and more, in our attempts to better understand and to manage our private and public affairs, at the same time, perhaps unwittingly, we are injecting more and more opacity into our lives (e.g., the average user of a cell phone may not care to know the intricacies of its operation). As is already the situation, AI is proving too difficult to fully understand. With this opacity, Shuldiner suggests an important tradeoff is taking place. Namely, human users (and maybe future machine or robot users) can focus their energy on operating AI systems or on understanding the technology in play, but maybe not both at the same time. Shuldiner proposes that useful IoE requires useful AI. But by embedding AI into IoE, particularly the intelligent infrastructure that will make up what he terms the "Internet of Big Things," humans and their technologists are creating a global operating system that is in a large sense opaque. To cope with this situation, he believes that we will have to accept a relationship with the smart things around us that is more akin to that of a parent with its child than to that of a user with its device. He concludes that we may come to understand our legacy problems better than in past years, but just as fast we are obscuring many aspects of the new world that we are building. The application of IoT to a human footbridge in a major metropolitan city by the author provides an early example of the unexpected uses of IoT and of the opacity that the developers of this "smart bridge" may encounter. With his sketch and privacy concerns about the use of IoT in everyday life, the author has skillfully characterized a future rapidly approaching.

Chapter 9, titled "Valuable Information and the Internet of Things," was written by Ira S. Moskowitz[12] of the Information Management and Decision Architectures Branch, Code 5580 at the Naval Research Laboratory in Washington, DC; and Stephen Russell of the Battlefield Information Processing Branch of the U.S. Army Research Laboratory in Adelphi, MD. Moskowitz is a mathematician at NRL and Russell is the Chief of the Battlefield Information Processing Branch at ARL. The authors investigated a theory for the value of information with respect to IoT and AI that is becoming innate to IoT. In an environment increasingly composed of ubiquitous computing and information, information's value has taken on a new and unexpected dimension. Moreover, when the system in which such information exists is itself becoming intelligent, the ability to elicit value, in context, will be more complicated but, from their perspective, more manageable with AI. Classical economic theory describes the relationship between value and information which, though moderated by demand, is highly correlated. According to the authors, in an environment where there is a wealth of information, such as is becoming reality with the IoT, the intelligence innate to the system will become a dominant moderator of demand (e.g., a self-adapting, self-operating, and self-protecting system; as an example, the system's ability to control access entry and exit at its portals). The authors begin their chapter with the perspective of Howard's value of information theory to illustrate mathematically that Howard's focus on maximizing value hid another important dimension: the guarantee of the value of information. Their insight is that IoT changes the perspective of how the value of information is obtained. This insight of theirs is based on the notion that Shannon's information theory is limited, forming an issue for a quantitative theory of the application of information to decision making in IoT. They rework Howard's contribution and extended it by asking about the value of information that they uncover at each step by ranking their results. They conclude that IoT provides a rich environment for almost all aspects of human behavior. With AI the fundamental notion of information will change as it is managed by AI. The authors construct a mathematical model of the value of information that will be very useful for themselves and for other AI researchers to help quantitatively in the management of future IoT systems. The authors offer a path forward for mathematical research as well as considerations that mathematicians must keep in mind as they go forward in their study of the IoT.

[12] Corresponding author: Ira.moskowitz@nrl.navy.mil.

Chapter 10, written by Shu-Heng Chen,[13] poses this question: "Would IOET Make Economics More Neoclassical or More Behavioral? Richard Thaler's Prediction, A Revisit." Shu-Heng Chen is at the National Chengchi University in Taipei, Taiwan, where he is a Distinguished Professor in its Department of Economics, Director of its AI-ECON Research Center, and its Vice President. He is Editor-in-Chief (Economics) of the journal of *New Mathematics and Natural Computation* and the *Journal of Economic Interaction and Coordination*; he is an Editor at *Economia Politica*, the *Global and Local Economic Review*, and the *International Journal of Financial Engineering and Risk Management*; and he is an Associate Editor for *Computational Economics* and for *Evolutionary and Institutional Economics Review*. The author for this chapter approaches IoE by providing a thoughtful study of what it means economically. In his view as an economist, the fundamental question pursued by economists today is the impact of IoE on the theory of how economics works, that is, namely how rational individual humans are from the perspective of economic theory or from the perspective of the history of economic analysis. To this end, for IoE, the author examines individual human economic behavior based on the earlier era of conventional economic theory and from the more modern individual human economic behavior as IoE dawns. The comparison that he draws motivates economists and readers as he sketches the future of individual behavior in economic theory. For IoE, the Nobel Laureate Richard Thaler would have proposed two possibilities two decades ago hinging on this branching point: Homo economicus, as human individuals are depicted in neoclassical economics, and Homo sapiens, as humans are articulated in behavioral economics. Thaler was not aware of IoE. Despite this lack of an awareness of IoE, Thaler would have predicted that behavioral economics, the latter, would be the trend that we would observe as the IoE develops and becomes central in our economic lives. In this chapter, on the macro and micro levels, even with arguments presented for both sides, and depending on whether collective intelligence raises or lowers, the author addresses his prediction based on Thaler's work for the coming age of IoE. He addresses the following two possibilities, namely, trend reversal and trend sustaining. He concludes with a warning that recurring social problems can be aggravated depending on the road that humans take to either check (free markets) or not check (socialism) the decisions that they make, a long-running argument that continues (e.g., Gilder, 1981/2012). The author offers a panoramic view of human behavior with IoE. He sees no easy answers but

---

[13] Corresponding author: chen.shuheng@gmail.com.

provides excellent cautions for readers and users of IoE. The author sees an increasing, well-deserved interest about IoE occurring among economists.

Chapter 11, titled "Accessing Validity of Argumentation of Agents of the Internet of Everything," was written by Boris Galitsky[14] of the Oracle Corporation in Redwood Shores, CA. Galitsky is a natural language specialist at Oracle who has trained in AI. In Galitsky's view, agents operating in IoE will make message exchanges between them, will make certain decisions based on those messages, and will need arguments provided to them to justify the decisions that they have made. When arguments are exchanged in the IoE, environment, validation of the arguments or the validity of the patterns in an argumentation message, including the truthfulness of a message, its authenticity and its consistency; all of these qualities become essential. The author formulates a problem of the domain-independent assessment of argumentation validity based on analyses of the rhetoric in text messages. He articulates a model where he is able to discover the structure of an argument; he makes these discoveries based on the structure of an argument with discourse trees extended with edges where the communicative actions entailed are labeled. He is then able to have the argumentation structures extracted represented in defeasible logic programs that can be revised or challenged and are otherwise open to dialectical analyses; with this representation and structure, in the search for the main claim being communicated among the agent exchanges of messages, the author is able to test and to establish the validity of the arguments for the main claim. The author evaluates the accuracy after each processing step in the argumentation pipeline that he has constructed as well as its overall performance among agents. He is able to determine illogical and emotional arguments. One of the needs with texts is to be able to mine them for the logic behind the arguments being made by humans and, in the near future, AI agents. The author provides an excellent introduction to the problem and a master class in advancing the science of understanding (text) language logically. The author advances the science of validating the logic in the messages exchanged between agents, including those intense arguments containing emotion.

Chapter 12, titled "Distributed Autonomous Energy Organizations: Next-Generation Blockchain Applications for Energy Infrastructure," was written by Michael Mylrea.[15] The author is a Senior Advisor for Cyber

---

[14] Corresponding author: boris.galitsky@oracle.com.
[15] Corresponding author: michael.mylrea@pnnl.gov.

Security and Energy Technology and Blockchain Lead at the Pacific Northwest National Laboratory (PNNL) in Richland, WA. In his chapter, Mylrea writes that blockchain technology combines cryptography and distributed computing with a more secure multiparty consensus algorithm to reduce the need for third-party intermediaries (e.g., bankers, meter readers, accountants, lawyers, etc.). Blockchain helps securely automate exchanges of value between parties in a more efficient and secure way that, he predicts, may give impetus to organizations known as "Distributed Autonomous Energy Organizations" (DAEO). In this chapter, the author applies the blockchain research that he developed while he was at the Pacific Northwest National Laboratory in combination with a new theoretical approach that allows him and others to explore how blockchain technology might be able to help users to construct a more distributed, more autonomous, and more cyber-resilient energy organization that can more autonomously respond to evolving cyber-physical threats. In the face of these threats, blockchain may help increase the resiliency and efficiency of energy utilities by linking producers securely with consumers and to create a new class of consumers combined with producers known as "prosumers." DAEO will give prosumers increased flexibility and control of how they consume and exchange energy and trade energy credits while securing data from the critical communications required for these complex transactions. The author offers an innovative approach for more autonomous and secure energy transactions that replaces third-party intermediaries with blockchain technology in a way that could potentially increase the efficiency and resilience of electric utilities. Blockchain-enabled distributed energy markets may unlock new value, empowering "prosumers" and replacing some third-party intermediaries with a distributed ledger consensus algorithm. However, many blockchain regulatory, policy, and technology obstacles ahead could potentially challenge this innovative change for the energy sector.

Chapter 13, titled "Compositional Models for Complex Systems," was written by Spencer Breiner,[16] Ram D. Sriram, and Eswaran Subrahmanian of the National Institute of Standards and Technology (NIST), Information Technology Lab, Gaithersburg, MD. Breiner is a specialist in graphical methods in the CyberInfrastructure Group at NIST; Sriram is currently the Chief of the Software and Systems Division of the Information Technology Laboratory at NIST; Subrahmanian, a Fellow of the American Association of Advancement of Science (AAAS), is also part of the

---

[16] Corresponding author: spencer.breiner@nist.gov.

CyberInfrastructure Group at NIST and is with the Carnegie Mellon University's Engineering and Public Policy, Institute for Complex Engineered Systems in Pittsburgh, PA. In this chapter the authors propose an argument for the use of representations from category theory to support better models for complex systems (to better understand the stability of mathematical structures and as an alternative to set theory, "category" theory was devised to consist of labeled directed subgraphs with arrows that associate, and objects with unique arrows, such as $A \rightarrow B \rightarrow C \rightarrow A$); the authors provide examples of what an application of category theory might look like. Their approach is based on the well-known observation that the design of complex systems is fundamentally recursive, formalized in computer science with structures known as algebras, coalgebras, and operads,[17] the mathematical structures that happen to be closely linked to labeled tree representations. Next, the authors construct two small examples from computer science to illustrate the functional aspects and use of the categorical approach. Their first example, a common HVAC heating and air conditioning system, defines a logical semantics of contracts that they use to organize the different requirements that may occur at the different scales in hierarchical systems. The second example that the authors offer concerns the integration of AI models into a preexisting human-driven process. The approach by the authors is used by them to characterize the complexity of systems (e.g., heterogeneity, open interactions, multiple perspectives of jointly cognitive agents). The authors conclude that category theory is hampered by the belief held by others that it is too abstract and cumbersome, an obstacle that the authors are striving to overcome by demonstrating its utility with the examples they provide and by concluding that the theory is well-linked across many domains (e.g., physics, computer science, data science, etc.).

Chapter 14, titled "Meta-agents: Using Multiagent Networks to Manage Dynamic Changes in the Internet of Things," was written by Hesham Fouad[18] and Ira S. Moskowitz of the Information Management and Decisions Architecture Branch, Code 5580, at the Naval Research Laboratory in Washington, DC. Fouad is a computer scientist with a strong background in both academic research and commercial software development (e.g., SoundScape3D and VibeStation, used in the VR Laboratory at NRL);

---

[17] To create reusable proofs, algebras provide a uniform language that generalize, for example, groups, rings, lattices and monoids; coalgebras are duals used to represent classes and objects; and operads model properties of mathematical structures of compositional architectures such as commutativity and anti-commutativity (e.g., Jacobs, 2016).

[18] Corresponding author: hesham.fouad@nrl.navy.mil.

Moskowitz is a mathematician at NRL (who holds three patents). The authors explore the idea of creating and deploying online agents as their way of crafting emergent configurations (EC). As part of this structure, their method entails the management of complexity through the use of dynamically emergent meta-agents forming a holonic system. From their perspective, in the context of their research, these meta-agents are agents existing inside of a software paradigm where they are able to reason and utilize their reasoning to construct and deploy other agents with special purposes for which they are able to form an EC. As the authors note, the kind of reasoning models that can support the idea of meta-agents in the context of an EC have not been well explored, which they proceed to perform and report on in their chapter. To realize an EC using meta-agents, the authors first discuss the management of the complexity that a problem creates, then they develop a multiagent framework capable of supporting meta-agents, and, finally, the authors explore and review known reasoning models. They give an example with a service-oriented architecture (SOA), they test it with an automated evaluation process, and they introduce holon agents. Holonic agents are intelligent agents able to work independently and as part of a hierarchy. They are simultaneously complete in and of themselves and are able to interact independently with the environment, yet they can also be a part of a hierarchy. A holon is something that is simultaneously a whole and a part. The idea of a holon began with Koestler (1967/1990), who introduced it as part of a duality between emotion and reason. As the authors note, the number of IoT devices is expected to exceed a billion, making computations and searches among the devices complex and difficult. With their approach they hope to simplify the process. The authors recommend the development of standards in the searches to be made for the discovery of IoT devices.

## REFERENCES

Babcock, C. (2006). What's the greatest software ever written? Witness the definitive, irrefutable, immutable ranking of the most brilliant software programs ever hacked. *InformationWeek*. August 11. From https://www.informationweek.com/whats-the-greatest-software-ever-written/d/d-id/1046033.

Chambers, J. (2014). Are you ready for the Internet of everything? *World Economic Forum*. January 15. From https://www.weforum.org/agenda/2014/01/are-you-ready-for-the-internet-of-everything/.

Datta, T., Aphorpe, N., & Feamster, N. (2018). A developer-friendly library for smart home IoT privacy-preserving traffic obfuscation. *arXiv*. August 22. From https://arxiv.org/pdf/1808.07432.pdf.

Freedberg, S. J., Jr. (2018). New tests prove IBCS missile defense network does work: Northrop. "There's a real capability that can be deployed as soon as the government says it can be," Northrop Grumman's Rob Jassey told me, possibly even in "months". *Breaking Defense.* August 15. From https://breakingdefense.com/2018/08/new-tests-prove-ibcs-missile-defense-network-does-work-northrop/.

Gasior, W., & Yang, L. (2013). Exploring covert channel in Android platform. *2012 International Conference on Cyber Security* (pp. 173–177). https://doi.org/10.1109/CyberSecurity.2012.29.

Gershenfeld, N. (1999). *When things start to think.* New York: Henry Holt & Co.

Gia, T. N., Ali, M., Dhaou, I. B., Rahmani, A. M., Westerlund, T., Liljeberg, P., et al. (2017). IoT-based continuous glucose monitoring system: a feasibility study. *Procedia Computer Science, 109,* 327–334.

Gilder. (1981/2012). *Wealth and poverty: A new edition for the twenty-first century.* Washington, DC: Regnery Publishing.

Goldberg, K. (2017). The robot-human alliance. Call it multiplicity: diverse groups of people and machines working together. *Wall Street Journal.* June 11. From https://www.wsj.com/articles/the-robot-human-alliance-1497213576.

Jacobs, B. (2016). *Introduction to coalgebra: Towards mathematics of states and observation (Cambridge tracts in theoretical computer science).* Cambridge, UK: Cambridge University Press.

King, R. (2017). Dell bets $1 billion on "internet of things". Computing giant seeking new avenues of growth amid a shift in corporate spending to the cloud. *Wall Street Journal.* October 10. From https://www.wsj.com/articles/dell-bets-1-billion-on-internet-of-things-1507647601.

Koestler, A. (1967/1990). *The ghost in the machine.* New York: Penguin Books.

Lawless, W. F. (2016). Preventing (another) Lubitz: the thermodynamics of teams and emotion. In H. Atmanspacher, T. Filk, & E. Pothos (Eds.), *Quantum interactions. LNCS 9535* (pp. 207–215). Switzerland: Springer International.

Martyushev, L. M. (2013). Entropy and entropy production: old misconceptions and new breakthroughs. *Entropy, 15,* 1152–1170.

McHale. (2018). Military AI/machine learning speeds decision-making and efficiency for warfighters. *Military Embedded Systems.* May 29. From http://mil-embedded.com/articles/military-learning-speeds-decision-making-efficiency-warfighters/.

Moskowitz, I. S. (2017). *Personal communication, May 23.*

Munro, K. (2017). *How to beat security threats to "internet of things".* May 23. From http://www.bbc.com/news/av/technology-39926126/how-to-beat-security-threats-to-internet-of-things.

Niedermeyer, E. (2018). "Autonomy" review: fast-tracking a driverless car. A period of remarkable progress seems to be giving way to a host of challenges that can't be solved with engineering talent alone. Edward Niedermeyer reviews "Autonomy" by Lawrence D. Burns with Christopher Shulgan. *Wall Street Journal.* August 27. From https://www.wsj.com/articles/autonomy-review-fast-tracking-a-driverless-car-1535412237.

NOC. (2018). Integrated air and missile defense battle command system extends hundreds of miles to enable the multi-domain battlespace. *Northrup.* August 15. From https://news.northropgrumman.com/news/releases/northrop-grummans-missile-defense-battle-manager-shares-integrated-air-picture-over-vast-distances.

NTSB. (2016). *Railroad accident report: Derailment of Amtrak Passenger Train 188 Philadelphia, Pennsylvania May 12, 2015; National Transportation Safety Board, Accident Report NTSB/RAR-16/02 PB2016-103218.* From https://www.ntsb.gov/investigations/AccidentReports/Reports/RAR1602.pdf.

NTSB. (2018). NTSB issues investigative update on Washington state Amtrak derailment. *National Transportation Safety Board.* January 25. From https://www.ntsb.gov/news/press-releases/Pages/mr20180125.aspx.

Stankovic, J. A. (2014). Research directions for the internet of things. *IEEE Internet of Things Journal, 1*(1), 3–9. https://doi.org/10.1109/JIOT.2014.2312291.

Suri, N., Tortonesi, M., Michaelis, J., Budulas, P., Benincasa, G., Russell, S., et al. (2016). Analyzing the applicability of internet of things to the battlefield environment. In *Military Communications and Information Systems (ICMCIS), 2016 International Conference on* (pp. 1–8): IEEE.

Wissner-Gross, A. D., & Freer, C. E. (2013). Causal entropic forces. *Physical Review Letters,* *110*(168702), 1–5.

Zakrzewski, C. (2017). The cybersecurity risks from the internet of things. Former Justice Department official John Carlin says smarter devices bring increased risks, and the world isn't ready. *Wall Street Journal.* December 17. From https://www.wsj.com/articles/the-cybersecurity-risks-from-the-internet-of-things-1513652760.

# CHAPTER 2

# Uncertainty Quantification in Internet of Battlefield Things

**Brian Jalaian, Stephen Russell**
US Army Research Laboratory, Adelphi, MD, United States

## 2.1 INTRODUCTION

The battlefield of the future will comprise a vast array of heterogeneous computational capable sensors, actuators, devices, information sources, analytics, humans, and infrastructure, with varying intelligence, capabilities, and constraints on energy, power, computing, and communication resources. To maintain information dominance, the future army must far surpass the ability of future opposing forces, kinetic and nonkinetic alike, to ensure mission success and minimize risks. This vision can only be achieved if systems progress from a state of total dependence on human control to autonomous and, ultimately, autonomic behavior. A highly adaptive and autonomous future will depend upon foundational algorithms, theories, and methods that do not fully exist today. There are many challenges in ensuring that the delegated mission goals are accomplished regardless of the immediate availability of human presence in the control loop or the partial attrition of mission assets.

During the past decade, there has been a tremendous growth in the field of machine learning (ML). Large datasets combined with complex algorithms, such as deep neural networks, have allowed for huge advances across a variety of disciplines. However, despite the success of these models there has not been as much focus on uncertainty quantification (UQ); that is, quantifying a model's confidence in its predictions. In some situations, UQ may not be a huge priority (e.g., Netflix recommending movie titles). But in situations where the wrong prediction is a matter of life or death, UQ is crucial. For instance, if army personnel in combat are using an ML algorithm to make decisions, it is vital to know how confident the given algorithm is in its predictions. Personnel may observe a data point in the field that is quite different from the data the algorithm was trained on, yet the algorithm will just supply a (likely poor) prediction, potentially resulting in a catastrophe.

*Artificial Intelligence for the Internet of Everything*
https://doi.org/10.1016/B978-0-12-817636-8.00002-8

19

In this chapter we first provide a background and motivation scenario in Section 2.2. In Section 2.4, we discuss how to be able to quantify *and* minimize the uncertainty with respect to training an ML algorithm. This leads us to the field of stochastic optimization, which is covered broadly in this section. In Section 2.4, we discuss UQ in ML. Specifically, we study how to develop ways for a model to *know what it doesn't know*. In other words we study how to enable the model to be especially cautious for data that is different from that on which it was trained. Section 2.5 explores the recent emerging trends on adversarial learning, which is a new application of UQ in ML in Internet of Battlefield Things (IoBT) in an offensive and defensive capacity. Section 2.6 concludes the chapter.

## 2.2 BACKGROUND AND MOTIVATING IOBT SCENARIO

In recent years the Internet of Things (IoT) technologies have seen significant commercial adoption. For IoT technology, a key objective is to deliver intelligent services capable of performing both analytics and reasoning over data streams from heterogeneous device collections. In commercial settings IoT data processing has commonly been handled through cloud-based services, managed through centralized servers and high-reliability network infrastructures.

Recent advances in IoT technology have motivated the defense community to research IoT architecture development for tactical environments, advancing the development of the IoBT for use in C4ISR applications (Kott, Swami, & West, 2016). Toward advancing IoBT adoption, differences in military versus commercial network infrastructures become an important consideration. For many commercial IoT architectures, cloud-based services are used to perform needed data processing, which rely upon both stable network coverage and connectivity. As observed in Zheng and Carter (2015), IoT adoption in the tactical environment faces several technical challenges: (i) limitations on tactical network connectivity and reliability, which impact the amount of data that can be obtained from IoT sensor collections in real time; (ii) limitations on interoperability between IoT infrastructure components, resulting in reduced infrastructure functionality; and (iii) availability of data analytics components accessible over tactical network connections, capable of real-time data ingest over potentially sparse IoT data collections.

Challenges such as these limit the viability of cloud-based service usage in IoBT infrastructures. Hence, significant changes to existing commercial IoT architectures become necessary to ensure their applicability, particularly in the context of ML applications. To help illustrate these challenges, a motivating scenario is provided.

## 2.2.1 Detecting Vehicle-Borne IEDs in Urban Environments

As part of an ongoing counterinsurgency operation by coalition forces in the country of Aragon, focus is placed on monitoring of insurgent movements and activities. Vehicle-borne improvised explosive devices (VBIEDs) have become more frequently used by insurgents in recent months, requiring methods for quick detection and interception. Recent intelligence reports have provided details on the physical appearance of IED-outfitted vehicles in the area. However, due to the time constraints in confirming detections of VBIEDs, methods for autonomous detection become desirable. To support VBIED detection, an IoBT infrastructure has been deployed by coalition forces consisting of a mix of unattended ground sensors (UGSs) and unmanned aerial systems (UASs). In turn, supervised learning methods are employed over sensor data gathered from both sources.

Recent intelligence has indicated that VBIEDs may be used in a city square during the annual Aragonian Independence Festival. A local custom for this festival involves decoration of vehicles with varying articles (including flags and Christmas tree lighting). A UAS drone is tasked with patrolling the airspace over one of the inbound roadways and recoding images of detected vehicles. However, due to the decorations present on many civilian vehicles, confidence in VBIED classification by the UAS is significantly reduced. To mitigate this, the drone flies along a 3-mile stretch of road for 10 minutes to gather new images of the decorated vehicles. In each case the drone generates a classification of each vehicle as VBIED or not, each with a particular confidence value. For low-confidence readings, the drone contacts a corresponding UGS to do the following: (i) take a high-resolution image, and (ii) take readings for presence of explosives-related chemicals in the air nearby, where any detectable explosives confirms the vehicle is a VBIED. Since battery power for the UGS is limited, along with available network bandwidth, the UAS should only request UGS readings when especially necessary. Following receipt of data from a UGS, the UAS performs retraining of the classifier to improve the accuracy of future VBIED classification attempts. Over a short period, the UAS has gathered additional training data to support detection of VBIEDs. Eventually, the drone passes over a 1-mile stretch of road lacking UGSs. At this point the UAS must classify detected vehicles without UGS support (Fig. 2.1).

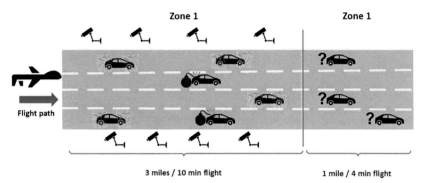

**Fig. 2.1** Diagram of drone flight over a roadway.

This example scenario highlights several research issues specific to IoBT settings, as reflected in prior surveys (e.g., Suri et al., 2016; Zheng & Carter, 2015): (i) a needed capability to quickly gather training data reflecting unforeseen learning/classification tasks; (ii) a needed capability to incrementally learn over the stream of field-specific data (e.g., increasing the accuracy of classifying VBIEDs by learning over the stream of pictures of decorated cars collected over 10 minutes of flight time); and (iii) management of limited network bandwidth and connectivity between assets (e.g., between the UAS and UGS along the road) requiring selective asset use to obtain classifier-relevant data that increases the classifier knowledge.

Each of these issues requires the selection of learning and classification methods appropriate to stream-based data sources. Prior research (Bottou, 1998 b; Bottou & Cun, 2004; Vapnik, 2013) demonstrates the equivalence of learning from stream-based data in real time with learning from *infinite* samples. From this work it follows that statistical-learning methods adept to large-scale data sources may be applicable for stream-based data.

This chapter opens with a survey of classical and modern statistical-learning theory, and how numerical optimization can be used to solve the resulting mathematical problems. The objective of this chapter is to encourage the IoT and ML research communities to revisit the underlying mathematical underpinnings of stream-based learning, as they apply to IoBT-based systems.

## 2.3 OPTIMIZATION IN MACHINE LEARNING

Behind the scenes of any ML algorithm is an optimization problem. To maximize a likelihood or a posterior distribution, or minimize a loss function, one must rely on mathematical optimization.

Of course the optimization literature provides numerous algorithms including gradient descent, Newton's method, Quasi-Newton methods, and nonlinear CG. In many applications these methods have been widely used for some time with much success. However, the size of contemporary datasets as well as complex model structure make traditional optimization algorithms ill suited for contemporary ML problems. For example, consider the standard gradient descent algorithm. When the objective function is strongly convex, the training uncertainty (or training error), $f(x_k) - f(x^*)$, is proportional to $e^{n-k}$, where $n$ is the amount of training data and $k$ is the number of iterations of the algorithm. Thus the training uncertainty grows *exponentially* with the size of the data. For large datasets, gradient descent clearly becomes impractical.

Stochastic gradient descent (SGD), on the other hand, has training uncertainty proportional to $1/k$. Although this error decreases more slowly in terms of $k$, it is *independent* of the sample size, giving it a clear advantage in a modern settings. Moreover, in a stochastic optimization setting, SGD actually achieves the optimal complexity rate in terms of $k$. These two features, as well as SGD's simplicity, have allowed it to become the standard optimization algorithm for most large-scale ML problems, such as training neural nets. However, SGD is not without its drawbacks. In particular, it performs poorly for badly scaled problems (when the Hessian is ill conditioned) and can have high variance with its step directions. While SGD's performance starts off particularly strong, its convergence to the optimum quickly slows. Although no stochastic algorithm can do better than SGD in terms of error uncertainty (in terms of $k$), there is certainly potential to improve the convergence rate up to a constant factor.

With regard to uncertainty, we would like to achieve a sufficiently small error for our model as quickly as possible. In the next section we discuss the formal stochastic optimization problem, the standard SGD algorithm, along with two popular variants of SGD. In Section 2.3 we propose an avenue for the development of an SGD variant that seems especially promising and discuss avenues of research for UQ in model predictions.

## 2.3.1 Optimization Problem

The standard stochastic optimization problem is:

$$\min_{w} f(w) = \mathbb{E}[F(w;\xi)] \tag{2.1}$$

where expectation is taken with respect to the probability distribution of $\xi = (X, Y)$, the explanatory, and response variables. In ML, $F(w;\xi)$ is typically of the form:

$$F(w;\xi) = \ell(h(X, w) - Y)$$

where $\ell$ is some loss function, such as $\|\cdot\|_2$. Most optimization algorithms attempt to optimize what is called the *sample-path* problem, the solution of which is often referred to as the empirical risk minimizer (ERM). This strategy attempts to solve an approximation to $f(w)$ using a finite amount of training data:

$$\min_w \hat{f}(w) = \frac{1}{n}\sum_{i=1}^{n} \ell(h(x_i, w) - y_i)$$

This is the problem that the bulk of ML algorithms attempt to minimize. A particular instance is maximum likelihood estimation, perhaps the most widely used estimation method among statisticians. For computer scientists minimizing a loss function (such as $\ell_2$ loss) without an explicit statistical model is more common.

Although it may go without saying that minimizing $\hat{f}(w)$ is not the end goal. Ideally we wish to minimize the true objective, $f(w)$. For finite sample sizes one runs into issues of overfitting to the sample problem. An adequate solution to the sample problem may not generalize well to future predictions (especially true for highly complex, over-parameterized models). Some ways of combating this problem include early-stopping, regularization, and Bayesian methods. In a large data setting, however, we can work around this issue. Due to such large sample sizes, we have an essentially infinite amount of data. Additionally, we are often in an online setting where data are continuously incoming, and we would like our model to continuously learn from new data. In this case we can model data as coming from an *oracle* that draws from the true probability distribution $P_\xi$ (such a scheme is fairly standard among the stochastic optimization community, but is more rare in ML). In this manner we can optimize the *true* risk (1) with respect to the objective function, $f(w)$.

## 2.3.2 Stochastic Gradient Descent Algorithm

Algorithm 2.1 shows a generic SGD algorithm to be used to solve (1). The direction of each iteration, $g(x_k, \xi_k)$ depends on the current iterate $x_k$ as well as a random draw $\xi_i \sim P_\xi$.

---

**Algorithm 2.1 Generic SGD**

1: Initialize $x_0$

2: **for** $k = 1, 2, \ldots$ **do**

3:    Choose batch size $n_k \in \mathbb{N}$

4:    Generate i.i.d sample $\xi_k \sim P_\xi$ from oracle

5:    Compute stochastic direction $g(x_k, \xi_k)$

6:    Generate stepsize $\alpha_k$

7:    $w_{k+1} \leftarrow w_k - \alpha_k g(w_k, \xi_k)$

8: **return** $x_{k+1}$

---

The basic SGD algorithm sets $n_k = 1$, $\alpha_k = \mathbb{O}(1/k)$ and computes the stochastic direction as:

$$w_{k+1} = w_k - \alpha_k \nabla F(w_k, \xi_k)$$

This is essentially the full-gradient method only evaluated for one sample point. Using the standard full-gradient method would require $n$ gradient evaluations every iteration, but the basic SGD algorithm only requires the evaluation of one. We briefly discuss an implementation for logistic regression.

## 2.3.3 Example: Logistic Regression

To make this algorithm more concrete, consider the case of binary logistic regression. When the amount of data is manageable, a standard way (Hastie, Tibshirani, & Friedman, 2009) to find the optimal parameters is to apply Newton's method (since there is no closed-form solution) to the log-likelihood for the model:

$$\ell(w; x, y) = \sum_{i=1}^{n} y_i w^T x_i - \log\left(1 + e^{w^T x_i}\right)$$

However, when $n$ is large, this quickly becomes unfeasible. Instead, we could use a simple SGD implementation. In this case we set the stochastic

---

**Algorithm 2.2 Basic SGD for Logistic Regression**

1: Initialize $x_0$

2: Set batch size $n \leftarrow 1$

3: **for** $k = 1, 2, \dots$ **do**

4:     Generate i.i.d sample $\xi_k \sim P_\xi$ from oracle

5:     Compute stochastic direction $g(x_k, \xi_k) \leftarrow x_k \left( y_k - \frac{e^{\beta^T x_k}}{1 + e^{\beta^T x_k}} \right)$

6:     Generate stepsize $\alpha_k \leftarrow 1/k$

7:     $w_{k+1} \leftarrow w_k - \alpha_k g(w_k, \xi_k)$

8: **return** $x_{k+1}$

---

direction to be a random gradient evaluated at $\xi_k = (X_k, Y_k)$, which is sampled from the oracle:

$$
\begin{aligned}
g(x_k, \xi_k) &= \nabla F(w_k, \xi_k) \\
&= \nabla \ell(w_k; x_k, y_k) \\
&= x_k \left( y_k - \frac{e^{w^T x_k}}{1 + e^{w^T x_k}} \right)
\end{aligned}
\tag{2.2}
$$

The implemented algorithm is then (Algorithm 2.2):

Again, note that for each iteration only a *single* training point is evaluated. On the other hand the full-gradient method would have to use the entire dataset for every iteration.

## 2.3.4 SGD Variants

As mentioned in Section 2.1, the basic SGD algorithm has some room for improvement. In this section we introduce two popular SGD variants: mini-batch SGD and SGD with momentum. Each variant gives a different yet useful way of improving upon the basic SGD algorithm.

### 2.3.4.1 Mini-Batch SGD

One of the major issues with SGD is that its search directions have high variance. Instead of moving downhill as intended, the algorithm may wander around randomly more than we would like. A natural idea is to use a larger sample size for the gradient estimates. The basic SGD uses a sample size of $n = 1$, so it makes sense that we might wish to use more draws from the oracle to reduce the variance. Specifically, we would reduce the variance in gradient estimates by a factor of $\frac{1}{n}$, where $n$ is the batch size. The *mini-batch* algorithm is implemented as shown in Algorithm 2.3.

It is shown in Bottou, Curtis, and Nocedal (2016) that under assumptions of smoothness and strong convexity, standard SGD (sample size $n = 1$ with fixed $\alpha$) achieves an error rate of:

$$\mathbb{E}(f(x_k) - f(x^*)) \leq \frac{\alpha LM}{2c\mu} + (1 - \alpha c\mu)^{k-1}\left(f(x_1) - f(x^*) - \frac{\alpha LM}{2c\mu}\right)$$

This convergence rate has several assumption-dependent constants such as the Lipschitz constant $L$ and strong-convexity parameter $c$. However, the defining feature of that algorithm is the $(\cdot)^{k-1}$ term, which implies that the error decreases exponentially to the constant $\frac{\alpha LM}{2c\mu}$. Using mini-batch SGD, on the other hand, yields the following bound:

$$\mathbb{E}(f(x_k) - f(x^*)) \leq \left(\frac{1}{n}\right)\frac{\alpha LM}{2c\mu} + (1 - \alpha c\mu)^{k-1}\left(f(x_1) - f(x^*) - \left(\frac{1}{n}\right)\frac{\alpha LM}{2c\mu}\right)$$

Thus the mini-batch algorithm converges at the same rate, but to a smaller error constant. This is certainly an improvement in terms of the error bound,

---

**Algorithm 2.3 Mini-Batch SGD**

1: Initialize $x_0$

2: Choose batch size $n \in \mathbb{N}$

3: **for** $k = 1, 2, \ldots$ **do**

4:     Generate i.i.d sample of size $n$, $\xi_k \sim P_\xi$ from oracle

5:     Compute stochastic direction $g(x_k, \xi_k) \leftarrow \frac{1}{n}\sum_{i=1}^{n} \ell(h(x_i, w) - y_i)$

6:     Generate stepsize $\alpha_k$

7:     $w_{k+1} \leftarrow w_k - \alpha_k g(w_k, \xi_k)$

8: **return** $x_{k+1}$

---

but of course requires $n - 1$ more samples at each iteration than the standard SGD. Thus it is not entirely clear which algorithm is better. If one could perform mini-batch in parallel with little overhead cost, the resulting algorithm would achieve the described bound without the cost of sampling $n$ draws sequentially. Otherwise, the tradeoff is somewhat ambiguous.

### 2.3.4.2 SGD With Momentum

Another issue with standard SGD is that it does not take into account scaling of the parameter space (which would require second-order information). A particular situation where this is an issue is when the objective function has very narrow level curves. Here, a standard gradient descent method tends to zigzag back and forth, moving almost perpendicular to the optimum. A common solution in the deterministic case is to use gradient descent with momentum, which has a simple yet helpful addition to the descent step. The stochastic version is:

$$w_{k+1} = w_k - \alpha_k \nabla F(w_k, \xi_k) + \beta(w_k - w_{k-1})$$

where the last term is the momentum term.

As the name implies, this algorithm is motivated by the physical idea of the inertia, for example, of a ball rolling down a hill. It might make sense to incorporate the previous step length this way into the next search direction. In this sense, the algorithm "remembers" all previous step distances, in the form of an exponentially decaying average. Momentum helps SGD avoid getting stuck in narrow valleys and is popular for training neural networks. Unfortunately, convergence for momentum is not as well understood. An upper bound for a convex, nonsmooth objective is given by Yang, Lin, and Li (2016) in the form of:

$$\mathbb{E}[f(\bar{x}_k) - f(x^*)] \leq \frac{\beta\epsilon_0}{(1-\beta)(k+1)} + \frac{(1-\beta)(\epsilon_0^x)^2}{2C\sqrt{(k+1)}} + \frac{C(L^2 + \delta^2)}{2(1-\beta)\sqrt{k+1}}$$

Note here that the error is given in terms of the average of the iterate $\bar{x}_k = 1/k \sum_{i=1}^{k} x_i$. For problems in this class the optimal convergence rate is $O(1/\sqrt{k})$, which this algorithm achieves.

## 2.3.5 Nesterov's Accelerated Gradient Descent

Nesterov's accelerated gradient descent (NAGD) algorithm for deterministic settings has been shown to be optimal for a variety of problem assumptions. For example, in the case where the objective is smooth and strongly convex, NAGD achieves the lower complexity bound, unlike standard gradient descent (Nesterov, 2004). Currently, there has not been a lot of attention given to NAGD in the stochastic setting (though, see Yang et al., 2016). We would like to extend NAGD to several problem settings in a stochastic context. Additionally, we would like to incorporate adaptive sampling (using varying batch sizes) into a stochastic NAGD. Adaptive sampling has shown promise, yet has not received a lot of attention.

The development of a more-efficient SGD algorithm would reduce uncertainty in the training of ML models at a faster rate than current algorithms. This is especially important for online learning, where it is crucial that algorithms adapt efficiently to newly observed data in the field.

## 2.3.6 Generalized Linear Models

The first and simplest choice of estimator function class is $\mathcal{F} = \mathbb{R}^p$. In this case, the estimator is a generalized linear model (GLM): $\hat{\mathbf{y}}(\mathbf{x}) = \mathbf{w}^T\mathbf{x}$ for some parameter vector $\mathbf{w} \in \mathbb{R}^p$ (Nelder & Baker, 1972). In this case optimizing the statistical loss is the stochastic convex optimization problem, stated as:

$$\min_{\mathbf{w} \in \mathbb{R}^p} \mathbb{E}_{\mathbf{x},\mathbf{y}}[\ell(\mathbf{w}^T\mathbf{x}, \mathbf{y})] \tag{2.3}$$

Observe that to optimize Eq. (2.3), assuming a closed-form solution is unavailable, a gradient descent or Newton's method must be used (Boyd & Vanderberghe, 2004). However, either method requires computing the gradient of $L(\mathbf{w}) := \mathbb{E}_{\mathbf{x},\mathbf{y}}[\ell(\mathbf{w}^T\mathbf{x}, \mathbf{y})]$, which requires infinitely many realizations $(\mathbf{x}_n, \mathbf{y}_n)$ of the random pair $(\mathbf{x}, \mathbf{y})$, and thus has infinite complexity. This computational bottleneck has been resolved through the development of stochastic approximation (SA) methods (Bottou, 1998 a; Robbins & Monro, 1951), which operate on subsets of data examples per step. The most common SA method is the SGD, which involves descending along the stochastic gradient $\nabla_\mathbf{w}\ell(\mathbf{w}^T\mathbf{x}_t, \mathbf{y}_t)$ rather than the true gradient at each step:

$$\mathbf{w}_{t+1} = \mathbf{w}_t - \eta_t \nabla_\mathbf{w}\ell(\mathbf{w}_t^T\mathbf{x}_t, \mathbf{y}_t) \tag{2.4}$$

Use of SGD (Eq. 2.4) is prevalent due to its simplicity, ease of use, and the fact that it converges to the minimizer of Eq. (2.3) almost certainly, and in expectation at a $\mathcal{O}(1/\sqrt{t})$ rate when $L(\mathbf{w})$ is convex and a sublinearly $\mathcal{O}(1/t)$ when it is strongly convex. Efforts to improve the mean convergence rate to $\mathcal{O}(1/t^2)$ through the use of Nesterov acceleration (Nemirovski, Juditsky, Lan, & Shapiro, 2009) have also been developed, whose updates are given as:

$$\begin{aligned} \mathbf{w}_{t+1} &= \mathbf{v}_t - \eta_t \nabla_\mathbf{w}\ell(\mathbf{v}_t^T\mathbf{x}_t, \mathbf{y}_t) \\ \mathbf{v}_{t+1} &= (1 - \gamma_t)\mathbf{w}_{t+1} + \gamma_t \mathbf{w}_t \end{aligned} \tag{2.5}$$

A plethora of tools have been proposed specifically to minimize the empirical risk (sample size $N$ is finite) in the case of GLMs, which achieve even faster *linear* or superlinear convergence rates. These methods are either based on reducing the variance of the SA (data-subsampling) error of the stochastic gradient (Defazio, Bach, & Lacoste-Julien, 2014; Johnson & Zhang, 2013; Schmidt, Roux, & Bach, 2013) or by using approximate second-order (Hessian) information (Goldfarb, 1970; Shanno & Phua, 1976). This thread has culminated in the fact that quasi-Newton methods (Mokhtari, Gürbüzbalaban, & Ribeiro, 2016) outperform variance reduction methods (Hu, Pan, & Kwok, 2009) for finite-sum minimization when $N$ is large scale. For specifics on stochastic quasi-Newton updates, see Mokhtari and Ribeiro (2015) and Byrd, Hansen, Nocedal, and Singer (2016). However, as $N \to \infty$, the analysis that yields linear or superlinear learning rates breaks down, and the best one can hope for is Nesterov's $\mathcal{O}(1/t^2)$ rate (Nemirovski et al., 2009).

### 2.3.7 Learning Feature Representations for Inference

Transformations of data domains have become widely used in the past decades, due to their ability to extract useful information from input signals as a precursor to solving statistical inference problems. For instance, if the signal dimension is very large, dimensionality reduction is of interest, which may be approached with principal component analysis (Jolliffe, 1986). If instead one would like to conduct multiresolution analysis, wavelets (Mallat, 2008) may be more appropriate. These techniques, which also include a $k$-nearest neighbor, are known as unsupervised or signal representation learning (Murphy, 2012). Recently, methods based on learned representations, rather than those fixed a priori, have gained traction in pattern recognition (Elad & Aharon, 2006; Mairal, Elad, & Sapiro, 2008). A special case of data-driven representation learning is dictionary learning (Mairal, Bach, Ponce, Sapiro, & Zisserman, 2008), the focus of this section.

Here we address finding a dictionary (signal encoding) that is well adapted to a specific inference task (Mairal, Bach, & Ponce, 2012). To do so, denote the coding $\alpha(\tilde{\mathbf{D}};\mathbf{x}) \in \mathbb{R}^k$ as a feature representation of the signal $\mathbf{x}_t$ with respect to some dictionary matrix $\tilde{\mathbf{D}} \in \mathbb{R}^{p \times k}$. Typically, $\alpha(\tilde{\mathbf{D}};\mathbf{x})$ is chosen as the solution to a lasso regression or approximate solution to an $\ell_0$ constrained problem that minimizes some criterion of distance between $\mathbf{D}^T\alpha$ and $\mathbf{x}$ to incentivize codes to be sparse. Further introduce the classifier $\mathbf{w} \in \mathbb{R}^k$ that is used to predict target variable $\mathbf{y}_t$ when given the signal encoding $\alpha(\tilde{\mathbf{D}};\mathbf{x})$. The merit of the classifier $\mathbf{w} \in \mathcal{W} \subset \mathbb{R}^k$ is measured by the smooth loss function

$\ell(\boldsymbol{\alpha}^*(\mathbf{w}^T\boldsymbol{\alpha}(\tilde{\mathbf{D}};\mathbf{x});(\mathbf{x}_t,\mathbf{y}_t)))$ that captures how well the classifier $\mathbf{w}$ may predict $\mathbf{y}_t$ when given the coding $\boldsymbol{\alpha}(\tilde{\mathbf{D}};\mathbf{x}_t)$. Note that $\alpha$ is computed using the dictionary $\tilde{\mathbf{D}}$. The task-driven dictionary learning problem is formulated as the joint determination of the dictionary $\tilde{\mathbf{D}}\in\mathcal{D}$ and classifier $\mathbf{w}\in\mathcal{W}\subset\mathbb{R}^k$ that minimize the cost $\ell(\boldsymbol{\alpha}(\tilde{\mathbf{D}};\mathbf{x}_t),\mathbf{w};(\mathbf{x}_t,\mathbf{y}_t))$ averaged over the training set:

$$(\tilde{\mathbf{D}}^*,\mathbf{w}^*) := \underset{\tilde{\mathbf{D}}\in\mathcal{D},\mathbf{w}\in\mathcal{W}}{\text{argmin}}\ \mathbb{E}_{\mathbf{x},\mathbf{y}}[\ell(\mathbf{w}^T\boldsymbol{\alpha}(\tilde{\mathbf{D}};\mathbf{x}_t);(\mathbf{x}_t,\mathbf{y}_t))] \qquad (2.6)$$

In Eq. (2.6) we specify the estimator $\hat{\mathbf{y}}(\mathbf{x})=\mathbf{w}^T\boldsymbol{\alpha}^*(\tilde{\mathbf{D}};\mathbf{x})$, which parameterizes the function class $\mathcal{F}$ as the product set $\mathcal{W}\times\mathcal{D}$. For a given dictionary $\tilde{\mathbf{D}}$ and signal sample $\mathbf{x}_t$, we compute the code $\boldsymbol{\alpha}^*(\tilde{\mathbf{D}};\mathbf{x}_t)$ as per some lasso regression problem, for instance, and then predict $\mathbf{y}_t$ using $\mathbf{w}$, and measure the prediction error with the loss function $\ell(\mathbf{w}^T\boldsymbol{\alpha}(\tilde{\mathbf{D}};\mathbf{x}_t),;(\mathbf{x}_t,\mathbf{y}_t))$. The optimal pair $(\tilde{\mathbf{D}}^*,\mathbf{w}^*)$ in Eq. (2.6) is the one that minimizes the cost averaged over the given sample pairs $(\mathbf{x}_t,\mathbf{y}_t)$. Observe that $\boldsymbol{\alpha}^*(\tilde{\mathbf{D}};\mathbf{x}_t)$ is not a variable in the optimization in Eq. (2.6) but a mapping for an implicit dependence of the loss on the dictionary $\tilde{\mathbf{D}}$. The optimization problem in Eq. (2.6) is not assumed to be convex—this would be restrictive because the dependence of $\ell$ on $\tilde{\mathbf{D}}$ is, partly, through the mapping $\boldsymbol{\alpha}^*(\tilde{\mathbf{D}};\mathbf{x}_t)$ defined by some sparse-coding procedure. In general, only local minima of Eq. (2.6) can be found. This formulation has, nonetheless, been successful in solving practical pattern recognition tasks in vision (Mairal et al., 2012) and robotics (Koppel, Fink, Warnell, Stump, & Ribeiro, 2016).

The lack of convexity of Eq. (2.6) means that attaining statistical consistency for supervised dictionary learning methods is much more challenging than for GLMs. To this end, the prevalence of nonconvex stochastic programs arising from statistical learning based on nonlinear transformations of the feature space $\mathcal{X}$ has led to a renewed interest in nonconvex optimization methods through applying convex techniques to nonconvex settings (Boyd & Vanderberghe, 2004). This constitutes a form of simulated annealing (Bertsimas & Tsitsiklis, 1993) with successive convex approximation (Facchinei, Scutari, & Sagratella, 2015). A compelling achievement of this recent surge is the hybrid convex-annealing approach, which has been shown to be capable of finding a global minimizer (Raginsky, Rakhlin, & Telgarsky, 2017). However, the use of these methods for addressing the training of estimators defined by nonconvex stochastic programs requires far more training examples to obtain convergence than convex problems and requires further demonstration in practice.

## 2.4 UNCERTAINTY QUANTIFICATION IN MACHINE LEARNING

Most standard ML algorithms only give a single output: the predicted value $\hat{y}$. While this is a primary goal of ML, as discussed in Section 2.1, it is important in many scenarios to also have a measure of model confidence. In particular, we would like the model to take into account variability due to new observations being "far" from the data on which the model was trained. This is particularly interesting for tactical application in which the human decision makers rely on the confidence of the predictive model to make actionable decisions. Unfortunately, this area has not been widely developed. We explore two ways of UQ in the context of ML: explicit and implicit uncertainty measures.

By *explicit* measures we mean methods that, in addition to a model's prediction $\hat{y}$, perform a separate computation to determine the model's confidence in that particular point. These methods often measure some kind of distance between a new data point and the training data. New data that are far away from the training data give reason to proceed with caution. A naive way to measure confidence explicitly would be to output an indicator variable that tells whether the new data points fall within the convex hull of the training data. If a point does not fall within the convex hull, the user would have reason to be suspicious of that prediction. More complicated methods can be applied using modern outlier detection theory (model-based methods, proximity-based methods, etc.). In particular, these methods can give more indicative measures of confidence, as opposed to a simple 1 or 0, and are more robust to outliers *within* the training data.

Another approach to UQ is incorporating the uncertainty arising from new data points in the ML model *implicitly*. A natural way of doing this is using a Bayesian approach: we can use a Gaussian process (GP) to model our beliefs about the function that we wish to learn. Predictions have a large variance in regions where little data has been observed, and smaller variance in regions where the observed data are more dense. However, for large, high-dimensional datasets, GPs become difficult to fit. Current methods that approximate GPs in some way that show promise include variational inference methods, dropout neural networks (Das, Roy, & Sambasivan, 2017), and neural network ensembles (Lakshminarayanan, Pritzel, & Blundell, 2017).

We explore the above techniques for UQ in intelligent battlefield systems. We believe that the development of ways to measure UQ could be of great use in areas that use ML or artificial intelligence to make risk-informed decisions, particularly when poor predictions come with a high cost.

## 2.4.1 Gaussian Process Regression

Gaussian process regression (GPR) is a framework for nonlinear, nonparametric, Bayesian inference (Rasmussen, 2004) (kriging; Krige, 1951). GPR is widely used in chemical processing (Kocijan, 2016), robotics (Deisenroth, Fox, & Rasmussen, 2015), and ML (Rasmussen, 2004), among other applications. One of the main drawbacks of GPR is its complexity, which scales cubically $N^3$ with the training sample size $N$ in batch setting.

GPR models the relationship between random variables $\mathbf{x} \in \mathcal{X} \subset \mathbb{R}^p$ and $y \in \mathcal{Y} \subset \mathbb{R}$, that is, $\hat{y} = f(\mathbf{x})$ by function $f(\mathbf{x})$, which should be estimated upon the basis of $N$ training examples $\mathcal{S} = \{\mathbf{x}_n, y_n\}_{n=1}^N$. Unlike in ERM, GPR does not learn this estimator by solving an optimization problem that assesses the quality of its fitness, but instead assumes that this function $f(\mathbf{x})$ follows some particular parameterized family of distributions, in which the parameters need to be estimated (Krige, 1951; Rasmussen, 2004).

In particular, for GPs, a uniform *prior* on the distribution of $\mathbf{f}_\mathcal{S} = [f(\mathbf{x}_n), \ldots, f(\mathbf{x}_N)]$ is placed as a Gaussian distribution, namely, $\mathbf{f}_\mathcal{S} \sim \mathcal{N}(\mathbf{0}, \mathbf{K}_N)$. Here $\mathcal{N}(\boldsymbol{\mu}, \boldsymbol{\Sigma})$ denotes the multivariate Gaussian distribution in $N$ dimensions with mean vector $\boldsymbol{\mu} \in \mathbb{R}^N$ and covariance $\boldsymbol{\Sigma} \in \mathbb{R}^{N \times N}$. In GPR, the covariance $\mathbf{K}_N = [\kappa(\mathbf{x}_m, \mathbf{x}_n)]_{m,n=1}^{N,N}$ is constructed from a distance-like kernel function $\kappa : \mathcal{X} \times \mathcal{X} \to \mathbb{R}$ defined over the product set of the feature space. The kernel expresses some prior about how to measure distance between points, a common example of which is itself the Gaussian, $[\mathbf{K}_N]_{mn} = \kappa(\mathbf{x}_m, \mathbf{x}_n) = \exp\{-\|\mathbf{x}_m - \mathbf{x}_n\|^2 / c^2\}$ with bandwidth hyperparameter $c$.

In standard GPR, a Gaussian prior on the noise will be placed that corrupts $\mathbf{f}_\mathcal{S}$ to form the observation vector $\mathbf{y} = [y_1, \ldots, y_N]$, that is, $\mathbb{P}(\mathbf{y} \mid \mathbf{f}_\mathcal{S}) = \mathcal{N}(\mathbf{f}_\mathcal{S}, \sigma^2 \mathbf{I})$ where $\sigma^2$ is some variance parameter. The prior can be integrated on $\mathbf{f}_\mathcal{S}$ to obtain the marginal likelihood for $\mathbf{y}$ as:

$$\mathbb{P}(\mathbf{y} \mid \mathcal{S}) = \mathcal{N}(\mathbf{0}, \mathbf{K}_N + \sigma^2 \mathbf{I}) \tag{2.7}$$

Upon receiving a new data point $\mathbf{x}_{N+1}$, a Bayesian inference $\hat{y}_{N+1}$ can be made, not by simply setting a point estimate $f(\mathbf{x}_{N+1}) = \hat{y}_{N+1}$. Instead, the entire *posterior* distribution can be formulated for $y_{N+1}$ as:

$$\mathbb{P}(y_{N+1} \mid \mathcal{S} \cup \mathbf{x}_{N+1}) = \mathcal{N}(\boldsymbol{\mu}_{N+1 \mid \mathcal{S}}, \boldsymbol{\Sigma}_{N+1 \mid \mathcal{S}})$$

$$\boldsymbol{\mu}_{N+1 \mid \mathcal{S}} = \mathbf{k}_{\mathcal{S}}(\mathbf{x}_{N+1})[\mathbf{K}_N + \sigma^2 \mathbf{I}]^{-1} \mathbf{y}_N$$

$$\boldsymbol{\Sigma}_{N+1 \mid \mathcal{S}} = \kappa(\mathbf{x}_{N+1}, \mathbf{x}_{N+1}) - \kappa(\mathbf{x}_{N+1}, \mathbf{x}_{N+1}) \mathbf{k}_{\mathcal{S}}(\mathbf{x}_{N+1})$$

$$[\mathbf{K}_N + \sigma^2 \mathbf{I}]^{-1} \mathbf{k}_{\mathcal{S}} + \sigma^2 \qquad (2.8)$$

While this approach to sequential Bayesian inference provides a powerful framework for fitting a mean and covariance envelope around observed data, it requires for each $N$ the computation of $\boldsymbol{\mu}_{N+1 \mid \mathcal{S}}$ and $\boldsymbol{\Sigma}_{N+1 \mid \mathcal{S}}$, which crucially depend on computing the inverse of the kernel matrix $\mathbf{K}_N$ every time a new data point arrives. It is well known that matrix inversion has cubic complexity $\mathcal{O}(N^3)$ in the variable dimension $N$, which may be reduced through use of Cholesky factorization (Foster et al., 2009) or subspace projections (Banerjee, Dunson, & Tokdar, 2012) combined with various compression criteria such as information gain (Seeger, Williams, & Lawrence, 2003), mean square error (Smola & Bartlett, 2001), integral approximation for Nyström sampling (Williams & Seeger, 2001), probabilistic criteria (Bauer, van der Wilk, & Rasmussen, 2016; McIntire, Ratner, & Ermon, 2016), and many others (Bui, Nguyen, & Turner, 2017).

## 2.4.2 Neural Network

While the mathematical formulation of convolutional neural networks and their variants have been around for decades (Haykin, 1998), their use has only become widespread in recent years as computing power and data pervasiveness has made them not impossible to train. Since the landmark work (Krizhevsky, Sutskever, & Hinton, 2012) demonstrated their ability to solve image recognition tasks on much larger scales than previously addressable, they have permeated many fields, such as speech (Graves, Mohamed, & Hinton, 2013), text (Jaderberg, Simonyan, Vedaldi, & Zisserman, 2016), and control (Lillicrap et al., 2015). An estimator function class $\mathcal{F}$ can be defined by the composition of many functions of the form $g_k(\mathbf{x}) = \mathbf{w}_k \sigma_k(\mathbf{x})$. $\sigma_k$ is a nonlinear "activation function," which can be, for example, a rectified linear unit $\sigma_k(a) = \max(a, 0)$, a sigmoid $\sigma_k(a) = 1/(1 + e^a)$, or a hyperbolic tangent $\sigma_k(a) = (1 - e^{-2a})/(1 + e^{-2a})$. Specifically, for a $K$-layer convolutional neural network, the estimator is given as:

$$\hat{\mathbf{y}}(\mathbf{x}) = g_1 \circ g_2 \circ \cdots g_K(\mathbf{x}) \tag{2.9}$$

and typically one tries to make the distance between the target variable and the estimator small by minimizing their quadratic distance:

$$\min_{\mathbf{w}_1, \ldots, \mathbf{w}_K} \mathbb{E}_{\mathbf{x}, \mathbf{y}} (\mathbf{y} - g_1 \circ g_2 \circ \cdots g_K(\mathbf{x}))^2 \tag{2.10}$$

where each $\mathbf{w}_k$ is a vector whose length depends on the number of "neurons" at each layer of the network. This operation may be thought of as an iterated generalization of a convolutional filter. Additional complexities can be added at each layer, such as aggregating values output for the activation functions by their maximum (max pooling) or average. But the training procedure is similar: minimize a variant of the highly nonconvex, high-dimensional stochastic program (Eq. 2.10). Due to their high dimensionality, efforts to modify nonconvex stochastic optimization algorithms to be amenable to parallel computing architectures have gained salience in recent years. An active area of research is the interplay between parallel stochastic algorithms and scientific computing to minimize the clock time required for training neural networks—see Lian, Huang, Li, and Liu (2015), Mokhtari, Koppel, Scutari, and Ribeiro (2017), and Scardapane and Di Lorenzo (2017). Thus far, efforts have been restricted to attaining computational speedup by parallelization to convergence at a stationary point, although some preliminary efforts to escape saddle points and ensure convergence to a local minimizer have also recently appeared (Lee, Simchowitz, Jordan, & Recht, 2016); these modify convex optimization techniques, for instance, by replacing indefinite Hessians with positive definite approximate Hessians (Paternain, Mokhtari, & Ribeiro, 2017).

## 2.4.3 Uncertainty Quantification in Deep Neural Network

In this section we discuss UQ in neural networks through Bayesian methods, more specifically, posterior sampling. Hamiltonian Monte Carlo (HMC) is the best current approach to perform posterior sampling in neural networks. HMC is the foundation from which all other existing approaches are derived. HMC is an MCMC method (Brooks, Gelman, Jones, & Meng, 2011) that has been a popular tool in the ML literature to sample from complex probability distributions when random walk-based first-order Langevin samplers do not exhibit the desired convergence behaviors. Standard HMC approaches are designed to propose candidate samplers for a Metropolis-Hastings-based acceptance scheme with high acceptance probabilities; since calculation of these M-H ratios necessitates a pass through the entire dataset, scalability of HMC-based algorithms has been limited. This has been addressed recently with the development of stochastic approaches, inspired by the now ubiquitous SGD-based ERM algorithms, where we omit the M-H correction step and calculate the Hamiltonian gradients over random mini-batches of the training data (Chen, Fox, & Guestrin, 2014; Welling & Teh, 2011). Further improvements to these approaches have been done by incorporating Riemann manifold techniques to learn the critically important Hamiltonian mass matrices, both in the standard HMC (Girolami & Calderhead, 2011) and stochastic (Ma, Chen, & Fox, 2015; Roychowdhury, Kulis, & Parthasarathy, 2016) settings. These Riemannian approaches have been shown to noticeably improve the acceptance probabilities of samples following the methods of those proposed by Girolami and Calderhead (2011), and dramatically improve the convergence rates in the stochastic formulations as well (Roychowdhury et al., 2016).

Preliminary experiments show that HMC does not work well in practice. Thus one can identify two challenges with posterior sampling using HMC. First, HMC still has a hard time finding the different modes of the distribution (i.e., if it can escape metastable regions of the HMC Markov chain). Second, as stated earlier, the massive dimensionality of deep neural networks make the most of the posterior probability mass that resides in models with poor classification accuracy. Fig. 2.2 shows sampled neural network models as a function of HMC steps for CIFAR100 image classification task (using a LeNet CNN architecture). In as few as 100 HMC steps, the posterior-sampled models are significantly worse than the best models in both training and validation accuracies. Thus HMC posterior sampling is

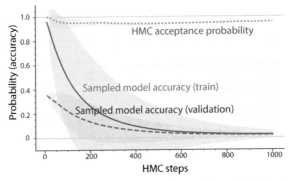

**Fig. 2.2** HMC samples produce inaccurate neural network models after a few HMC steps in the CIFAR100 image classification task.

impractical for deep neural networks, even as the HMC acceptance probability is high throughout the experiment.

It is an open avenue of research to explore a few mode exploration fixes. Here, traditional MCMC methods can be used, such as annealing and annealing importance sampling. Less traditional methods are also explored, such as stochastic initialization and model perturbation.

Regarding the important challenge of posterior sampling accurate models in an given posterior mode, mini-batch stochastic gradient Langevin dynamics (SGLD) (Welling & Teh, 2011) is increasingly credited to being a practical Bayesian method to train neural networks to find good generalization regions (Chaudhari et al., 2017), and it may help in improving parallel SGD algorithms (Chaudhari et al., 2017). The connection between SGLD and SGD has been explored in Mandt, Hoffman, and Blei (2017) for posterior sampling in small regions around a locally optimal solution. To make this procedure a legitimate posterior sampling approach, we explore the use of Chaudhari et al.'s (2017) methods to smooth out local minima and significantly extend the reach of Mandt et al.'s (2017) posterior sampling approach.

This smoothing out has connections to Riemannian curvature methods to explore the energy function in the parameter (weight) space (Poole, Lahiri, Raghu, Sohl-Dickstein, & Ganguli, 2016). The Hessian, which is a diffusion curvature, is used by Fawzi, Moosavi-Dezfooli, Frossard, and Soatto (2017) as a measure of curvature to empirically explore the energy function of learned model with regard to examples (the curvature with regard to the input space, rather than the parameter space). This approach is also related to the implicit regularization arguments of Neyshabur, Tomioka, Salakhutdinov, and Srebro (2017).

There is a need to develop an alternative SGD-type method for accurate posterior sampling of deep neural network models that is capable of giving the all-important UQ in the decision-making problem in C3I systems. Not surprisingly a system that correctly quantifies the probability that a suggested decision is incorrect inspires more confidence than a system that incorrectly believes itself to always be correct; the latter is a common ailment in deep neural networks. Moreover, a general practical Bayesian neural network method would help provide robustness against adversarial attacks (as the attacker needs to attack a family of models, rather than a single model), reduce generalization error via posterior-sampled ensembles, and provide better quantification of classification accuracy and root mean square error (RMSE).

## 2.5 ADVERSARIAL LEARNING IN DNN

Unfortunately these models have been shown to be very brittle and vulnerable to specially crafted adversarial perturbations to examples: given an input $x$ and any target classification $t$, it is possible to find a new input $x'$ that is similar to $x$ but classified as $t$. These adversarial examples often appear almost indistinguishable from natural data to human perception and are, as yet, incorrectly classified by the neural network. Recent results have shown that accuracy of neural networks can be reduced from close to 100% to below 5% using adversarial examples. This creates a significant challenge in deploying these deep learning models in security-critical domains where adversarial activity is intrinsic, such as IoBT, cyber networks, and surveillance. The use of neural networks in computer vision and speech recognition has brought these models into the center of security-critical systems where authentication depends on these machine-learned models. How do we ensure that adversaries in these domains do not exploit the limitations of ML models to go undetected or trigger an unintended outcome?

Multiple methods have been proposed in literature to generate adversarial examples as well as defend against adversarial examples. Adversarial example-generation methods include both white-box and black-box attacks on neural networks (Goodfellow, Shlens, & Szegedy, 2014; Papernot et al., 2017; Papernot, McDaniel, Jha, et al., 2016; Szegedy et al., 2013), targeting feed-forward classification networks (Carlini & Wagner, 2016), generative networks (Kos, Fischer, & Song, 2017), and recurrent neural networks (Papernot, McDaniel, Swami, & Harang, 2016). These methods leverage gradient-based optimization for normal examples to discover perturbations that lead to misprediction—the techniques differ in defining the neighborhood in which perturbation is permitted and the loss function used to guide the search. For example, one of the earliest attacks (Goodfellow et al., 2014) used a fast sign gradient method (FGMS) that looks for a similar image $x'$ in the $L^\infty$ neighborhood of $x$. Given a loss function $Loss(x, l)$ specifying the cost of classifying the point $x$ as label $l$, the adversarial example $x'$ is calculated as:

$$x' = x + \epsilon \cdot sign(\nabla_x Loss(x, l_x))$$

FGMS was improved to an iterative gradient sign approach (IGSM) in Kurakin, Goodfellow, and Bengio (2016) by using a finer iterative optimization strategy, where the attack performs FGMS with a smaller step-width $\alpha$ and clips the updated result so that the image stays within the $\epsilon$ boundary of $x$. In this approach, the $i$th iteration computes the following:

$$x'_{i+1} = clip_{\epsilon,x}(x'_i + \alpha \cdot sign(\nabla_x Loss(x, l_x)))$$

In contrast to FGSM and IGSM, DeepFool (Moosavi-Dezfooli, Fawzi, & Frossard, 2016) attempts to find a perturbed image $x'$ from a normal image $x$ by finding the closest decision boundary and crossing it. In practice, Deep-Fool relies on local linearized approximation of the decision boundary. Another attack method that has received a lot of attention is the Carlini attack, which relies on finding a perturbation that minimizes change as well as the hinge loss on the logits (presoftmax classification result vector). The attack is generated by solving the following optimization problem:

$$\min_{\delta} [\| \delta \|_2 + c \cdot \max (Z(x')_{l_x} - max Z(x')_i : i \neq l_x, -\kappa)]$$

where $Z$ denotes the logits, $l_x$ is the ground-truth label, $\kappa$ is the confidence (the raising of which will force the search for larger perturbations), and $c$ is a hyperparameter that balances the perturbation and the hinge loss. Another attack method is projected gradient method (PGM) proposed in Madry, Makelov, Schmidt, Tsipras, and Vladu (2017). PGD attempts to solve this constrained optimization problem:

$$\max_{\|x^{adv}-x\|_\infty \leq \epsilon} Loss(x^{adv}, l_x)$$

where $S$ is the constraint on the allowed perturbation, usually given as bound $\epsilon$ on the norm, and $l_x$ is the ground-truth label of $x$. Projected gradient descent is used to solve this constrained optimization problem by restarting PGD from several points in the $l_\infty$ balls around the data points $x$. This gradient descent increases the loss function $Loss$ in a fairly consistent way before reaching a plateau with a fairly well-concentrated distribution and the achieved maximum value is considerably higher than that of a random point in the dataset. In this chapter, we focus on this PGD attack because it is shown to be a universal first-order adversary (Madry et al., 2017), that is, developing detection capability or resilience against PGD also implies defense against many other first-order attacks.

Defense of neural networks against adversarial examples is more difficult compared to generating attacks. Madry et al. (2017) propose a generic saddle point formulation, where $\mathcal{D}$ is the underlying training data distribution and $Loss(\theta, x, l_x)$ is a loss function at data point $x$ with ground-truth label $l_x$ for a model with parameter $\theta$:

$$\min_{\theta} E_{(x,y) \sim \mathcal{D}} \left[ \max_{\|x^{adv}-x\|_\infty \leq \epsilon} Loss(\theta, x^{adv}, l_x) \right]$$

This formulation uses robust optimization over the expected loss for worst-case adversarial perturbation for the training data. The internal maximization corresponds to finding adversarial examples and can be approximated using IGSM (Kurakin et al., 2016). This approach falls into a category of defenses that use *adversarial training* (Shaham, Yamada, & Negahban, 2015). Instead of training with only adversarial examples, using a mixture of normal and adversarial examples in the training set has been found to be more effective (Moosavi-Dezfooli et al., 2016; Szegedy et al., 2013). Another alternative is to augment the learning objective with a regularizer term corresponding to the adversarial inputs (Goodfellow et al., 2014). More recently, logit pairing has been shown to be an effective approximation of adversarial regularization (Kannan, Kurakin, & Goodfellow, 2018).

Another category of defense against adversarial attacks on neural networks are defensive distillation methods (Papernot, McDaniel, Jha, et al., 2016). These methods modify the training process of neural networks to make it difficult to launch gradient-based attacks directly on the network. The key idea is to use distillation training technique (Hinton, Vinyals, & Dean, 2015) and hide the gradient between the presoftmax layer and the softmax outputs. Carlini and Wagner (2016) found methods to break this defense by changing the loss function, calculating gradient directly from presoftmax layer and transferring attack from an easy-to-attack network to a distilled network. More recently, Athalye, Carlini, and Wagner (2018) showed that it is possible to bypass several defenses proposed for the white-box setting (Fig. 2.3).

## 2.6 SUMMARY AND CONCLUSION

This chapter provided an overview of classical and modern statistical-learning theory, and of how numerical optimization can be used to solve the corresponding mathematical problems with an emphasis on UQ. We discussed how ML and artificial intelligence are the fundamental algorithmic building blocks of IoBT to address the decision-making problem that arises in the underlying control, communication, and networking within the IoBT infrastructure in addition to the inevitable part of almost all military-specific applications developed over IoBT. We studied UQ for ML and artificial intelligence within the context of IoBT, which is critical to provide an accurate measure of error over the output in addition to precise output in military settings. We studied how to quantify *and* minimize the uncertainty with respect to training an ML algorithm in Section 2.4,

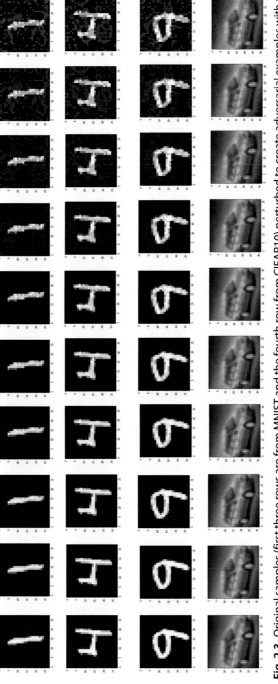

**Fig. 2.3** Original samples (first three rows are from MNIST and the fourth row from CIFAR10) perturbed to create adversarial examples with an increasing (*left* to *right*) norm bound in the PPM implemented within CleverHans system (Papernot, Carlini, et al., 2016).

which led to a broad discussion on stochastic optimization. Next, we discussed UQ in ML, specifically, how to develop ways for a model to *know what it doesn't know*. In other words, we want the model to be especially cautious of data that is different from that on which it was trained. Section 2.5 explored the recent emerging trends on adversarial learning, which is a new application of UQ in ML in IoBT in an offensive and defensive capacity.

## REFERENCES

Athalye, A., Carlini, N., & Wagner, D. (2018). *Obfuscated gradients give a false sense of security: Circumventing defenses to adversarial examples.* arXiv preprint arXiv:1802.00420.

Banerjee, A., Dunson, D. B., & Tokdar, S. T. (2012). Efficient Gaussian process regression for large datasets. *Biometrika, 100*(1), 75–89.

Bauer, M., van der Wilk, M., & Rasmussen, C. E. (2016). Understanding probabilistic sparse Gaussian process approximations. In *Advances in neural information processing systems* (pp. 1533–1541).

Bertsimas, D., & Tsitsiklis, J. (1993). Simulated annealing. *Statistical Science, 8*(1), 10–15.

Bottou, L. (1998a). Online algorithms and stochastic approximations. D. Saad (Ed.), *Online learning and neural networks.* Cambridge: Cambridge University Press.

Bottou, L. (1998b). Online learning and stochastic approximations. *On-Line Learning in Neural Networks, 17*(9), 142.

Bottou, L., & Cun, Y. L. (2004). Large scale online learning. In *Advances in neural information processing systems* (pp. 217–224).

Bottou, L., Curtis, F. E., & Nocedal, J. (2016). *Optimization methods for large-scale machine learning.* arXiv:1606.04838.

Boyd, S., & Vanderberghe, L. (2004). *Convex programming.* New York: Wiley.

Brooks, S., Gelman, A., Jones, G., & Meng, X. -L. (2011). *Handbook of Markov chain Monte Carlo.* London: CRC Press.

Bui, T. D., Nguyen, C., & Turner, R. E. (2017). Streaming sparse Gaussian process approximations. In *Advances in neural information processing systems* (pp. 3301–3309).

Byrd, R. H., Hansen, S. L., Nocedal, J., & Singer, Y. (2016). A stochastic quasi-Newton method for large-scale optimization. *SIAM Journal on Optimization, 26*(2), 1008–1031.

Carlini, N., & Wagner, D. (2016). *Towards evaluating the robustness of neural networks.* arXiv preprint arXiv:1608.04644.

Chaudhari, P., Baldassi, C., Zecchina, R., Soatto, S., Talwalkar, A., & Oberman, A. (2017). *Parle: Parallelizing stochastic gradient descent.* arXiv:1707.00424.

Chen, T., Fox, E., & Guestrin, C. (2014). Stochastic gradient Hamiltonian Monte Carlo. In *International conference on machine learning* (pp. 1683–1691).

Das, S., Roy, S., & Sambasivan, R. (2017). *Dropout as a Bayesian approximation: Representing model uncertainty in deep learning.* arXiv:1509.05142.

Defazio, A., Bach, F., & Lacoste-Julien, S. (2014). Saga: A fast incremental gradient method with support for non-strongly convex composite objectives. In *Advances in neural information processing systems* (pp. 1646–1654).

Deisenroth, M. P., Fox, D., & Rasmussen, C. E. (2015). Gaussian processes for data-efficient learning in robotics and control. *IEEE Transactions on Pattern Analysis and Machine Intelligence, 37*(2), 408–423.

Elad, M., & Aharon, M. (2006). Image denoising via sparse and redundant representations over learned dictionaries. *IEEE Transactions on Image Processing, 15*(12), 3736–3745. https://doi.org/10.1109/TIP.2006.881969.

Facchinei, F., Scutari, G., & Sagratella, S. (2015). Parallel selective algorithms for nonconvex big data optimization. *IEEE Transactions on Signal Processing, 63*(7), 1874–1889.

Fawzi, A., Moosavi-Dezfooli, S. -M., Frossard, P., & Soatto, S. (2017). *Classification regions of deep neural networks*. arXiv preprint arXiv:1705.09552.

Foster, L., Waagen, A., Aijaz, N., Hurley, M., Luis, A., Rinsky, J., et al. (2009). Stable and efficient Gaussian process calculations. *Journal of Machine Learning Research, 10*(Apr), 857–882.

Girolami, M., & Calderhead, B. (2011). Riemann manifold Langevin and Hamiltonian Monte Carlo methods. *Journal of the Royal Statistical Society: Series B (Statistical Methodology), 73*(2), 123–214.

Goldfarb, D. (1970). A family of variable metric updates derived by variational means. *Mathematics of Computation, 24*(109), 23–26.

Goodfellow, I. J., Shlens, J., & Szegedy, C. (2014). *Explaining and harnessing adversarial examples*. arXiv preprint arXiv:1412.6572.

Graves, A., Mohamed, A. -R., & Hinton, G. (2013). Speech recognition with deep recurrent neural networks. In *2013 IEEE international conference on acoustics, speech and signal processing (ICASSP)* (pp. 6645–6649).

Hastie, T., Tibshirani, R., & Friedman, J. (2009). *The elements of statistical learning*. New York: Springer-Verlag.

Haykin, S. (1998). *Neural networks: A comprehensive foundation* (2nd ed). NJ: Prentice Hall.

Hinton, G., Vinyals, O., & Dean, J. (2015). *Distilling the knowledge in a neural network*. arXiv preprint arXiv:1503.02531.

Hu, C., Pan, W., & Kwok, J. T. (2009). Accelerated gradient methods for stochastic optimization and online learning. In *Advances in neural information processing systems* (pp. 781–789).

Jaderberg, M., Simonyan, K., Vedaldi, A., & Zisserman, A. (2016). Reading text in the wild with convolutional neural networks. *International Journal of Computer Vision, 116*(1), 1–20.

Johnson, R., & Zhang, T. (2013). Accelerating stochastic gradient descent using predictive variance reduction. In *Advances in neural information processing systems* (pp. 315–323).

Jolliffe, I. T. (1986). *Principal component analysis*. New York: Springer-Verlag.

Kannan, H., Kurakin, A., & Goodfellow, I. (2018). *Adversarial logit pairing*. arXiv preprint arXiv:1803.06373.

Kocijan, J. (2016). *Modelling and control of dynamic systems using Gaussian process models*. New York: Springer.

Koppel, A., Fink, J., Warnell, G., Stump, E., & Ribeiro, A. (2016). Online learning for characterizing unknown environments in ground robotic vehicle models. In *2016 IEEE/RSJ international conference on intelligent robots and systems (IROS)* (pp. 626–633).

Kos, J., Fischer, I., & Song, D. (2017). *Adversarial examples for generative models*. arXiv preprint arXiv:1702.06832.

Kott, A., Swami, A., & West, B. J. (2016). The internet of battle things. *Computer, 49*(12), 70–75. https://doi.org/10.1109/MC.2016.355.

Krige, D. G. (1951). A statistical approach to some basic mine valuation problems on the witwatersrand. *Journal of the Southern African Institute of Mining and Metallurgy, 52*(6), 119–139.

Krizhevsky, A., Sutskever, I., & Hinton, G. E. (2012). Imagenet classification with deep convolutional neural networks. In *Advances in neural information processing systems* (pp. 1097–1105).

Kurakin, A., Goodfellow, I., & Bengio, S. (2016). *Adversarial examples in the physical world*. arXiv preprint arXiv:1607.02533.

Lakshminarayanan, B., Pritzel, A., & Blundell, C. (2017). Simple and scalable predictive uncertainty estimation using deep ensembles. *NIPS*, pp. 1–12 (Supplemental material, p. 13).

Lee, J. D., Simchowitz, M., Jordan, M. I., & Recht, B. (2016). Gradient descent only converges to minimizers. In *Conference on learning theory* (pp. 1246–1257).

Lian, X., Huang, Y., Li, Y., & Liu, J. (2015). Asynchronous parallel stochastic gradient for nonconvex optimization. In *Advances in neural information processing systems* (pp. 2737–2745).

Lillicrap, T. P., Hunt, J. J., Pritzel, A., Heess, N., Erez, T., Tassa, Y., et al. (2015). *Continuous control with deep reinforcement learning*. arXiv preprint arXiv:1509.02971.

Ma, Y. -A., Chen, T., & Fox, E. (2015). A complete recipe for stochastic gradient MCMC. In *Advances in neural information processing systems* (pp. 2917–2925).

Madry, A., Makelov, A., Schmidt, L., Tsipras, D., & Vladu, A. (2017). *Towards deep learning models resistant to adversarial attacks*. arXiv preprint arXiv:1706.06083.

Mairal, J., Bach, F., & Ponce, J. (2012). Task-driven dictionary learning. *IEEE Transactions on Pattern Analysis and Machine Intelligence, 34*(4), 791–804.

Mairal, J., Bach, F., Ponce, J., Sapiro, G., & Zisserman, A. (2008). Supervised dictionary learning. In *Advances in neural information processing systems 21, Proceedings of the twenty-second annual conference on neural information processing systems, Vancouver, British Columbia, Canada, December 8–11, 2008* (pp. 1033–1040).

Mairal, J., Elad, M., & Sapiro, G. (2008). Sparse representation for color image restoration. *Transaction on Image Processing, 17*(1), 53–69.

Mallat, S. (2008). In *A wavelet tour of signal processing: The sparse way* (3rd ed.). London: Academic Press.

Mandt, S., Hoffman, M. D., & Blei, D. M. (2017). Stochastic gradient descent as approximate Bayesian inference. *The Journal of Machine Learning Research, 18*(1), 4873–4907.

McIntire, M., Ratner, D., & Ermon, S. (2016). Sparse Gaussian processes for Bayesian optimization. In *Proceedings of the thirty-second conference on uncertainty in artificial intelligence* (pp. 517–526).

Mokhtari, A., Gürbüzbalaban, M., & Ribeiro, A. (2016). *Surpassing gradient descent provably: A cyclic incremental method with linear convergence rate*. arXiv preprint arXiv:1611.00347.

Mokhtari, A., Koppel, A., Scutari, G., & Ribeiro, A. (2017). Large-scale nonconvex stochastic optimization by doubly stochastic successive convex approximation. In *2017 IEEE international conference on acoustics, speech and signal processing (ICASSP)* (pp. 4701–4705).

Mokhtari, A., & Ribeiro, A. (2015). Global convergence of online limited memory BFGS. *Journal of Machine Learning Research, 16*, 3151–3181.

Moosavi-Dezfooli, S. -M., Fawzi, A., & Frossard, P. (2016). Deepfool: A simple and accurate method to fool deep neural networks. In *Proceedings of the IEEE conference on computer vision and pattern recognition* (pp. 2574–2582).

Murphy, K. (2012). *Machine learning: A probabilistic perspective*. Cambridge, MA: MIT Press.

Nelder, J. A., & Baker, R. J. (1972). Generalized linear models. *Encyclopedia of Statistical Sciences*.

Nemirovski, A., Juditsky, A., Lan, G., & Shapiro, A. (2009). Robust stochastic approximation approach to stochastic programming. *SIAM Journal on optimization, 19*(4), 1574–1609.

Nesterov, Y. (2004). *Introductory lectures on convex optimization*. New York: Springer US.

Neyshabur, B., Tomioka, R., Salakhutdinov, R., & Srebro, N. (2017). *Geometry of optimization and implicit regularization in deep learning*. arXiv preprint arXiv:1705.03071.

Papernot, N., Carlini, N., Goodfellow, I., Feinman, R., Faghri, F., Matyasko, A., et al. (2016). *cleverhans v2. 0.0: An adversarial machine learning library*. arXiv preprint arXiv:1610.00768.

Papernot, N., McDaniel, P., Goodfellow, I., Jha, S., Celik, Z. B., & Swami, A. (2017). Practical black-box attacks against machine learning. In *Proceedings of the 2017 ACM on Asia conference on computer and communications security* (pp. 506–519).

Papernot, N., McDaniel, P., Jha, S., Fredrikson, M., Celik, Z. B., & Swami, A. (2016). The limitations of deep learning in adversarial settings. In *2016 IEEE European symposium on security and privacy (EuroS&P)* (pp. 372–387).

Papernot, N., McDaniel, P., Swami, A., & Harang, R. (2016). Crafting adversarial input sequences for recurrent neural networks. In *Military communications conference, MILCOM 2016–2016 IEEE* (pp. 49–54).

Paternain, S., Mokhtari, A., & Ribeiro, A. (2017). *A second order method for nonconvex optimization.* arXiv preprint arXiv:1707.08028.

Poole, B., Lahiri, S., Raghu, M., Sohl-Dickstein, J., & Ganguli, S. (2016). Exponential expressivity in deep neural networks through transient chaos. In *Advances in neural information processing systems* (pp. 3360–3368).

Raginsky, M., Rakhlin, A., & Telgarsky, M. (2017). *Non-convex learning via stochastic gradient Langevin dynamics: A nonasymptotic analysis.* arXiv preprint arXiv:1702.03849.

Rasmussen, C. E. (2004). Gaussian processes in machine learning. In *Advanced lectures on machine learning* (pp. 63–71). New York: Springer.

Robbins, H., & Monro, S. (1951). A stochastic approximation method. *Annals of Mathematical Statistics, 22*(3), 400–407. https://doi.org/10.1214/aoms/1177729586.

Roychowdhury, A., Kulis, B., & Parthasarathy, S. (2016). Robust Monte Carlo sampling using Riemannian Nosé-Poincaré Hamiltonian dynamics. In *International conference on machine learning* (pp. 2673–2681).

Scardapane, S., & Di Lorenzo, P. (2017). *Stochastic training of neural networks via successive convex approximations.* arXiv preprint arXiv:1706.04769.

Schmidt, M., Roux, N. L., & Bach, F. (2013). *Minimizing finite sums with the stochastic average gradient.* arXiv preprint arXiv:1309.2388.

Seeger, M., Williams, C., & Lawrence, N. (2003). Fast forward selection to speed up sparse Gaussian process regression. *Artificial Intelligence and Statistics, 9*, 1–8 (Issue: EPFL-CONF-161318).

Shaham, U., Yamada, Y., & Negahban, S. (2015). *Understanding adversarial training: Increasing local stability of neural nets through robust optimization.* arXiv preprint arXiv:1511.05432.

Shanno, D. F., & Phua, K. H. (1976). Algorithm 500: Minimization of unconstrained multivariate functions [e4]. *ACM Transactions on Mathematical Software (TOMS), 2*(1), 87–94.

Smola, A. J., & Bartlett, P. L. (2001). Sparse greedy Gaussian process regression. In *Advances in neural information processing systems* (pp. 619–625).

Suri, N., Tortonesi, M., Michaelis, J., Budulas, P., Benincasa, G., Russell, S., et al. (2016). Analyzing the applicability of internet of things to the battlefield environment. In *2016 International conference on military communications and information systems (ICMCIS)* (pp. 1–8). https://doi.org/10.1109/ICMCIS.2016.7496574.

Szegedy, C., Zaremba, W., Sutskever, I., Bruna, J., Erhan, D., Goodfellow, I., & Fergus, R. (2013). *Intriguing properties of neural networks.* arXiv preprint arXiv:1312.6199.

Vapnik, V. (2013). *The nature of statistical learning theory.* New York: Springer Science & Business Media.

Welling, M., & Teh, Y. W. (2011). Bayesian learning via stochastic gradient Langevin dynamics. In *Proceedings of the 28th international conference on machine learning (ICML-11)* (pp. 681–688).

Williams, C. K., & Seeger, M. (2001). Using the Nyström method to speed up kernel machines. In *Advances in neural information processing systems* (pp. 682–688).

Yang, T., Lin, Q., & Li, Z. (2016). *Unified convergence analysis of stochastic momentum methods for convex and non-convex optimization.* arXiv preprint arXiv:1604.03257.

Zheng, D. E., & Carter, W. A. (2015). *Leveraging the internet of things for a more efficient and effective military,* Center for Strategic & International Studies (CSIS), A Report of the CSIS Strategic Technologies Program, Rowman & Littlefield, Lanham, MD.

# CHAPTER 3

# Intelligent Autonomous Things on the Battlefield

**Alexander Kott, Ethan Stump**
U.S. Army Research Laboratory, Adelphi, MD, United States

## 3.1 INTRODUCTION

The Internet of Battle Things (IoBT) is the emerging reality of warfare. A variety of networked intelligent systems—"things"—will continue to proliferate on the battlefield where they will operate with varying degrees of autonomy. Intelligent things will not be a rarity but a ubiquitous presence on the future battlefield (Scharre, 2014).

Most of these intelligent things will not be too dissimilar from the systems we see on today's battlefield, such as unattended ground sensors, guided missiles (especially the fire-and-forget variety) and, of course, unmanned aerial systems (UAVs). They will likely include physical robots ranging from a very small size (such as insect-scale mobile sensors) to large vehicles that can carry troops and supplies. Some will fly; others will crawl, walk or ride. Their functions will be diverse. Sensing (seeing, listening, etc.) the battlefield will be one common function. Numerous small, autonomous sensors can cover the battlefield and provide an overall awareness to warfighters that is reasonably complete and persistent (Fig. 3.1).

Other things might act as defensive devices, for example, autonomous active protection systems (Freedberg, 2016). Finally, there will be munitions that are intended to impose physical or cyber effects on the enemy. These will not be autonomous, instead they will be controlled by human warfighters. This assumes that the combatants of that future battlefield will comply with a ban on offensive autonomous weapons beyond meaningful human control. Although the US Department of Defense already imposes strong restrictions on autonomous and semi-autonomous weapon systems (Hall, 2017), nobody can predict what other countries might decide on this matter.

In addition to physical intelligent things, the battlefield—or at least the cyber domain of the battlefield—will be populated with disembodied cyber

*Artificial Intelligence for the Internet of Everything*
https://doi.org/10.1016/B978-0-12-817636-8.00003-X

**Fig. 3.1** Networked teams of intelligent things and humans will operate in an extremely complex, challenging environment that is unstructured, unstable, rapidly changing, chaotic, rubble-filled, adversarial, and deceptive useful.

robots. These will reside within various computers and networks, and will move and act in cyberspace. Just like physical robots, cyber robots will be employed in a wide range of roles. Some will protect communications and information (Stytz, Lichtblau, & Banks, 2005) or will fact-check, filter, and fuse information for cyber situational awareness (Kott, Wang, & Erbacher, 2014). Others will defend electronic devices from the effects of electronic warfare using actions such as the creation of informational or electromagnetic deceptions or camouflage. Yet others will act as situation analysts and decision advisers to humans or physical robots. In addition to these defensive or advisory roles, cyber robots might also take on more assertive functions, such as executing cyber actions against enemy systems (Fig. 3.2).

In order to be effective in performing these functions, battle things will have to collaborate with each other, and also with human warfighters. This collaboration will require a significant degree of autonomous self-organization and acceptance of a variety of relations between things and humans (e.g., from complete autonomy of an unattended ground sensor to the tight control of certain other systems), and these modes will have to change as needed. Priorities, objectives, and rules of engagement will change rapidly, and intelligent things will have to adjust accordingly (Kott, Swami, & West, 2016).

**Fig. 3.2** Networks of opponents will fight each other with cyber and electromagnetic attacks of great diversity and volume; most such offensive and defensive actions will be performed by autonomous cyber agents.

Clearly, these requirements imply a high degree of intelligence on the part of the things. Particularly important is the necessity to operate in a highly adversarial environment, i.e., an intentionally hostile and not merely randomly dangerous world. The intelligent things will have to constantly think about an intelligent adversary that strategizes to deceive and defeat them. Without this adversarial intelligence, the battle things will not survive long enough to be Fig. 3.1.

## 3.2 THE CHALLENGES OF AUTONOMOUS INTELLIGENCE ON THE BATTLEFIELD

The vision—or rather, the emerging reality—of the battlefield populated by intelligent things portends a multitude of profound challenges. The use of artificial intelligence (AI) for battlefield tasks has been explored on multiple occasions (e.g., Rasch, Kott, & Forbus, 2002), and though it makes things individually and collectively more intelligent, it also makes the battlefield harder to understand and manage. Human warfighters have to face a much more complex, more unpredictable world where things have a mind of their own and perform actions that may appear inexplicable to humans. Direct control of such intelligent things becomes impossible or limited to cases of decisions about whether to take a specific destructive action.

On the other hand, humans complicate the life for intelligent things. Humans and things think differently. Intelligent things, in the foreseeable future, will be challenged in understanding and anticipating human intent, goals, lines of reasoning, and decisions. Humans and things will remain largely opaque to each other and yet, things will be expected to perceive, reason, and act while taking into account the social, cognitive, and physical needs of their human teammates. Furthermore, things will often deal with humans who are experiencing extreme physical and cognitive stress, and may therefore behave differently from what can be assumed from observing humans under more benign conditions.

An intelligent thing will need to deal with a world of astonishing complexity. The sheer number and diversity of things and humans within the IoBT will be enormous. For example, the number of connected things within a future army brigade is likely to be several orders of magnitude greater than in current practice, and this is just the beginning. Consider that intelligent things belonging to such a brigade will inevitably interact—willingly or unwillingly—with things owned and operated by other parties, such as those of the adversary, or of the surrounding civilian population. If the brigade operates in a large city where each apartment building can contains thousands of things, the overall universe of connected things grows dramatically. Millions of things per square kilometer is not an unreasonable expectation (Fig. 3.2).

The above scenario also points to a great diversity of things within the overall environment of the battlefield. Things will come from different manufacturers; have different designs, capabilities, and purposes; be configured or machine-learned differently, etc. No individual thing will be able to use preconceived (preprogrammed, prelearned, etc.) assumptions about the behaviors or performance of other things it meets on the battlefield. Instead, behaviors and characteristics will have to be learned and updated autonomously and dynamically during the operations. This includes humans (yes, humans are a species of things, in a way) and therefore the behaviors and intents of humans, such as friendly warfighters, adversaries, civilians, and so on, will have to be continually learned and inferred.

The cognitive processes of both things and humans will be severely challenged in this environment of voluminous and heterogeneous information. Rather than the communications bandwidth, the cognitive bandwidth may become the most severe constraint. Both humans and things seek information that is well-formed, reasonably sized, essential in nature, and highly relevant to their current situation and mission. Unless information is useful, it does more harm than good. The trustworthiness of the information and the value of information arriving from different sources (especially other things) will be highly variable and generally uncertain. For any given intelligent thing, the incoming information could contain mistakes, erroneous observations or conclusions made by other things, or intentional distortions (deceptive information) produced by an adversary malware residing in friendly things or otherwise inserted into the environment. Both humans and things are susceptible to deception, and humans are likely to experience cognitive challenges when surrounded by opaque things that might be providing them with untrustworthy information (Kott & Alberts, 2017).

This situation reminds us that the adversarial nature of the battlefield environment is a concern of exceptional importance, above all others. The intelligent things will have to deal with an intelligent, capable adversary. The adversary will bring about physical destruction, either by means such as gunfire (also known as "kinetic" effects) or by using directed energy weapons. The adversary will jam the communication channels between things, and between things and humans. The adversary will deceive things by presenting them with misleading information. Recent research in adversarial learning comes to mind in this connection (Papernot et al., 2016). Perhaps most dangerously, the adversary will attack intelligent things by depositing malware on them.

## 3.3 AI WILL FIGHT THE CYBER ADVERSARY

A key assumption that must be made regarding the IoBT is that in a conflict with a technically sophisticated adversary, IoBT will be a heavily contested battlefield (Kott, Alberts, & Wang, 2015). Enemy software cyber agents, or malware, will infiltrate our networks and attack our intelligent things. To fight them, things will need artificial cyber hunters—intelligent, autonomous, mobile agents specialized in active cyber defense and residing on IoBT.

Such agents will stealthily patrol the networks, detect the enemy malware while remaining concealed, and then destroy or degrade the enemy malware. They will do so mostly autonomously, because human cyber experts will be always scarce on the battlefield. They will be adaptive because the enemy malware is constantly evolving. They will be stealthy because the enemy malware will try to find and kill them. At this time, such capabilities do not exist but are a topic of research (Theron et al., 2018). We will now explore the desired characteristics of an intelligent autonomous agent operating in the context of IoBT.

Under consideration is a thing—a simple senor or a complex military vehicle—on which one or more computers resides. Each computer contributes considerably to the operation of the thing or systems installed on the thing. One or more of the computers is assumed to have been compromised, where the compromise is either established as a fact or is suspected.

Due to the contested nature of the communications environment (e.g., the enemy is jamming the communications or radio silence is required to avoid detection by the enemy), communications between the thing and other elements of the friendly force can be limited and intermittent. Under some conditions, communications are entirely impossible.

Given the constraints on communications, conventional centralized cyber defense is infeasible. (Here, centralized cyber defense refers to an architecture where local sensors send cyber-relevant information to a central location, where highly capable cyber defense systems and human analysts detect the presence of malware and initiate corrective actions remotely.) It is also unrealistic to expect that human warfighters in the vicinity of the thing (if they exist) have the necessary skills or time available to perform cyber defense functions for that thing.

Therefore cyber defense of the thing and its computing devices must be performed by an intelligent, autonomous software agent. The agent (or multiple agents per thing) would stealthily patrol the networks, detect the enemy agents while remaining concealed, and then destroy or degrade the enemy malware. The agent must do so mostly autonomously, without the support or guidance of a human expert.

In order to fight the enemy malware deceptively deployed on the friendly thing, the agent often has to take destructive actions, such as deleting or quarantining certain software. Such destructive actions are carefully controlled by the appropriate rules of engagement and are allowed only on the computer where the agent resides. The agent may also be the primary mechanism responsible for defensive cyber maneuvering (e.g., a mobbing target defense), deception (e.g., redirection of malware to honeypots (De Gaspari, Jajodia, Mancini, & Panico, 2016)), self-healing (e.g., Azim, Neamtiu, & Marvel, 2014), and other such autonomous or semi-autonomous behavior (Jajodia, Ghosh, Swarup, & Wang, 2011).

In general, the actions of the agent cannot be guaranteed to preserve the integrity of the functions and data of friendly computers. There is a risk that an action of the agent may "break" the friendly computer, disable important friendly software, or corrupt or delete important data. In a military environment, this risk must be balanced against the death or destruction caused by the enemy if an agent's recommended action is not taken.

Provisions are made to enable a remote or local human controller to fully observe, direct, and modify the actions of the agent. However, it is recognized that human control is often impossible, especially because of intermittent communications. The agent is therefore able to plan, analyze, and perform most or all of its actions autonomously. Similarly, provisions are made for the agent to collaborate with other agents (residing on other computers); however, in most cases, because the communications are impaired or observed by the enemy, the agent operates alone.

The enemy malware and its associated capabilities and techniques evolves rapidly, as does the environment in general, together with the mission and constraints to which the thing is subject. Therefore the agent is capable of autonomous learning.

Because the enemy malware knows that the agent exists and is likely to be present on the computer, the enemy malware seeks to find and destroy the agent. Therefore the agent possesses techniques and mechanisms for maintaining a degree of stealth, camouflage, and concealment. More generally, the agent takes measures that reduce the probability of its detection by the enemy malware. The agent is mindful of the need to exercise self-preservation and self-defense.

It is assumed here that the agent resides on the computer where it was originally installed by a human controller or by an authorized process. We envision the possibility that an agent may move itself (or a replica of itself) to another computer. However, it is assumed that such propagation occurs only under exceptional and well-specified conditions and only within a friendly network—from one friendly computer to another friendly computer. This situation brings to mind the controversy about "good viruses." Such viruses were proposed, criticized, and dismissed earlier (Muttik, 2016). These criticisms do not apply here. This agent is not a virus because it only propagates under explicit conditions within authorized and cooperative nodes. Also, it is used only in military environments, where most of the usual concerns are irrelevant.

## 3.4 AI WILL PERCEIVE THE COMPLEX WORLD

Agents will have to become useful teammates—not tools—of human warfighters on a highly complex and dynamic battlefield. Fig. 3.1 depicts an environment wherein a highly dispersed team of human and intelligent agents (including but not limited to physical robots) is attempting to access a multitude of highly heterogeneous and uncertain information sources and use them to form situational awareness and make decisions (Kott, Singh, McEneaney, & Milks, 2011), while simultaneously trying to survive

**Fig. 3.3** AI-enabled agents—members of a human-agent team—will rapidly learn in ever-changing, complex environments, providing the team's commander with real-time estimates of enemy, reasoning on possible courses of action, and tactically sensible decision.

extreme physical and cyber threats. They must be effective in this unstructured, unstable, rapidly changing, chaotic, and rubble-filled adversarial environment; learning in real-time under extreme time constraints, with only a few observations that are potentially erroneous and with uncertain accuracy and meaning, or are even intentionally misleading and deceptive (Fig. 3.3).

It is clearly far beyond the current state of AI to operate intelligently in such an environment and with such demands. In particular machine learning, an area that has seen dramatic progress in the last decade, must experience major advances in order to become relevant to the real battlefield. Let's review some of the required advances.

Learning with a very small number of samples is clearly a necessity in an environment where friends and enemies continuously change their tactics and the environment itself is highly fluid, rich with details, dynamic, and changing rapidly. Furthermore, very few (if any) of the available samples will be labeled or, if so, not in a very helpful manner. This learning stands in stark contrast to the highly influential ImageNet dataset (Deng et al., 2009) that led to the advent of modern deep learning by providing a rich, labeled dataset for a massive 1000-class task. Whereas ImageNet data is labeled and provides one main class per image, real field data is fraught with partially occluded objects and ambiguous detections.

Dealing with limited samples means moving beyond the current state-of-the-art in deep learning that seeks to learn efficient representations for entire domains by only allowing each sample to influence the model a very small amount. Embracing classical nonparametric techniques that treat each piece of data as representative of its own local domain is one potential path to sample-efficient learning. Overcoming the never-ending growth of data required to define our model is an area of active research, but by allowing the system to trade accuracy for efficiency, it is possible to keep the cost of learning in check (Koppel, Warnell, Stump, & Ribeiro, 2017).

Truly intelligent agents, however, will not need to memorize data to make sense of the changing world; rather they will be able to investigate only a few examples in order to quickly learn how the current environment relates to their experience. This technique of *domain adaptation* (Patel, Gopalan, Li, & Chellappa, 2015) promises to allow models trained over exhaustive datasets of benign environments to remain useful on a dynamic battlefield. Whether by updating only a small portion of the model (Chu, Madhavan, Beijbom, Hoffman, & Darrell, 2016), appealing to the underlying geometry of the data manifolds (Fernando, Habrard, Sebban, & Tuytelaars, 2013; Gong, Shi, Sha, & Grauman, 2012), or turning the learning algorithms upon themselves to be trained how to adapt (Long, Cao, Wang, & Jordan, 2015), future agents will maintain flexible representations of their learned knowledge, amenable to reinterpretation and reuse.

Flexibility of learning and knowledge is crucial: it will undoubtedly be undesirable for an agent to enter a new environment with pretrained (preconceived) absolute notions of how it should perceive and act. Instead, an agent will always be formulating and solving learning problems; and the role of training is to teach the system how it can do this as efficiently as possible, perhaps even in one learning step (Finn, Abbeel, & Levine, 2017). This fascinating concept of *meta-learning*, or learning how to learn (Andrychowicz et al., 2016), allows the agent to finally take advantage of both its knowledge and experience to perceive and interact with the dynamic world and an evolving team and mission.

The domains that agents must learn and understand are vast and complex. A typical example might be a video snippet of events and physical surroundings for a robot, where the overwhelming majority of elements (e.g., pieces of rubble) are hardly relevant and potentially misleading for the purposes of learning. The information in the samples is likely to be highly heterogeneous in nature. Depending on circumstances, samples might consist of one or more of the following data: still images in various parts of the spectrum (IR, visible, etc.), video, audio, telemetry, solid models of the environment, records of communications between agents, and so on. Multiple modalities offer the potential to allow one type of data to help sort through ambiguities and unobservability in another modality. Moreover, complex and widespread events such as social movements can only truly be understood by aligning and composing these heterogeneous sources to detect underlying patterns (Giridhar, Wang, Abdelzaher, Al Amin, & Kaplan, 2017; Gui et al., 2017).

The danger is that some samples may be misleading in general, even if unintentionally (e.g., an action succeeds even though an unsuitable action is applied) and the machine-learning algorithms will have to make the distinction between the relevant and irrelevant, the instructive and misleading. In addition, some of the samples might be a product of intentional deception by the enemy. In general, issues of adversarial learning and adversarial reasoning are of great importance (Papernot et al., 2016). Although initial demonstrations that showed how to perturb an image to fool a trained model were seen as an amusement, later demonstrations have shown that not only can these attacks be used in the real environment (Kurakin, Goodfellow, & Bengio, 2016), they also do not require insider knowledge of the learning system (Papernot et al., 2017) and are exceedingly difficult to detect in isolation (Carlini & Wagner, 2017). Robustness to these adversarial actions will come about as the product of engineering principles that treat learning as part of a larger system of models and heterogeneous data that provide avenues to check and attest to the veracity of our models.

## 3.5 AI ENABLES EMBODIED AGENTS

Some intelligent things will be embodied so that they can actively explore and interact with the world, not merely constructs that protect our virtual environment or sensors that vigilantly observe and interpret. AI enables these interactions, allowing things to develop intuition about the laws of physics and to learn how to act optimally to accomplish their missions. In some cases, agents will take our traditional hand-crafted control paradigms and expand them through learning and artificial evolution; in other cases, agents will learn behaviors as a child does, developing motor skills through careful play. The agents will produce dramatic new behaviors that are perfectly suited for their tasks yet display the same adaptability that we find in their perception systems. These creative solutions to embodiment will accomplish another important goal: to find the inflection points in the design and control space where complex physical interactions of body and environment lead to mechanical advantage and efficient cycles that let systems overcome their fundamental limitations on weight and power.

Humans have developed many control schemes that allow us to bend natural processes to our will, and machines must continue these developments, tapping into a capacity for learning and adaptation to magnify these traditional techniques. In some cases, this means identifying pieces of our planning and control systems that are particularly hard to model and letting the system learn them (Richter, Vega-Brown, & Roy, 2015). In other cases we can take a more holistic view of learning to plan and control: recent advances in planning have allowed us to sidestep the challenge of thinking through all of the compounding choices by substituting enumeration with sampling and relying on the mechanisms of probability to give us a path to convergence and optimality (Karaman & Frazzoli, 2011; Tedrake, Manchester, Tobenkin, & Roberts, 2010). Intelligent systems will learn to guide their sampling over time as a way to realize the knowledge they have built about the world and their capabilities while still retaining the ability to be flexible in case their model is not quite right. Modeling probability distributions can be challenging, but learning to transform a simple distribution can accomplish the same goal and provide a path to learnable sampling-based control (Lenz, Knepper, & Saxena, 2015).

These planning and control approaches are founded on the ability to make predictions about the effect of our actions on the world, but, in a battlefield environment where conditions can deteriorate rapidly and intelligent things may need to continuously adapt to damage, forming these predictions is another task that AI must step in to perform. We can take inspiration from studies of how the human mind develops and learns in order to understand how agents can develop intuition about the physical world (Tenenbaum, Kemp, Griffiths, & Goodman, 2011); this intuition can be holistic or focused on understanding specific aspects of the world such as rigid body motion (Byravan & Fox, 2017) or how fluids behave (Schenck & Fox, 2016). Through observations and careful experimentation (Pinto, Gandhi, Han, Park, & Gupta, 2016), agents can treat physics as another application of perception algorithms that can take cause and effect data and learn to generalize (Hefny, Downey, & Gordon, 2015). These models then become an intimate part of the planning and control process (Boots, Siddiqi, & Gordon, 2011; Williams et al., 2017).

Traditional scientific and design methodology emphasizes the need to model and analyze the parts of a system in isolation, carefully controlling the variables so that the most concise and elegant description of a phenomenon or capability can be developed. In the future where components are the result of learning processes that can radically reshape their functionality, these traditional processes must also evolve. This evolution is already taking place with the advent of so-called *end-to-end learning* approaches that build and simultaneously train the entire processing and decision-making pipeline from perception to action (Bojarski et al., 2016; Levine, Finn, Darrell, & Abbeel, 2016). Simultaneously learning on many tasks at once keeps this process from overspecializing (Devin, Gupta, Darrell, Abbeel, & Levine, 2017)—another example of *meta-learning*. Eventually these techniques will be able to recapture the crucial feature of traditional systems engineering: being able to formally prove correctness (Aswani, Gonzalez, Sastry, & Tomlin, 2013).

Despite the future advances in embodied intelligence just discussed, the challenge of limited electrical power will remain a driving factor in deployment for the battlefield. Most successful AI relies on vast computing and electrical power resources including cloud-computing reach-back when necessary. The battlefield AI, on the other hand, must operate within the constraints of edge devices, such as small sensors, micro-robots, and the handheld radios of warfighters. This situation means that computer processors must be relatively light and small, and as frugal as possible in the use of electrical power. One might suggest that a way to overcome such limitations on computing resources available directly on the battlefield is to offload the computations via wireless communications to a powerful computing resource located outside of the battlefield (Kumar & Lu, 2010). Unfortunately, it is not a viable solution because the enemy's inevitable interference with friendly networks will limit the opportunities for use of reach-back computational resources. We must turn to techniques to trade precision for power to keep computing at the edge (Gupta, Mohapatra, Park, Raghunathan, & Roy, 2011; Iandola et al., 2016) or encode mature AI procedures directly into circuitry. Perhaps the systems will again lead the way, just as they did when they used meta-learning to learn adaptability by obtaining the correct balance between power and accuracy and tuning their own algorithms to realize it.

## 3.6 COORDINATION REQUIRES AI

It is essential that agents work collectively to sense and explore the battle-field: the size and scope of the challenge demand it and agents can fall prey to hazards or adversaries at any time. Humans are masters of coordination, able to work together to accomplish large tasks using an array of different modes of communication, from explicit instructions to codewords to an unspoken understanding of team roles. Coordination on the battlefield will require agents to use all of these mechanisms and more, taking inspiration from nature around us and also from applied logic to demonstrate the ability to share and sequence. Underlying all of this coordination will be the collective activity necessary to enable the communications networks upon which higher-level coordination will depend.

A certain amount of abstraction is required as teams become large and tracking and managing every agent's identity through changing and merging battlefield roles becomes impossible. These abstractions are exemplified by the complex emergent behavior of swarms of fish and birds that move with a purpose but have no explicit guidance. It has been shown that these phenomena can arise from the interactions of simple rules between neighboring agents (Jadbabaie, Lin, & Morse, 2003) and that they are robust, able to maintain cohesion even as neighbors come and go (Olfati-Saber & Murray, 2004; Ren & Beard, 2005; Tanner, Jadbabaie, & Pappas, 2007). Not only can these swarms move together, they can also explore and manipulate the world (Berman, Lindsey, Sakar, Kumar, & Pratt, 2011). These insights are grounded in application of graph theory to dynamic systems (Mesbahi & Egerstedt, 2010); all of this work on understanding and replicating swarms showed how we can synthesize and understand global properties by studying local ones.

It is not enough to just observe the emergent behavior; we must actively control the emergent behavior to realize the vision of coordination that can scale and adapt to meet battlefield challenges. The challenge lies in the fact that, at a suitable level of abstraction, agents have no identity, yet we must allocate and control them toward complex tasks. Again, the answers lie in stochasticity: allowing each agent to randomly determine its own actions but with probabilities proportional to the number of agents required breaks the need for identity by letting each agent self-determine whether it will help (Berman, Halász, Hsieh, & Kumar, 2009). These probabilities can be further adapted in a closed-loop fashion to shape the distributions (Mather & Hsieh, 2011).

The final step in controlling swarms is to embrace the heterogeneity of platforms and sensors that we can employ and let agents specialize to their suited tasks while still retaining a degree of anonymity (Kott & Abdelzaher, 2014).

A team that includes multiple warfighters and multiple artificial agents must be capable of distributed learning and reasoning. Besides distributed learning, these include such challenges as: multiple decentralized mission-level task allocations; self-organization, adaptation, and collaboration; space management operations; and joint sensing and perception. Commercial efforts to date have been largely limited to single platforms in benign settings. Military-focused programs, like Micro Autonomous Systems and Technology and Collaborative Technology Alliance (MAST CTA) (Piekarski et al., 2017), have been developing collaborative behaviors for UAVs. Ground vehicle collaboration is challenging and is largely still at the basic research level at present. In particular, to address such challenges, a new collaborative research alliance called Distributed and Collaborative Intelligent Systems and Technology (DCIST) has been initiated (https://dcist-cra.org/). Note that the battlefield environment imposes yet another complication: because the enemy interferes with communications, all of this collaborative, distributed AI must work well even with limited, intermittent connectivity.

## 3.7 HUMANS IN THE OCEAN OF THINGS

In this vision of the future warfare, a key challenge is to enable autonomous systems and intelligent agents to effectively and naturally interact across a broad range of warfighting functions. Human-agent collaboration is an active ongoing research area that must address such issues as trust and transparency, common understanding of shared perceptions, and human-agent dialog and collaboration (Kott & Alberts, 2017).

One seemingly relevant technology is question answering—the system's ability to respond with relevant, correct information to a clearly stated question. Successes of question-answering commercial technologies are indisputable. They work well for very large, stable, and fairly accurate volumes of data (e.g., encyclopedias). But such tools do not work for rapidly changing battlefield data, which is also distorted by an adversary's concealment and deception. They cannot support continuous, meaningful dialog in which both warfighters and AI agents develop a shared situational awareness and intent understanding. Research is being performed to develop human-robotic dialog technology for warfighting tasks using natural voice, which is critical for reliable battlefield teaming.

A possible approach to developing the necessary capabilities—both human and AI—is to train a human-agent team in immersive artificial environments. This training requires building realistic, intelligent entities in immersive simulations. Training (for humans) and learning (for agents) experiences must exhibit a high degree of realism to match operational demands. Immersive simulations for human training and machine learning must have physical and sociocultural interactions with high fidelity and a realistic complexity of the operational environment. These include realistic behaviors of human actors (friendly warfighters, enemies, noncombatants), and interactions and teaming with robots and other intelligent agents. In today's video games these interactions are limited and not suitable for simulating the real battlefield. Advances in AI are needed to drive character behaviors that are truly realistic, diverse, and intelligent.

To this end, some of the cutting-edge efforts in the computer-generation of realistic virtual characters are moving toward what would be needed to enable realistic interactions in an artificial immersive battlefield. For example, Hollywood studios sought out the army-sponsored Institute for Creative Technologies (http://ict.usc.edu/) on multiple occasions to create realistic avatars of actors. These technologies enable film creators to digitally insert an actor into scenes, even if that actor is unavailable, much older or younger, or deceased. This is how the actor Paul Walker was able to appear in "Fast and Furious 7," even though he died partway into filming (CBS News, 2017).

## 3.8 SUMMARY

Intelligent things—networked and teamed with human warfighters—will be a ubiquitous presence on future battlefields. Their appearances, roles and functions will be highly diverse. The AI required for such things will have to be significantly more sophisticated than that provided by today's AI and machine-learning technologies. The adversarial—strategically and not randomly dangerous—nature of the battlefield is a key driver of these requirements. Complexity of the battlefield, including the complexity of collaboration with humans, is another major driver. Cyber warfare will assume a far greater importance, and AI will have to fight cyber adversaries. Major advances in areas such as adversarial learning and adversarial reasoning will be required. Simulated immersive environments may help to train humans and AI.

## REFERENCES

Andrychowicz, M., Denil, M., Gomez, S., Hoffman, M. W., Pfau, D., Schaul, T., et al. (2016). Learning to learn by gradient descent by gradient descent. In *Advances in neural information processing systems* (pp. 3981–3989).

Aswani, A., Gonzalez, H., Sastry, S. S., & Tomlin, C. J. (2013). Provably safe and robust learning-based model predictive control. *Automatica, 49*(5), 1216–1226.

Azim, M. T., Neamtiu, I., & Marvel, L. M. (2014). Towards self-healing smartphone software via automated patching. In: In *Proceedings of the 29th ACM/IEEE international conference on automated software engineering* (pp. 623–628) ACM.

Berman, S., Halász, A. M., Hsieh, M. A., & Kumar, V. (2009). Optimized stochastic policies for task allocation in swarms of robots. *IEEE Transactions on Robotics, 25*, 927–937.

Berman, S., Lindsey, Q., Sakar, M. S., Kumar, V., & Pratt, S. (2011). Experimental study and modeling of group retrieval in ants as an approach to collective transport in swarm robotic systems. *Proceedings of the IEEE, 99*, 1470–1481.

Bojarski, M.; Del Testa, D.; Dworakowski, D.; Firner, B.; Flepp, B.; Goyal, P.; Jackel, L.D.; Monfort, M. Muller, U.; Zhang, J.; et al. End to end learning for self-driving cars. arXiv preprint arXiv:1604.07316, 2016.

Boots, B., Siddiqi, S. M., & Gordon, G. J. (2011). Closing the learning-planning loop with predictive state representations. *The International Journal of Robotics Research (IJRR), 30*(7), 954–966.

Byravan, A., & Fox, D. (2017). SE3-nets: learning rigid body motion using deep neural networks. In: *Proceedings of the IEEE international conference on robotics & automation (ICRA)*.

Carlini, N., & Wagner, D. (2017). Adversarial examples are not easily detected: bypassing ten detection methods. In: In *Proceedings of the 10th ACM workshop on artificial intelligence and security* (pp. 3–14) ACM.

CBS News. (2017). *Digital doubles: bringing actors back to life*. February 26, 2017 https://www.cbsnews.com/news/digital-doubles-bringing-actors-back-to-life/.

Chu, B., Madhavan, V., Beijbom, O., Hoffman, J., & Darrell, T. (2016). Best practices for fine-tuning visual classifiers to new domains. In *European conference on computer vision*, (pp. 435–442). Cham: Springer (pp. 435–442).

De Gaspari, F., Jajodia, S., Mancini, L. V., & Panico, A. (2016). AHEAD: a new architecture for active defense. In *Proceedings of the 2016 ACM workshop on automated decision making for active cyber defense* (pp. 11–16). Vienna, Austria: ACM.

Deng, J., Dong, W., Socher, R., Li, L., Li, K., & Fei-Fei, L. (2009). Imagenet: a large-scale hierarchical image database. In *IEEE conference on computer vision and pattern recognition* (pp. 248–255).

Devin, C., Gupta, A., Darrell, T., Abbeel, P., & Levine, S. (2017). Learning modular neural network policies for multi-task and multi-robot transfer. In *International conference on robotics and automation (ICRA)*.

Fernando, B.; Habrard, A.; Sebban, M.; and Tuytelaars, T. Unsupervised visual domain adaptation using subspace alignment. In Computer vision (ICCV), 2013 IEEE international conference on, pp. 2960-2967. IEEE, 2013.

Finn, C., Abbeel, P., & Levine, S. (2017). Model-agnostic meta-learning for fast adaptation of deep networks. In *International conference on machine learning (ICML)*.

Freedberg, S. J., Jr. (2016). *Missile defense for tanks: Raytheon quick kill vs. Israeli trophy*. Breakingdefense.com.

Giridhar, P., Wang, S., Abdelzaher, T. F., Al Amin, T., & Kaplan, L. M. (2017). Social fusion: integrating twitter and instagram for event monitoring. In *2017 IEEE International Conference on Autonomic Computing (ICAC)* (pp. 1–10).

Gong, B., Shi, Y., Sha, F., & Grauman, K. (2012). Geodesic flow kernel for unsupervised domain adaptation. In *Computer vision and pattern recognition (CVPR), 2012 IEEE conference on* (pp. 2066–2073). IEEE.

Gui, H., Liu, J., Tao, F., Jiang, M., Norick, B., Kaplan, L. M., et al. (2017). Embedding learning with events in heterogeneous information networks. *IEEE Transactions on Knowledge and Data Engineering, 29*, 2428–2441.

Gupta, V., Mohapatra, D., Park, S. P., Raghunathan, A., & Roy, K. (2011). IMPACT: IMPrecise adders for low-power approximate computing. In *IEEE/ACM international symposium on low power electronics and design* (pp. 409–414).

Hall, B.K. 2017. Autonomous weapons systems safety, Joint Force Quarterly 86, 86-93, Online at http://ndupress.ndu.edu/JFQ/Joint-Force-Quarterly-86/Article/1223911/autonomous-weapons-systems-safety/.

Hefny, H., Downey, C., & Gordon, G. J. (2015). Supervised learning for dynamical system learning. In *Vol. 28. Proceedings on advances in neural information processing systems (NIPS)*.

Iandola, F.N.; Han, S.; Moskewicz, M.W.; Ashraf, K.; Dally, W.J.; and Keutzer, K. SqueezeNet: AlexNet-level accuracy with 50x fewer parameters and $< 0.5$ MB model size. arXiv preprint arXiv:1602.07360 (2016).

Jadbabaie, A., Lin, J., & Morse, S. (2003). Coordination of groups of mobile autonomous agents using nearest neighbor rules. *IEEE Transactions on Automatic Control, 48*(6), 988–1001.

Jajodia, S., Ghosh, A. K., Swarup, V., & Wang, X. S. (Eds.), (2011). *Vol. 54. Moving target defense: Creating asymmetric uncertainty for cyber threats*: Berlin/Heidelberg: Springer Science & Business Media.

Karaman, S., & Frazzoli, E. (2011). Sampling-based algorithms for optimal motion planning. *International Journal of Robotics Research, 30*(7), 846–894.

Koppel, A., Warnell, G., Stump, E., & Ribeiro, A. (2017). Parsimonious online learning with kernels via sparse projections in function space. In: *Proceedings on international conference on acoustics speech signal process* [submitted].

Kott, A., & Abdelzaher, T. (2014). Resiliency and robustness of complex systems and networks. *Adaptive, Dynamic, and Resilient Systems, 67*, 67–86.

Kott, A., & Alberts, D. S. (2017). How do you command an army of intelligent things? *Computer, 12*, 96–100.

Kott, A., Alberts, D. S., & Wang, C. (2015). Will cybersecurity dictate the outcome of future wars? *Computer, 48*(12), 98–101.

Kott, A., Singh, R., McEneaney, W. M., & Milks, W. (2011). Hypothesis-driven information fusion in adversarial, deceptive environments. *Information Fusion, 12*(2), 131–144.

Kott, A., Swami, A., & West, B. J. (2016). The internet of battle things. *Computer, 49*(12), 70–75.

Kott, A., Wang, C., & Erbacher, R. F. (Eds.), (2014). *Cyber defense and situational awareness.* New York: Springer.

Kumar, K., & Lu, Y. -H. (2010). Cloud computing for mobile users: can offloading computation save energy? *Computer, 43*, 51–56.

Kurakin, A.; Goodfellow, I.J.; and Bengio, S. Adversarial examples in the physical world. arXiv preprint arXiv:1607.02533, 2016.

Lenz, I., Knepper, R., & Saxena, A. (2015). DeepMPC: learning deep latent features for model predictive control. In *Robotics: Science and systems*.

Levine, S., Finn, C., Darrell, T., & Abbeel, P. (2016). End-to-end training of deep visuomotor policies. *Journal of Machine Learning Research, 17*, 1334–1373.

Long, M.; Cao, Y.; Wang, J.; and Jordan, M.I. Learning transferable features with deep adaptation networks. arXiv preprint arXiv:1502.02791 (2015).

Mather, T. W., & Hsieh, M. A. (2011). Distributed robot ensemble control for deployment to multiple sites. In: *Robotics: Science and systems VII*.

Mesbahi, M., & Egerstedt, M. (2010). *Graph theoretic methods in multiagent networks, Vol. 33.* USA: Princeton University Press.

Muttik, I. (2016). *Good viruses. Evaluating the risks, talk at DEFCON-2016 conference* Online at, https://www.defcon.org/images/defcon-16/dc16-presentations/defcon-16-muttik.pdf.

Olfati-Saber, R., & Murray, R. M. (2004). Consensus problems in networks of agents with switching topology and time-delays. *IEEE Transactions on Automatic Control, 49*(9), 1520–1533.

Papernot, N., McDaniel, P., Goodfellow, I., Jha, S., Celik, Z. B., & Swami, A. (2017). Practical black-box attacks against machine learning. In *Proceedings of the 2017 ACM on Asia conference on computer and communications security* (pp. 506–519). ACM.

Papernot, N., McDaniel, P., Jha, S., Fredrikson, M., Celik, Z. B., & Swami, A. (2016). The limitations of deep learning in adversarial settings. In *In Security and privacy (EuroS&P), 2016 IEEE European symposium* (pp. 372–387) IEEE.

Patel, V. M., Gopalan, R., Li, R., & Chellappa, R. (2015). Visual domain adaptation: a survey of recent advances. *IEEE Signal Processing Magazine, 32*(3), 53–69.

Piekarski, B., Mathis, A., Nothwang, W., Baran, D., Kroninger, C., Sadler, B., et al. (2017). *Micro autonomous systems and technology (MAST) 2016 annual report for program Capstone.* Technical Report ARL-SR-0377, US Army Research Laboratory: Adelphi, MD.

Pinto, L., Gandhi, D., Han, Y., Park, Y. -L., & Gupta, A. (2016). *The curious robot: Learning visual representations via physical interactions* (pp. 3–18). Cham: Springer International Publishing.

Rasch, R., Kott, A., & Forbus, K. D. (2002). AI on the battlefield: an experimental exploration. In *Proceedings of the fourteenth innovative applications of artificial intelligence conference on artificial intelligence.* Alberta, Canada: Edmonton.

Ren, W., & Beard, R. W. (2005). Consensus seeking in multiagent systems under dynamically changing interaction topologies. *IEEE Transactions on Automatic Control, 50*(5), 655–661.

Richter, C., Vega-Brown, W., & Roy, N. (2015). Bayesian learning for safe high-speed navigation in unknown environments. In *ISRR.*

Scharre, P. (2014). *Robotics on the battlefield part II: the coming swarm.* Report Washington, DC: Center for a New American Security.

Schenck, C., & Fox, D. (2016). Towards learning to perceive and reason about liquids. In *Proceedings of the international symposium on experimental robotics (ISER).*

Stytz, M. R., Lichtblau, D. E., & Banks, S. B. (2005). *Toward using intelligent agents to detect, assess, and counter cyberattacks in a network-centric environment.* Report, Alexandria, VA: Institute for Defense Analyses.

Tanner, H. G., Jadbabaie, A., & Pappas, G. J. (2007). Flocking in fixed and switching networks. *IEEE Transactions on Automatic Control, 52*(5), 863–868.

Tedrake, R., Manchester, I., Tobenkin, M., & Roberts, J. (2010). LQR-trees: feedback motion planning via sums-of-squares verification. *International Journal of Robotics Research, 29*(8), 1038–1052.

Tenenbaum, J. B., Kemp, C., Griffiths, T. L., & Goodman, N. D. (2011). How to grow a mind: statistics, structure, and abstraction. *Science, 331*(6022), 1279–1285.

Theron, P., Kott, A., Drašar, M., Rzadca, K., LeBlanc, B., & Pihelgas, M. (2018). Towards an active, autonomous and intelligent cyber defense of military systems: The NATO AICA reference architecture. *2018 International Conference on Military Communications and Information Systems (ICMCIS) (pp. 1–9),* IEEE.

Williams, G., Wagener, N., Goldfain, B., Drews, P., Rehg, J. M., Boots, B., et al. (2017). Information theoretic MPC for model-based reinforcement learning. In *Robotics and automation (ICRA), 2017 IEEE international conference on* (pp. 1714–1721). IEEE.

## FURTHER READING

Kott, A., Ground, L., Budd, R., Rebbapragada, L., & Langston, J. (2002). Toward practical knowledge-based tools for battle planning and scheduling. In *AAAI/IAAI* (pp. 894–899).

Marcin, A., Denil, M., Colmenarejo, S. G., Hoffman, M. W., Pfau, D., Schaul, T., et al. (2016). Learning to learn by gradient descent by gradient descent. In *NIPS*.

Pinto, L., Davidson, J., Sukthankar, R., & Gupta, A. (2017). Robust adversarial reinforcement learning. *International conference on machine learning (ICML)*.

Zhengdong, Z., Suleiman, A., Carlone, L., Sze, V., & Karaman, S. (2017). Visual-inertial odometry on chip: an algorithm-and-hardware co-design approach. In *Robotics: Science and systems*.

# CHAPTER 4

# Active Inference in Multiagent Systems: Context-Driven Collaboration and Decentralized Purpose-Driven Team Adaptation

**Georgiy Levchuk, Krishna Pattipati, Daniel Serfaty, Adam Fouse, Robert McCormack**
Aptima Inc., Woburn, MA, United States

## 4.1 INTRODUCTION

Autonomous intelligent systems are no longer a fancy of science fiction writers; instead, they are quickly becoming part of our everyday lives. These devices, from heart monitoring implants to home-heating control systems, make our lives easier. Commercial technology developers make these devices "smarter" every day. While most of the currently deployed Internet of Things (IoT) systems perform simple tasks, like environment monitoring and human-guided control for smart homes, hospitals, or assembly plants, it is not difficult to envision a near future in which the intelligence and authority of these devices expand well beyond their current applications.

Most research in the area of IoT intelligence has been focused on the devices, including hardware–software interoperability (Al-Fuqaha, Guizani, Mohammadi, Aledhari, & Ayyash, 2015), standards and architectures (Perera, Zaslavsky, Christen, & Georgakopoulos, 2014), and operational challenges for individual devices or networks of homogeneous IoT components (Whitmore, Agarwal, & Da Xu, 2015). However, increasing interdependencies between component devices, data, physical systems, and human users prompted researchers and practitioners to explore the implications of emergent device intelligence on broader aspects of our everyday lives (Evans, 2012), forming the field of the Internet of Everything (IoE). Such studies allow the development of models to extract the highest potential from multiple autonomous and heterogeneous intelligent systems, including human–machine teaming recently identified as the defense technology of the future (Pellerin, 2015).

*Artificial Intelligence for the Internet of Everything*
https://doi.org/10.1016/B978-0-12-817636-8.00004-1

In this chapter we address two fundamental issues in IoE. First, we describe a **general framework of adaptive multiagent behavior** based on *minimizing a team's free energy*. This framework explains how multiple autonomous agents can produce team-optimal context-aware behaviors by performing collaborative perception and control. Second, we present a mechanism for IoE agents to **instantiate adaptive behaviors** by *intelligently sampling their environment* and *changing their organization structure*. This structure adaptation modifies the agents' roles and relations, which encode and constrain their decision responsibilities and interactions, and is computed in a distributed manner without a central authority. Energy optimization formally enables locally computed but globally optimal decisions by using approximate variational inference. The agents make local decision and communicate by passing belief messages in peer-to-peer manner. By providing the formal mapping between adaptive decisions, goal-driven actions, and perception, this model prescribes foundational functional requirements for developing IoE entities and networks that can efficiently operate in the complex, dynamic, and uncertain environments of the future.

## 4.2 ENERGY-BASED ADAPTIVE AGENT BEHAVIORS

### 4.2.1 Free Energy Principle

Recently, Friston proposed a theory, called the *free energy principle*, that describes how the agents and biological systems (such as a cell or a brain) adapt to the uncertain environments by reducing the information-theoretic quantity known as "variational free energy" (Friston, 2010; Friston, Thornton, & Clark, 2012). This theory brings Bayesian, information-theoretic, neuroscientific, and machine-learning approaches into a single formal framework. The framework prescribes that agents reduce their free energy in three ways: (1) by changing sensory inputs (*control*); (2) by changing predictions of the hidden variables and future sensory inputs (*perception*); and (3) by changing the model of the agent, such as its form, representation of environment, and structure of relations with other agents (*learning* and *reorganization*).

Variational free energy is defined as a function of sensory outcomes and a probability density over their (hidden) causes. This function is an upper bound on *surprise*, a negative log of the model evidence representing the difference between an agent's predictions about its sensory inputs, and the observations it actually encounters. Since the long-term average of surprise is entropy, an agent acting to minimize free energy will implicitly place an upper bound on the entropy of its outcomes—or the sensory states—it samples. Consequently, the free energy principle provides a mathematical foundation to explain how agents maintain order by restricting themselves to a limited number of states. This framework gives a formal mechanism to design decentralized purpose-driven behaviors, where multiple agents can operate autonomously to resist disorder without supervised control by external agents but have a potential for peer-to-peer collaboration and competition.

## 4.2.2 Adaptive Behavior and Context

Free energy generalizes to learning and cognition, prescribing the acquisition of any form of knowledge as an attempt to reduce surprise. Moreover, a fundamental property of this formulation, as can be seen below with its mathematical derivations, is that both free energy and the surprise it bounds are highly contextual. First, surprise is a function of sensations and the agent predicting them, existing only in relation to model-based expectations. Surprise-minimizing agents attempt to adapt to the context contained in their observations. Second, the free energy principle suggests that agents harvest the sensory signals they can predict, keeping to consistent subspaces of the physical and physiological variables that define their existence (Friston, Thornton, & Clark, 2012). When the perceptions about the world are constant, minimization of the energy makes the agents change their actions to maximize the entropy of the sensations (and, accordingly, self-information) they receive. In other words, the adaptive behaviors prescribed by the free energy principle tightly couple the environment and the agents that populate it and conform to the expectations of those behaviors.

Further, the minimization of surprise suggests that the selected adaptive actions cannot be deterministic. These reflections provide a key differentiation between the behaviors based on the free-energy principle and the classical control formulations where utility or cost functions are optimized. Essentially, the contextual information encoded by free energy produces stochastic actions to achieve a boundedly rational behavior.

The concept of surprise minimization is the basis for many modern estimation theories, system identification, anomaly detection, and adaptive control (e.g., Bar-Shalom, Li, & Kirubarajan, 2004; Ljung & Glad, 1994). Ideas similar to the free-energy principle have also been pursued in manual control and normative-descriptive models of human decision making. For example, the internal model control (IMC) principles of control theory state that every good regulator/controller of a system must be a model of that system (Conant & Ross Ashby, 1970; Smith, 1959). The basic assumption underlying human decision making in dynamic contexts is that well-trained and motivated humans behave in a normative, rational manner subject to their sensory and neuro-motor limitations, as well as perceived task objectives (e.g., Kleinman, Baron, & Levison, 1971; Pattipati, Kleinman, & Ephrath, 1983).

## 4.2.3 Formal Definitions

Given an agent and its generative model of environment $m$, we formally assert that a purpose-driven adaptive system "behaves rationally" if it maximizes the *model evidence*, a probability distribution $p(o|m)$ over observations $o$ conditioned on the model of the environment $m$, or equivalently minimizes a measure of surprise:

$$\text{Surprise}(o, m) = - \ln p(o|m).$$

A direct optimization of model evidence or surprise is intractable due to marginalization over all possible hidden states of the world (Friston, 2012). Recently, researchers conjectured that the only tractable way to optimize surprise is to minimize the variational free energy $F(o, b)$, an information-theoretic function of outcomes $o$, and an internal state of the agent defined as a probability density $b$ over (hidden) causes of these outcomes (Friston, Thornton, & Clark, 2012):

$$F(o, b) = \underbrace{E_q[- \ln p(s, o|m)]}_{\text{average energy}} - \underbrace{H[q(s|b)]}_{\text{entropy}},$$

where:
- $p(s, o|m)$ is a *generative density* representing the joint probability of world states $s$ and observations $o$ based on an agent model $m$;
- $q(s|b)$ is a *recognition density* that defines an agent's beliefs about the hidden states $s$ given internal state of agent $b$;
- $E_q[\cdot]$ is the expected value over recognition density, i.e., $E_q[-\ln p(s, o|m)] = - \sum_s q(s|b) \ln p(s, o|m)$; and
- $H[\cdot]$ is the entropy of the recognition density, i.e., $H[q(s|b)] = - \sum_s q(s|b) \ln q(s|b)$.

By rewriting the free energy function, we can obtain several interpretations of how adaptive agents "behave." First, free energy is equal to the sum of surprise and divergence, obtaining that free energy is an **upper bound on surprise**:

$$F(o, b) = \underbrace{- \ln p(o \mid m)}_{\text{surprise}} + \underbrace{D_{\mathrm{KL}}[q(s \mid b) \| p(s \mid o, m)]}_{\text{divergence}} \geq - \ln p(o \mid m),$$

where $D_{\mathrm{KL}}[q(s \mid b) \| p(s \mid o, m)]$ is the Kullback-Leibler divergence between the recognition density $q(s \mid b)$ and the true *posterior* of the world states $p(s \mid o, m) = p(s \mid o)$. Consequently, the minimization of free energy achieves the approximate minimization of surprise, at which point the perceptions $q(s \mid b)$ are equal to the posterior density $p(s \mid o, m)$.

Second, we can rewrite the free energy as the difference between complexity and accuracy:

$$F(o, b) = \underbrace{D_{\mathrm{KL}}[q(s \mid b) \| p(s \mid m)]}_{\text{complexity}} - \underbrace{E_q[\ln p(o(a) \mid s, m)]}_{\text{accuracy}}$$

Here, $D_{\mathrm{KL}}[q(s \mid b) \| p(s \mid m)]$ is a measure of divergence between the recognition density $q(s \mid b)$ and *prior* beliefs about the world $p(s \mid m)$, interpretable as a measure of complexity; the second component is the expectation about the observations $o$ to be received after performing an action $a$, which represents accuracy. This result means that the agent modifies its sensory outputs $o = o(a)$ through action $a$ to achieve the most accurate explanation of data under fixed complexity costs. Accordingly, we can now define the free energy minimization using two sequential phases that separate estimation and control:

- *Perception* phase finds beliefs $b^* = \arg \min_b F(o, b)$; and
- *Control* phase finds actions $a^* = \arg \min_a F(o(a), b^*)$.

The control phase produces a policy for an agent to generate observations that entail, on average, the smallest free energy. This result ensures that the individual actions produced over time are not deterministic, and that the control phase can be converted into a sampling process $a^* \sim Q(a, b, o)$ as a function of exploration bonus plus expected utility (Friston et al., 2013) or average free energy (Friston, Samothrakis, & Montague, 2012). Further, the free energy is dependent on the agent's model $m$, which can be adapted to minimize its free energy via an evolutionary or neurodevelopmental optimization. This process is distinct from perception; it entails changing the form and architecture of the agent (Friston, Thornton, & Clark, 2012). This change means that the free energy function can be used to compare two or more agents (models) to each other (a better agent is the one that has the smaller free energy), and thus is an ultimate measure of *fitness*, or *congruence*, or *match* between the agent and its environment.

## 4.2.4 Behavior Workflow and Computational Considerations

Fig. 4.1 depicts a simplified schematic of the resulting cycle of sensing, control, and perception in adaptive agents, where posterior expectations (about the hidden causes of observation inputs) minimize free energy and prescribe actions. A team of agents differs from a single agent model by distributing the observations, perceptions, and actions among multiple agents, while allowing the agents to communicate to achieve team-level goals.

The key benefit of using the information-theoretic free-energy principle for modeling dynamical systems is that the function $-\ln p(s, o \,|\, m)$ can have a simple mathematical structure when generative density $p(s, o \,|\, m)$ factors out:

$$p(s, o \,|\, m) = \frac{1}{Z}\prod_i \varphi_i(s_i, o_i),$$

where $\{s_i, o_i\}$ represent the subsets of state and observation variables, $\varphi_i$ are factor functions encoding dependency relations among the corresponding variables, and $Z$ is the normalization constant. Usually functions $\varphi_i(\cdot)$ are simple, typically describing the relations among one to four variables at a time. Then the agent, or team, or agents can minimize their energy with respect to internal state (recognition density $q(s \,|\, b)$) using a generalized belief propagation (BP) algorithm (Friston et al., 2013), an iterative procedure based on message passing. Moreover, using a standard BP algorithm, derived from a Bethe approximation to the variational free energy (Yedidia, Freeman, & Weiss, 2005), the agents can obtain the approximating density in

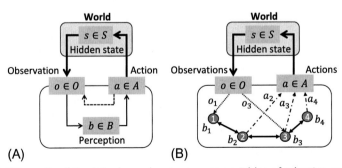

(A)                                (B)

**Fig. 4.1** Schematic of the interdependencies among variables of adaptive agent and team models. (A) Model of a single agent. (B) Model of a team of agents.

a peer-to-peer manner with low computational complexity. While standard BP does not guarantee convergence, it performs well in practice.

The free energy principle does not dictate the specifics of a generative process, i.e., the structure/components of the generative density $p(s, o \mid m)$ required to define the free-energy function. Nor does it prescribe the algorithms that need to be employed to minimize free energy. However, it provides a unifying framework that can be tailored to specific environments and systems. Next, we apply the free-energy formalisms to the design of adaptive multiagent teams, defining appropriate abstractions, and discussing their implications for the IoE functional requirements.

## 4.3 APPLICATION OF ENERGY FORMALISM TO MULTIAGENT TEAMS

### 4.3.1 Motivation

A team consisting of human and machine agents is a decentralized purpose-driven system. One of the main challenges in defining adaptive team behavior is in realizing global team-level perception and control, and corresponding optimization processes, into local inferences and decisions produced by individual agents without external control.

In our previous work we showed how free-energy minimization can be applied to define adaptive behavior in teams that execute given multitask missions (Levchuk, Pattipati, Fouse, & Serfaty, 2017). Examples of teams include military organizations, manufacturing teams, and many other project-based organizations. These teams interact with their environment by jointly assigning and executing tasks; optimal teams have the highest task execution accuracy and/or the fastest execution times. In the domain of project-based teams, we considered team members (agents) to possess high levels of intelligence, and thus assumed that agent-to-task assignment decision-making processes should not be externally controlled. We defined observations as the outcomes of task execution, and treated task assignments as a world state variable hidden from the agent. Consequently, the perception phase estimated the probability of agent-to-task assignments, while the control phase defined a team's organization structure, including the roles and relationships that constrain the tasks that agents could assign and execute, specifying a formal process for the team to resist its disorder.

In this chapter we review an instantiation of energy-minimizing adaptive behavior in a distributed decision-making setting. This entails a more general setup than project-based teams, motivated by the following. First, we wanted to understand how intelligent adaptive behaviors are related to the formal dynamics and structures among agents. We studied how organizational structure influences the processes of searching for sets of good decisions and stabilizing around good decisions once they are discovered (Rivkin & Siggelkow, 2003). The search and stability issues are conceptually identical to the exploration-exploitation tradeoffs afforded by free-energy minimization, allowing us to examine the alignments between energy-based computational mechanisms and discrete human decision-making processes analyzed by Rivkin and Siggelkow.

Second, we posit that the free-energy principle explains the empirically observed behaviors of business organizations. Unlike network-based theories of cities (e.g., Schläpfer et al., 2014), which are developed and tested using extensive quantitative data about social and economic transactions, development of behavior models for business organizations has lagged behind since the data on operations of business enterprises (e.g., communication channels, personnel assignments, and task outcomes) is often proprietary and not available. However, it has been empirically observed that as companies mature and grow, they attempt to maximize profits (utility) at the expense of innovation (entropy, disruption or disorder), placing increasing emphasis on rules, regulations, and other forms of bureaucratic control over its members, impeding market adjustments and leading to their eventual demise (West, 2017). The free-energy principle explains how placing more emphasis on utility versus entropy makes the system brittle and unable to adapt to a changing environment.

Finally, we wanted to identify what implications the free-energy minimization principle had on the design of agents that constitute the effective members of a high-performance team.

### 4.3.2 Problem Definition

The formal definition of a distributed decision-making problem (Rivkin & Siggelkow, 2003) is as follows. Assume that a team of $M$ agents seeks an $N$-dimensional binary decision vector $\boldsymbol{d} = [d_1, \ldots, d_N]$, where $d_i \in \{0, 1\}$, to maximize its additive objective function, i.e.,

$$\boldsymbol{d}^* = \arg\max_{\boldsymbol{d} \in \{0,1\}^N} C(\boldsymbol{d}) = \sum_{j=1}^{P} c_j(\boldsymbol{d}_j),$$

where $\boldsymbol{d}_j$ is a subset of decision variables, and $P$ is the number of these subsets. Component reward functions $c_j(\boldsymbol{d}_j)$ encode dependencies between decisions in subset $\boldsymbol{d}_j$ (such as local and team-level rewards). The general additive form of the objective function $C(d)$ represents many real-world search and inference problems. Relationships among the reward functions and decision variables can be expressed using a factor graph or a function-to-decision adjacency matrix (Fig. 4.2).

As the number $N$ of decision variables increases, the space of possible decision outcomes $d$ grows exponentially.[1] As a result, the optimal solution to the above maximization problem cannot be achieved by an exhaustive search of the values of joint reward function $C(d)$. Instead, an intelligent search in the space of all possible decisions needs to be conducted by the team of agents. To constrain the actions and enable agent collaboration, the organizational structure $m$ among the agents is defined using two variables (Fig. 4.3):

- *Decision decomposition*, prescribing subsets of decisions and cost functions assigned to each agent; and
- *An agent network*, prescribing superior-subordinate relations among the agents.

Each agent is locally aware of and controls only a subset of decisions and reward functions, giving rise to potential local-global decision inconsistencies. Accordingly, to produce team optimal decisions (maximizing the team objective function $C(d)$), agents have to collaborate.

Rivkin and Siggelkow (2003) defined a version of the decision-making and collaboration processes that mimicked the human decision making that occurs in business organizations. Subordinate agents generate a set of discrete decision vectors, rank these vectors with local payoffs, and communicate the ranked vectors to a superior agent (indicated as CEO in Fig. 4.3B). The

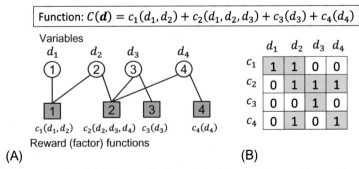

**Fig. 4.2** An example of defining a distributed decision-making problem with a factor graph and an adjacency matrix. (A) Factor graph. (B) Adjacency matrix.

---

[1] This is a so-called NP-hard problem, meaning that there are no known polynomial-time algorithms to solve this problem.

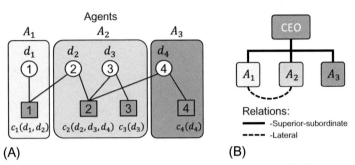

**Fig. 4.3** Variables of team structure. (A) Decision decomposition. (B) Agent network.

superior agent combines the vectors of subordinates into a set of candidate team-level decision vectors, evaluates them against a team's objective function, and communicates the best vector to the subordinates for implementation. The number of decision vector values the agents can evaluate during a specified time period is constrained by internal capacity. Lateral relationships can also be defined among the agents, allowing one agent to inform another about their local decisions vectors.

The decision-making process (Rivkin & Siggelkow, 2003) presents a heuristic solution to a distributed optimization problem, but provides no guarantees of convergence or efficacy even with the introduction of global incentives for agents. This heuristic also does not explain the causes of an underlying behavior, nor prescribes an adaptive behavior for the team or its members. We can still evaluate and compare the behaviors of teams of agents using these heuristics in terms of the time it takes to produce their solution, its proximity to the true maximum, and the amount of exploration versus exploitation in the state space of all decision vectors the agents jointly generate. In the following, we offer a formal optimization process that solves this problem in a distributed manner using free energy–minimization principles, along with the concomitant adaptive team behaviors exhibited by the team members during a search process. We show that an energy-based search provides a mechanism to adapt the multiagent behaviors and significantly outperforms the discrete optimization heuristics by Rivkin and Siggelkow, described in the previous section.

### 4.3.3 Distributed Collaborative Search Via Free Energy Minimization

We recast the problem described above as a joint inference over a factorized objective function in Section 4.2.4. In the distributed search problem of

Section 4.3.2, the environment is fully observable, hence we omit the observation notation from the rest of the exposition. We define the adaptive behavior for a team of agents based on the free-energy principle using three processes:

- *Perception* will find the beliefs $b$ representing the probability distribution $q(d \mid m)$;
- *Control* will produce the next decision $d$ by sampling the state space to minimize surprise; and
- *Reorganization* will adapt the structure $m$ among agents in terms of decision decompositions and the agent network.

Formally, we define a generative probability distribution for a decision variable $d$ as:

$$p(d \mid m) \cong \frac{1}{Z} e^{C(d)} = \frac{1}{Z} \prod_{j=1}^{P} \varphi_j(d_j),$$

where $\varphi_j(d_j) = e^{c_j(d_j)}$. We can then write the variational free energy as a function of beliefs $b$ and of the team structure $m$:

$$F(b, m) = E_q[-\ln p(d \mid m)] - H[q(d \mid b)].$$

Then minimizing the variational free energy $F(b, m)$ with respect to probability functions $q(d \mid b)$ becomes an exact procedure for bounding surprise and recovering $p(d \mid m)$. Exact minimization, however, is intractable for general forms of $q(d \mid m)$ due to the curse of dimensionality.

When the generative probability is factorizable, as we described in Section 4.2.4, generalized belief propagation is used to find the marginal probability distributions (Yedidia et al., 2005) that form the basis for generating decision points stochastically. This method, however, requires a difficult decision decomposition step and incurs high computational cost in an optimal message aggregation step.

Two features can help us address these challenges. First, we note that maximizing a global team decision cost function is equivalent to maximizing the joint decision probability function. This process, known as maximum a-posteriori (MAP) estimation, requires obtaining max-marginal probability values rather than marginal probabilities. Second, instead of the exact computation of belief distributions, we use an approximate solution produced by the standard belief propagation algorithm (Yedidia et al., 2005), based on the Bethe approximation of the free-energy function. We use the max-product algorithm to reduce a space of the distributions to analyze, lowering the computational complexity. The max-product belief propagation algorithm computes max-marginal distributions by iteratively passing belief messages between variable and factor nodes in the factor graph (Fig. 4.4A) using the following update equations:

- *Variable-to-factor* message updates involve multiplication of all except one of the incoming beliefs:

$$m_{i \to j}(d_i) = \prod_{c \in N(i) \setminus j} m_{c \to i}(d_i)$$

- *Factor-to-variable* message updates are conducted by maximizing component functions:

$$m_{j \to i}(d_i) = \max_{d_j \setminus d_i} \varphi_j(d_j) \prod_{v \in N(j) \setminus i} m_{v \to j}(d_v)$$

In the above, $N(i)$ denotes the neighbor nodes of node $i$ in a factor graph. For a team of agents, some of the computations above are conducted locally by a single agent, while the message passing across the links between variables and factors that are assigned to different agents need to be physically passed among the agents (Fig. 4.4B). These messages define formal local-global decision making, while the collaborative process is formally specified as the belief messages sent between connected agents.

Variable-to-factor messages contain the beliefs about the variable, interpreted as **experience messages**. Factor-to-variable messages are the probability distributions over decision values at a corresponding variable node, corresponding to **influence messages**. The free energy principle and approximate inference with a max-product algorithm only requires the agents to understand the dependencies of their local decisions on the decisions of other agents; they must also be capable of creating, sharing and interpreting the experience and influence messages.

After a max-product algorithm converges, the agents obtain the max-marginal probability distributions, and use these distributions to sample

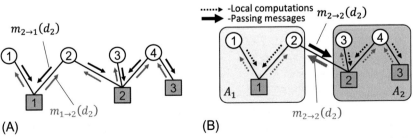

**Fig. 4.4** Message passing in belief propagation. (A) Passing beliefs in factor graph. (B) Collaboration by message passing.

the space of decision vectors *locally* (i.e., each agent samples its own subset of decision vector variables). Max-marginal estimates include variable marginals used by agents to sample the decision space:

$$b_i(d_i) = \max_{d \backslash \{d_i\}} p(d \mid b) \propto \prod_{j \in N(i)} m_{j \to i}(d_i),$$

as well as factor marginals, used to adapt a team's structure:

$$b_j(d_j) = \max_{d \backslash \{d_j\}} p(d \mid b) \propto \varphi_j(d_j) \prod_{i \in N(j)} m_{i \to j}(d_i)$$

With these quantities, we compute a *Bethe approximation* to the free-energy function (Yedidia et al., 2005):

$$F_{\text{Bethe}}(b, m) = E_{\text{Bethe}}(b, m) - H_{\text{Bethe}}(b, m),$$

where the first component is a negative expected utility computed as $E_{\text{Bethe}}(b, m) = -\sum_{d_j} b_j(d_j) c_j(d_j)$, and the second component is the entropy $H_{\text{Bethe}}(b, m) = (n_i - 1) \sum_i \sum_{d_i} b_i(d_i) \ln b_i(d_i) - \sum_j \sum_{d_j} b_j(d_j) \ln b_j(d_j)$, where $n_i = |N(i)|$ is the number of factors $d_j$ that the variable $i$ is involved in. Minimizing the free energy is achieved when the team finds all possible (maximally varying) marginals with the highest utility.

## 4.3.4 Adapting Team Structure

The team structure is represented by a model variable $m$, which affects the perceptions and decisions the team jointly produces. In addition, this structure also constrains how the information flows and is incorporated in the organization, including where the belief message can be sent, what communication delays and transmission errors are incurred, which of the messages are used to update decisions, and the concomitant computation workload incurred by team agents. This problem of team structure design can be formulated (and solved) as a network design problem (Feremans, Labbé, & Laporte, 2003).

Decision decomposition and the corresponding BP message calculations represent the *internal computational workload* incurred by agents, representing the collaboration process required to solve a decision problem. Specification of the messages passed between decision and factor nodes in a factor graph define the *external communication workload* of the agents. The problem of structuring a team can be formulated as the alignment of decision decomposition ("the task network") and the agent network ("team structure") to properly balance internal and external workloads. We model the impact

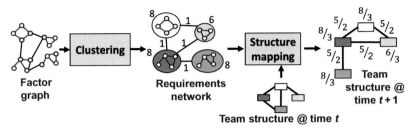

**Fig. 4.5** A notional team structure adaptation workflow.

of internal and external workloads on a team's perception and action processes using delay models and/or message transmission errors (the classic "delay-accuracy" tradeoff in team performance). Schematically, the team structuring problem can be decomposed in two steps (Fig. 4.5). First, we aggregate the decision and factor nodes to balance the internal and external workloads via cluster analysis by minimizing the inter-cluster links, subject to constraints on the workload capacities of agents. Second, we use this network as a set of requirements, and map it to the current agent network, realigning agent network parameters (i.e., capacities) as the factor graph evolves (e.g., changes its decision reward parameters).

## 4.4 VALIDATION EXPERIMENTS

### 4.4.1 Experiment Setup

We conducted several studies to validate our proposed adaptive team behavior model. First, we generated a collection of synthetic distributed decision-making problems by randomly generating the values for the joint reward function. We manipulated the density of dependencies between variables using a parameter $K$ defined as the average number of variables influencing a factor node. We computed several assessment metrics, including the percent of trials where a team converged to an optimal solution (determined as producing a vector with a reward value within a small threshold of the optimal value), and a normalized payoff (computed as the fraction of the discovered decision payoff compared to the optimal one). We evaluated team performance over time, as well as using a time-averaged payoff. Second, we introduced random periodic variations of the parameters in the joint reward function to evaluate how quickly the teams can recover from these changes. The latter analysis enables us to quantify the attributes of resilience in a team: (1) capacity to absorb changes, (2) recoverability, and (3) adaptive capacity (Francis & Bekera, 2014).

Using these generated datasets, we conducted several evaluations, comparing the discrete decision-making model (Rivkin & Siggelkow, 2003) with two alternative decision processes: perception-maximizing decisions (selecting decisions as a maximum of the max-marginal probabilities), and energy minimization (selecting a decision by sampling max-marginals to minimize surprise). We also analyzed the impact a specific team structure (models) had on the ability of the team to find correct solutions.

### 4.4.2 Discrete Decision Making Versus Free Energy

In our first evaluation, we compared the performance of distributed discrete decision making (D3M) heuristics with our model, where the decision vector minimizes a free-energy function. Fig. 4.6 shows the normalized payoff achieved at the 100th iteration by the best of D3M policies (Rivkin & Siggelkow, 2003) versus payoffs of one of the teams defined by our energy-optimizing model. While the free-energy solution provides only a marginal improvement compared to the D3M model (2%–10%), our model achieves convergence much faster than the D3M heuristics (usually at 15 iterations versus 50–80 iterations for D3M), and maintains high convergence for increasing objective function complexity (parameter $K$), while the performance of D3M consistently decreases with $K$. As a result, we continued to compare only energy-based adaptation processes.

In the next set of experiments we analyzed the ability of a team to adapt to changes in the environment, defined as random regeneration of an objective function's parameters (without changing the topology of the factor graph) introduced at every 20 decision iterations.

### 4.4.3 Impact of Agent Network Structure

We compared the effects of three different agent network topologies (Fig. 4.7) on the quality of the search process and the ability of a team to

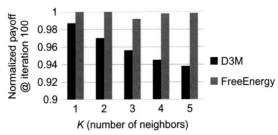

**Fig. 4.6** Comparing performance of the D3M heuristic versus free-energy minimization.

adapt. We also analyzed different behaviors at the root node (CEO agent) in the hierarchy: "active" refers to the agent that passes indirect messages among subordinate agents and "passive" accounts for ignoring those messages completely.

From the average payoff values in Fig. 4.8, we concluded that organizations with stronger subordinates ("lateral" and "fully connected") performed better, while the relative benefit of such teams is highest for medium dependencies between decisions ($K = 2$–$3$). In these situations the benefit of lateral coordination appears to outweigh the cost of managing multiple communications. The relative benefit of fully connected networks reduces as the dependencies become more complex ($K > 3$), mostly due to the suboptimality of a distributed solution when there are many dependencies (i.e., large $K$) among the decision variables.

### 4.4.4 Impact of Decision Decomposition

Finally, we studied the effect of decision decomposition (the assignment of decision and factor nodes to agents) on team performance. We computed a score on the quality of a current decision as the value of an objective function at the max-marginal vector $\hat{\boldsymbol{d}} = \{\hat{d}_i\}$, where,

$$\hat{d}_i = \arg\max b_i(d_i).$$

We found that using optimized versus random decomposition improved the solutions achieved by a team, with a larger effect for lateral structures (Fig. 4.9).

Due to space limitations we omitted an analysis of (a) how team structures affect performance; (b) correlation between free energy and the reward function improvement; (c) internal/external workload metrics and how they impact the decision quality; and (d) measures of resilience. These will be included in a future manuscript.

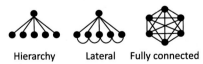

Hierarchy    Lateral    Fully connected

**Fig. 4.7** Considered team structures.

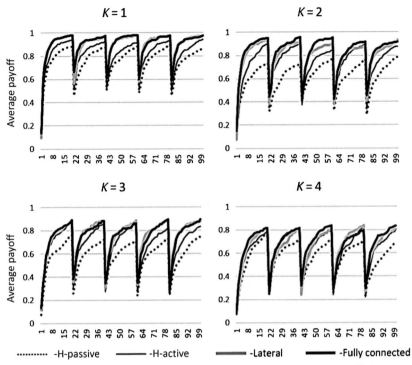

Fig. 4.8 Comparison of effect of team structure on average payoff (H-active/ passive = hierarchy with active or passive CEO). *K* represents increasing complexity *of decision problem.*

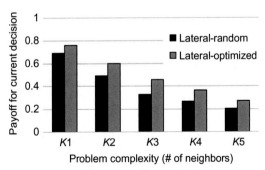

Fig. 4.9 Example of the effects of decision decomposition on the quality of a current solution with a lateral team structure.

## 4.5 CONCLUSIONS

In this chapter we studied the problem of generating adaptive behaviors for cooperating agents. We presented an application of the free energy–minimization principle to generate decentralized purpose-driven teams of agents. Experiments with synthetic data establish that energy-based behavior results in a higher performance on a distributed search task compared to discrete decision-making heuristics. The minimum free-energy formalism provides a mathematically sound mechanism for coupling perception and action selection processes. Finally, the decisions to affect the environment through actions, adapt by modifying perception, and adjust the architecture of a team in terms of organizational structure among the agents can all be executed in a distributed collaborative manner without the need for external controlling agents.

One of the key innovations of our work is that it prescribes two general interfaces that the intelligent adaptive agents must possess: generating, communicating, and incorporating *experience* and *influence* messages. Neither of these interfaces alone can allow multiple agents to achieve the required team-optimal decisions using distributed local computations. Our current work is focused on defining a precise free-energy function that the encodes the effects of team structure on decisions and communications, studying the convergence properties of distributed perception and control processes, obtaining the collaborative adaptation mechanisms for project-based teams, and deriving high-level corollaries with general trends from lower-level free energy–minimizing processes.

## REFERENCES

Al-Fuqaha, A., Guizani, M., Mohammadi, M., Aledhari, M., & Ayyash, M. (2015). Internet of things: a survey on enabling technologies, protocols, and applications. *IEEE Communication Surveys and Tutorials, 17*(4), 2347–2376.

Bar-Shalom, Y., Li, X. R., & Kirubarajan, T. (2004). *Estimation with applications to tracking and navigation: Theory algorithms and software.* John Wiley & Sons.

Conant, R. C., & Ross Ashby, W. (1970). Every good regulator of a system must be a model of that system. *International Journal of Systems Science, 1*(2), 89–97.

Evans, D. (2012). *The internet of everything: How more relevant and valuable connections will change the world:* (pp. 1–9). Cisco IBSG.

Feremans, C., Labbé, M., & Laporte, G. (2003). Generalized network design problems. *European Journal of Operational Research, 148*(1), 1–13.

Francis, R., & Bekera, B. (2014). A metric and frameworks for resilience analysis of engineered and infrastructure systems. *Reliability Engineering & System Safety, 121,* 90–103.

Friston, K. (2010). The free-energy principle: a unified brain theory? *Nature Reviews Neuroscience, 11*(2), 127–138.

Friston, K. (2012). A free energy principle for biological systems. *Entropy*, *14*(11), 2100–2121.

Friston, K., Samothrakis, S., & Montague, R. (2012). Active inference and agency: optimal control without cost functions. *Biological Cybernetics*, *106*(8–9), 523–541.

Friston, K., Schwartenbeck, P., FitzGerald, T., Moutoussis, M., Behrens, T., & Dolan, R. J. (2013). The anatomy of choice: active inference and agency. *Frontiers in Human Neuroscience*, *7*, 1–18, Article 598.

Friston, K., Thornton, C., & Clark, A. (2012). Free-energy minimization and the dark-room problem. *Frontiers in Psychology*, *3*, 1–7, Article 130.

Kleinman, D., Baron, S., & Levison, W. (1971). A control theoretic approach to manned-vehicle systems analysis. *IEEE Transactions on Automatic Control*, *16*(6), 824–832.

Levchuk, G., Pattipati, K., Fouse, A., & Serfaty, D. (2017). Application of free energy minimization to the design of adaptive multi-agent teams. In *Disruptive technologies in sensors and sensor system*. SPIE DSO.

Ljung, L., & Glad, T. (1994). *Modeling of dynamic systems*. Englewood Cliffs, NJ: Prentice Hall.

Pattipati, K. R., Kleinman, D. L., & Ephrath, A. R. (1983). A dynamic decision model of human task selection performance. *IEEE Transactions on Systems, Man, and Cybernetics*, *2*, 145–166.

Pellerin, C., 2015. Work: human-machine teaming represents defense technology future. Department of Defense News. , Retrieved from https://www.defense.gov/News/Article/Article/628154/work-human-machine-teaming-represents-defense-technology-future/. Accessed 3 January 2018.

Perera, C., Zaslavsky, A., Christen, P., & Georgakopoulos, D. (2014). Context aware computing for the internet of things: a survey. *IEEE Communication Surveys and Tutorials*, *16*(1), 414–454.

Rivkin, J. W., & Siggelkow, N. (2003). Balancing search and stability: interdependencies among elements of organizational design. *Management Science*, *49*(3), 290–311.

Schläpfer, M., Bettencourt, L. M., Grauwin, S., Raschke, M., Claxton, R., Smoreda, Z., et al. (2014). The scaling of human interactions with city size. *Journal of the Royal Society Interface*, *11*(98), 20130789.

Smith, O. J. (1959). A controller to overcome dead time. *ISA Journal*, *6*, 28–33.

West, G. (2017). *Scale: The universal laws of growth, innovation, sustainability, and the pace of life in organisms, cities, economies, and companies*. Penguin.

Whitmore, A., Agarwal, A., & Da Xu, L. (2015). The internet of things—a survey of topics and trends. *Information Systems Frontiers*, *17*(2), 261–274.

Yedidia, J. S., Freeman, W. T., & Weiss, Y. (2005). Constructing free-energy approximations and generalized belief propagation algorithms. *IEEE Transactions on Information Theory*, *51*(7), 2282–2312.

## FURTHER READING

Siggelkow, N., & Rivkin, J. W. (2005). Speed and search: designing organizations for turbulence and complexity. *Organization Science*, *16*(2), 101–122.

# CHAPTER 5

# Policy Issues Regarding Implementations of Cyber Attack: Resilience Solutions for Cyber Physical Systems

**Barry M. Horowitz**
Systems and Information Engineering, University of Virginia, Charlottesville, VA, United States

## 5.1 INTRODUCTION: CONTEXT

A resilient cyber physical system is one that maintains state awareness and an accepted level of operational normalcy in response to disturbances, including threats of an unexpected and malicious nature (Rieger, Gertman, & McQueen, 2009). Responding to cyber attacks against cyber-physical systems such as automated vehicles, weapon systems, and manufacturing systems requires addressing cyber-attack risks that can potentially include consequences such as injuries or death. The amplified severity of these consequences compared with those of information-system cyber attacks necessitates new policy considerations related to cybersecurity. However, as was the case for the integration of information systems through the Internet, unless special attention is paid to this matter early on, security will likely be dominated by responses to actual attacks, rather than anticipatory solutions designed to reduce the risks.

Over the past 7 years the author has been leading a technology-focused research effort that addresses cyber-attack resilience for physical systems (Jones, Luckett, Beling, & Horowitz, 2013; Horowtiz & Pierce, 2013; Bayuk & Horowitz, 2011; Gay, Horowitz, Bobko, Elshaw, & Kim, 2017; Babineau, Jones, & Horowitz, 2012; Jones, Nguyen, & Horowitz, 2011; Horowitz, 2016; Horowitz & Scott Lucero, 2017). Unlike cyber-attack defense solutions, resilience solutions involve monitoring to detect successful cyber attacks and support for rapid reconfiguration of the attacked system for continued operation with contained consequences.

*Artificial Intelligence for the Internet of Everything*
https://doi.org/10.1016/B978-0-12-817636-8.00005-3

The reconfigurations can include modifications in the roles and procedures for human system operators as well as technology related adjustments. The monitoring subsystem(s), referred to as a Sentinel, for detection of attacks and derivation of potential reconfigurations must, in turn, be very highly secured to avoid becoming an attractive target for attacks. Resilience solutions can serve as a deterrent to attackers since they promise to reduce the highest risk consequences of potential cyber attacks. As an example of cyber-attack resiliency consider an automobile equipped with an automated collision-avoidance capability. A variety of cyber attacks have been demonstrated in which an automobile could be automatically directed toward a possible collision with another nearby vehicle. Monitoring the automobile's sensor outputs, control system inputs and outputs, and driver inputs through the acceleration and brake pedals, would provide a basis for recognition of an inconsistency potentially caused by a cyber attack impacting the control system. However, the control error could also be the result of erroneous sensor inputs. Comparing measurements from a diverse set of sensors would provide a basis for detecting and responding to either a failed or cyber attacked sensor subsystem. Integration of the alternate explanations for the control error provides the opportunity to automatically correct the situation or, alternately, provide an opportunity for the driver to respond. Note that a resilience solution impacts the effectiveness of a variety of possible cyber attacks that would create common symptoms.

The technology-focused research effort has included a number of prototyping projects involving protection of currently available, highly automated physical systems that are being cyber-attacked. These prototyping activities have served to demonstrate the importance of, and potential for, cyber-attack resiliency solutions. Specific operational prototyping activities have included: (1) a DoD-sponsored effort involving cyber defense of an unmanned air vehicle (UAV) conducting surveillance missions (including in-flight evaluations, Miller, 2014a); (2) defending automobiles (including Virginia State Police exercises with unsuspecting policemen driving cyber-attacked police cars, NBC.29, 2015; Higgins, 2015a); and (3) a National Institute of Standards sponsored effort involving the defense of a 3D printer through the monitoring of its motors, temperature controllers, and other physical component controllers, while in the process of printing defective parts due to cyber attacks on the machine's internal technology components. These real-world cases have served to illuminate a number of important and complex policy issues made visible to government and industry participants involved with the prototype projects. These policy issues are the subject of this paper.

## 5.2 THE NEED TO ADDRESS CYBERSECURITY FOR PHYSICAL SYSTEMS

Two important, closely related technology trends are occurring simultaneously; however, the two trends are not reinforcing.

Trend 1: The integration of technology-based automation capabilities associated with physical systems. This trend includes:

- the development of autonomous and highly automated vehicles for transportation (air, ground, and sea);
- the development of increasingly capable 3D printers and robots for manufacturing;
- the use of network-based access to physical systems to enable remote control and/or monitoring (e.g., physical system maintenance plans based upon measured conditions of use, customized patient health care–related responses based upon collected information from on-body sensors); and
- emergent Internet of Things (IoT) opportunities that relate to consumer products, the home, smart cities, etc.

Trend 2: The increasing recognition of the potential risks related to cyber attacks on physical systems, particularly with regard to human safety, not typically associated with cyber attacks on conventional information systems. While attacks on physical systems have not yet emerged as a high risk, various technology demonstrations have shown the potential threat of these types of attacks. Such demonstrations include the following:

- Recent automobile attacks (Higgins, 2015b) showing the feasibility of cyber attacks to cause physical harm;
- Actual high visibility cyber attacks on physical systems, such as the Stuxnet attacks (Falliere, Murchu, & Chien, 2011) highlighting the potential for other attacks of this kind. The Stuxnet attacks impacted a large number of Iranian nuclear-enrichment centrifuges, serving as a warning that industrial computer-controlled physical systems are vulnerable to attack; and
- Less publicized attacks on physical systems that have also occurred. For example, a German government security report indicated that an unnamed steel plant suffered an attack that impacted its blast furnace, causing significant damage (CART, 2013; Kovacs, 2014).

To-date, the cybersecurity engineering community has principally been focused on information systems, an area where the risks are different and the technical factors regarding cyber defense pose significantly different challenges.

## 5.2.1 Historic Patterns for Addressing Cybersecurity

While cybersecurity experts point to the fact that incorporating anticipatory cyber-security features into the design of systems provides a pathway for achieving better security, historically most solutions have been add-ons to systems in response to actual attacks (Miller, 2014b). The reasons for this are economic. When new innovations are in their early development phase (such as autonomous vehicles), designers are consumed with achieving a working system, and security is treated as something that will follow. When the innovation is ready to be brought to the market, concern about the cost impacts the security of the new products' prices and further delays security implementation. When the new products are selling, but significant attacks have yet to occur, there is no pressing demand to anticipate attacks. When attacks start occurring, and there are already large numbers of existing systems in use, responsive patching becomes the de-facto solution.

For existing information systems the major consequences of cyber attacks have been financial in nature or related to privacy. Should human safety become a primary risk of cyber attacks in the future, new societal patterns may emerge that demand stronger anticipatory solutions. Anticipatory solutions must be designed not only on the basis of prior attacks, but also based upon predictions of what cyber attackers might target in the future and how they might implement these attacks. Prediction of attacker behavior is quite complex, requiring considerations such as: (1) historic attacks; (2) attacker motivations; (3) attack complexity and corresponding attacker skill requirements; (4) costs of design and implementation; (5) risks of attacks failing; and (6) risks of getting caught. This situation is exacerbated by the need for competitors to share information (e.g., historic attack information) in order to have a more complete basis for making predictions and to provide the opportunity to derive a common framework for considering solutions that are related to a domain of similar products. Furthermore, for physical systems classes that include rapidly changing automation features, predictions can be unstable (e.g., the increasing rate for adding new automation features in automobiles points to the need for annual reconsideration of potential cyber attacks and the corresponding defenses). This situation is further complicated by the fact that it would be difficult to measure the success of resilience solutions serving to deter attacks, since deterrence is not directly observable. For all of these reasons one can expect that managing the design of anticipatory defenses would be quite difficult. Furthermore, should successful, high-visibility cyber attacks occur, confidence in anticipatory solutions serving as a deterrent would likely suffer, thereby resulting in reconsiderations regarding their effectiveness.

In the event that more emphasis is placed on implementing anticipatory solutions to cyber attacks, questions arise regarding the roles of industry and government in deciding on specific resilience requirements. With its superior knowledge of physical system design details and the potential means of exploiting those details, industry is in a much stronger position than government to address the selection of anticipatory solutions. On the other hand, with its access to information regarding actual cyber attacks, and considering our country's history of relying on government for implementing safety measures, government does possess some advantages. This suggests a shared role, but a variety of cybersecurity-specific complications, discussed in the following section, emerge when dividing accountabilities.

To demonstrate policy issues regarding the anticipation of cyber attacks, we return to the automobile collision avoidance–system scenario described in the initial section of this article. Note that this automobile example is pertinent to other classes of physical systems. Assume that a collision event was to actually occur as a result of the earlier-described cyber attack. Members of the law-enforcement community would be the principal investigators as to the cause, but they would have no basis for determining the cause as being a cyber attack. Doing so would likely require access to a portion of the stored data from the involved automobiles' onboard systems. Depending on the specific manufacturers and models of the involved automobiles, the data required to identify the cause as a cyber attack would likely vary from vehicle to vehicle. Due to these variations the costs associated with necessary field tools and officer training would be driven up. This may suggest standardization as the required solution, but the standardization of pertinent data implies corresponding commonalities in the designs of automation features, which creates issues related to competition. To further complicate matters, the cyber-security community recognizes risks associated with "monoculture solutions"; i.e., common designs are vulnerable to common cyber attacks, enabling undesirable reuse opportunities by those who employ or sell software that accomplishes cyber attacks. In addition, the automobile companies and individual drivers may be reticent to provide such data (e.g., intellectual property–protection reasons, and privacy reasons unrelated to the incident). This very complex set of circumstances will require significant attention and government and industry collaboration. Yet without evidence that cyber attacks on automobiles are actually occurring, it would take very strong leadership to push through measures allowing law enforcement to address cyber attacks on automobiles in an anticipatory manner.

Recognizing the natural desire to avoid the costs associated with anticipating cyber-security need, perhaps historical roles in safety regulation can provide a starting point for government involvement. Historically, with certain exceptions, safety analyses have not considered cyber attacks to be a safety issue. The trend of advancing highly automated physical systems into general use raises the issue of whether or not the safety communities (government and industry) should start to address this intersection. In doing so, it becomes necessary to understand and account for the relationships between the systems at risk and other interconnected and interrelated systems that can be a pathway for generating a cyber attack. If one starts down this path, some new and complex issues arise.

## 5.2.2 Mission-Based Cybersecurity

In this section, an integrated set of interconnected systems' combined mission is considered as the point of departure regarding anticipation of cyber attacks. The technology-focused research efforts that the author has been engaged in have addressed a number of illuminating scenarios. For example, as part of addressing UAV cybersecurity solutions, a variety of potential cyber attacks were considered as potential concerns that call for defensive capabilities. For illustration purposes consider cyber attacks aimed at modifying a UAV's flight path, adversely impacting its ability to carry out its safety-related surveillance mission (e.g., monitoring an oil or gas pipeline). Such an attack could, for example, accompany a physical attack on the pipeline. One way for an attacker to accomplish this outcome is to modify mission-related waypoints that have been entered into the navigation system on board the aircraft. One possible solution addresses a cyber-attack in which the ground-based portion of the UAV system is utilized by the attacker to automatically send surveillance-disrupting changes to the navigation waypoints loaded on board the aircraft. These changes would cause the aircraft to be routed in a manner that prevents gathering of the critical information the mission was intended to collect. A potential solution could involve monitoring the aircraft's navigation system and the pilot's data-entry system (e.g., key stroke monitoring). If, when a change in a waypoint is detected on the aircraft, there is no corresponding pilot data input, then a cyber attack is a possible cause. In response, the aircraft could transmit information to designated personnel who could then take actions to confirm and address the cyber-attack possibility. This example highlights the fact that certain attack detections require coordinating information retrieved from multiple subsystems at different locations. If one considers air traffic control systems, a parallel set of circumstances can occur involving ground-based subsystems (e.g., surveillance, communications, navigation, air traffic controller support systems) and corresponding airborne subsystems. Implementation of solutions would require decisions regarding the perceived level of risk, solution costs, the allocation of costs to subsystems, and decisions regarding the sources for paying for the solutions. Furthermore, for certain attacks that can create the same outcomes through different points of insertion, our technology-focused research efforts have shown that the ease of attack on one subsystem can be very different from that of another subsystem, providing opportunities to address the minimization of total costs when dealing with high-priority targets. However, lowering total costs can be accompanied by controversial cost-allocation issues, requiring policies that manage such situations. As stated earlier, without prior data that provides evidence that relevant cyber attacks are actually occurring, it will take very strong leadership to address the issues of anticipating safety-related outcomes and cost allocation for the implementation of solutions.

### 5.2.3 Education of Engineers and Policy-Makers

The discussions presented above do not address what may be the most critical issue in implementing cyber security for physical systems, namely the education of both our engineering and policy-making communities. Teams that include mechanical, electrical, and system engineers design physical systems. Engineering schools do not integrate computer security courses into the individual curriculums of these engineering disciplines. As a result, there are a very limited number of physical system–design engineers who have the requisite knowledge to design systems that better account for cyber-security considerations. Furthermore, educators in these areas of engineering have no historic basis for engaging in the cyber security–related aspects of their fields. As a result, our colleges and universities need to consider this emergent need and develop cross-department programs that are responsive to this new, important requirement. Development of new programs can be influenced by industry taking a strong position in calling upon the education system to provide such programs, including providing financial support for the development of new integrated programs, student internships, and professional-education programs that support their current workforce. Similar to the issues discussed earlier, it will take strong industry leadership to support such programs without prior data providing evidence that cyber attacks on physical systems are occurring.

A similar situation faces the policy-making community. As part of structuring resilience-related prototyping efforts, researchers have to address project-specific safety issues associated with conducting experiments. This requirement calls for interactions with a variety of policy organizations. Based on such interactions it became clear to the author that the imagination of policy makers with regards to what cyber attacks could potentially accomplish far exceeded reality. Furthermore, discussions surrounding particular cyber attacks and their consequences, as well as the solutions to be evaluated, made it clear that the requisite technology-related knowledge became an issue in deriving safety controls. Interestingly, in some cases, the policy outcomes could have been unnecessarily conservative and in others, not conservative enough. Another important finding was that the policy community found that the security community was greatly steeped in specialized technical jargon, providing a barrier to beneficial discussions regarding solutions and policies.

Of course, addressing this particular issue would require an education element for both policy makers and cyber-security engineers who engage in policy matters.

Perhaps a side issue, but one that could greatly influence matters, is that the demonstrations of cyber attacks on physical systems and their impacts can be interpreted as a consequence of the manufacturers or industrial users of those physical systems not being sufficiently sensitive to cyber security/safety-related outcomes in their products and system designs. As a result, in carrying out projects, the issue arises regarding reporting on the cybersecurity risks of current systems and the undue reputation impact it could have on the companies whose systems are being used for experimentation. It is not generally understood that the risks are emergent and that the nature of these findings would be expected across all current software-controlled physical systems that have safety-related outcome potentials. A need exists to address this topic, including defining professional behavior for engineers regarding reporting on the results of their work involving current commercial systems and cyber attacks, and its relationship to the related companies' reputations.

The author of this article has recently served as a Commissioner for Cybersecurity for the Commonwealth of Virginia, which, with strong support from the Governor, has been engaged in strategy development regarding cyber security (CyberVirginia, 2015). The 11-person Cybersecurity Commission for Virginia, working with Virginia's Cabinet members, has made strong recommendations regarding education programs, and the state has developed budgets to start addressing this need. This state-level initiative is the type of anticipatory action that will be required in order to prepare for the cyber attack of physical systems that could materialize.

## 5.3 CYBERSECURITY ROLE AND CERTIFICATION OF THE OPERATORS OF PHYSICAL SYSTEMS

An important aspect of the defense of physical systems from cyber attacks is that immediate system-reconfiguration responses to attack detections (including system shut-downs, which can be very expensive) may be necessary in order to provide the desired level of safety. This aspect calls for doctrine regarding immediate responses. Doctrine must include: (1) the allocation of decision-making and response-control roles to specified personnel, (2) selection criteria for and training of those people, (3) exercising for preparedness, and (4) addressing the possibilities of unanticipated confusion regarding operator judgments related to the possibility of missed or incorrect attack detections (including zero-day attacks).

Part of the author's research on physical system defense included human involvement in cyber attack scenarios. In the UAV case, a desktop simulation environment was used to gain an initial understanding of operator responses to a monitoring system that detects cyber attacks and provides suggested responses to the UAV pilots. In the State Police case, a controlled exercise was conducted involving unsuspecting policemen being dispatched and their cars being attacked and failing to operate properly. The results of these activities highlighted the point that the doctrinal processes to be developed must recognize the fact that cyber attacks on physical systems are an area where people do not and will not have practical experience to rely upon. Furthermore, since attacks are very unlikely to occur, responses may stray from what operators are trained for. The research efforts showed that operators, based on their past experiences, can usually imagine other causes for observed consequences of a cyber attack and, as a result, may not be as responsive to automated decision support as expected.

Consider the case in which a Sentinel detects a cyber attack that consists of an improper digital control message preventing a car from operating properly. From the operator's perspective there can be many different causes for the car not operating properly (e.g., a failed battery), and these are typically causes they have previously experienced. Consequently, under the immediate pressure of needing to take decisive action, the operator may be more likely to assume these causes of failure, rather than a never-experienced cyber attack. Research results showed that even when an operator accepts a Sentinel's input as being correct, uncertainty remains regarding the possibility for additional elements of the cyber attack having yet to emerge. This element of uncertainty is escalated when there are high consequences associated with an operator's decisions, and the operator's accountability for those decisions can impact behavior, including asking for access to cybersecurity experts before making a critical decision. Of course, such calls for help can potentially delay decision making to an undesirable degree. As a result of these scenarios actually emerging during our research experiments, a significant effort has been initiated to better understand human behavior in uncertain circumstances that are likely to exist in scenarios regarding cyber attacks on physical systems. From a policy vantage point, research efforts are needed to address questions regarding selection, certification, and readiness training requirements for operators of physical systems for which cyber attacks could have serious consequences.

## 5.4 DATA CURATION

Data curation can be defined as the active and ongoing management of data through its lifecycle of interest and usefulness. If one assumes that a critical step in vigorously addressing cyber security for physical systems is the need for early evidence that cyber attacks are actually occurring, significant issues emerge regarding curation of the data that would provide the needed evidence. Based on the automobile-focused State Police project referred to above, an important next step would be the development of accepted policies and processes regarding the collection, storage, security, sharing, analysis, and supplementation of data. For example, consider the case of distribution of specific data that were to be collected at the scene of an automobile incident and, based upon analysis, indicated a possible cyber attack. Recognizing the international manufacturing base for automobiles and the international sales of automobiles, information would need to be shared across the world. It would be important that worldwide law-enforcement agencies, national governments engaged in addressing automobile cyber security, automobile companies, and numerous others gain access to that data. As a result, international curation policies and processes would be called for. Organizations such as INTERPOL could potentially play a key role in creating the needed international orientation.

## 5.5 MARKET INCENTIVES

In February 2014, the National Institute of Standards and Technology (NIST) released Version 1 of White House Executive Order 13636—Cybersecurity Framework, an initial structure for organizations, government, and customers to use in considering comprehensive cyber-security programs (WH, 2013). In April 2015 a NIST presentation provided a status report on the evolving framework (NIST, 2015). The framework broadly addresses the specific needs that are discussed in the previous section, but without the required specificity to illuminate the complexity associated with anticipatory physical system solutions. Past efforts to establish market incentives for improved information system cyber security illustrate the consequences of inaction, and also demonstrate the uncertainties and difficulties surrounding anticipatory actions. The example provided by information systems highlights the importance of initiating early data collection efforts so that incidents can be assessed for potential cyber attacks and confirmed attacks can be documented. With this evidence in hand, it will be easier to evaluate next-step responses and incentives for anticipatory forms of cyber security will be increased. As emphasized above, it will be difficult to motivate anticipatory solutions without confirmation that attacks on physical systems are actually occurring. The National Highway Safety Traffic System (NHTSA), through guidance that they are providing for improving automobile-related cybersecurity, has taken encouraging steps to anticipate some of the needs addressed above (USDOT, 2016). A potential sequence of events is that data collection starts early and provides incontrovertible evidence of attacks on physical systems, which then drives the development of the needed government, industry, and consumer relationships that underpin market incentives for investment in anticipatory cyber security. As suggested above, attacks on physical systems generally pose a much greater risk to human safety than attacks on information systems. Therefore it may be easier to motivate firms and policymakers to invest in physical system security, since potential consequences are so severe. The development of data curation processes that could promote the involvement of appropriate government, industry, and consumer groups appears to be a critical early step towards achieving market incentives.

## 5.6 CONCLUSIONS AND RECOMMENDATIONS

This article emphasizes the point that due to the risk of injuries and deaths associated with cyber attacks on physical systems, anticipatory cybersecurity solutions are likely to be desired, potentially much more so than has been the case for information-system cyber security. In addition, a number of examples have been provided that illuminate both the complexity of addressing anticipation and the difficulties associated with selecting and applying the most critical solutions. This complexity includes recognizing the impacts of subsystem interconnections in critical systems, such as air traffic control systems. It has been suggested that managing the implementation of anticipatory solutions will require teams of government and industrial organizations, both to address the consequences of attacks and to design systems for detecting and responding to attacks. The examples highlight the fact that this is an international issue, involving government as well as the relevant industries. The examples also demonstrate that standardization solutions have to consider their monoculture implications in addition to the normal factors that relate to standardization. In order to make progress, our education system needs to prioritize addressing cyber security across a broader set of education programs than is currently the practice.

Additionally, it appears likely that evidence of actual cyber attacks on physical systems will be a necessary precursor for anticipatory solutions; due to the associated costs, it is unlikely that self-motivation will be sufficient to drive investment in cyber security for physical systems. The creation of market incentives for investment in cybersecurity for physical systems will require the engagement of government, industry, and consumer organizations. Since they are first on the scene for incidents of the kind being addressed here, the law-enforcement community would seemingly be a logical choice for collecting the needed data. Consequently, the first step in post-event data analysis is equipping law-enforcement officers with applicable equipment, so that they can identify the events caused by cyber attacks. It is also suggested that industry members engage with the law-enforcement community to determine the data requirements to identify a cyber attack. Once a number of instances are documented, the policy responses suggested above will likely increase in priority. Hopefully, with appropriate engagement of consumer groups, anticipatory solutions will arise. In order for a rapid response to be possible, an early emphasis must be placed on supporting relevant research and education.

An interesting side note related to this paper is that technology-focused, system prototype experiments served to create early interactions between technologists and policy makers that illuminated a number of important issues related to policy. It would appear that prototype-based projects that serve to couple government and industry would be a valuable method for accelerating the partnerships necessary for identifying and addressing critical policy issues. A preliminary strategy would include identifying safety-related domains that demand the rapid integration of fast-changing technologies into their physical systems. This article provides examples related to advanced air traffic control and automated automotive systems.

## ACKNOWLEDGMENTS

This material is based upon work supported, in whole or in part, by the US Department of Defense through the Systems Engineering Research Center under Contract HQ0034-13-0004. The SERC is a federally funded University Affiliated Research Center managed by Stevens Institute of Technology, Hoboken, NJ, USA. Any opinions, findings, and conclusions or recommendations expressed in this material are those of the authors and do not necessarily reflect the views of the US Department of Defense.

## REFERENCES

Babineau, G. L., Jones, R. A., & Horowitz, B. M. (2012). A system-aware cyber security method for shipboard control systems with a method described to evaluate cyber security solutions. In *2012 IEEE international conference on technologies for homeland security (HST)*.

Bayuk, J. L., & Horowitz, B. M. (2011). An architectural systems engineering methodology for addressing cyber security. *Systems Engineering, 14*, 294–304.

CyberVirginia. (2015). About the Commission. Available from: https://www.cyberva.virginia.gov/about-the-commission/.

Cyber Security Research Alliance (CART). (2013). *Designed-in cyber security for cyber-physical systems*. Workshop report.

Falliere, N., Murchu, L. O., & Chien, E. (2011). *W32.Stuxnet Dossier*. Symantec Security Response.

Gay, C., Horowitz, B., Bobko, P., Elshaw, J., & Kim, I. (2017). Operator suspicion and decision responses to cyber-attacks on unmanned ground vehicle systems. In *HFES 2017 international annual meeting, Austin, TX*.

Higgins, K. J. (2015a). State trooper vehicles hacked. *Dark Reading*. September.

Higgins, K. J. (2015b). Car hacking shifts into high gear. *Dark Reading*. July.

Horowitz, B. M. (2016). *AFCEA SIGNAL—cybersecurity for unmanned aerial vehicle missions*. April (pp. 40–43).

Horowitz, B. M., & Scott Lucero, D. (2017). System-aware cybersecurity: a systems engineering approach for enhancing cybersecurity. *INCOSE INSIGHT*. https://doi.org/10.1002/inst.12165.

Horowtiz, B. M., & Pierce, K. M. (2013). The integration of diversely redundant designs, dynamic system models, and state estimation technology to the cyber security of physical systems. *Systems Engineering, 16*(4), 401–412.

Jones, R. A., Luckett, B., Beling, P., & Horowitz, B. M. (2013). Architectural scoring framework for the creation and evaluation of system-aware cyber security solutions. *Journal of Environmental Systems and Decisions, 33*(3), 341–361.

Jones, R. A., Nguyen, T. V., & Horowitz, B. M. (2011). System-aware security for nuclear power systems. In *2011 IEEE international conference on technologies for homeland security (HST)*, pp. 224–229.

Kovacs, E. (2014). Cyberattack on German steel plant caused significant damage: report. *Security Week*. December.

Miller, P. C. (2014a). University of Virginia research protects UAS from cyber-attackers. *UAS Magazine*. December.

Miller, P. C. (2014b). Dual knowledge for UAS Cybersecurity. *UAS Magazine*. December.

NBC29.com. (2015). *Va. CyberSecurity research working to protect first responders*. Press Release from the Office of Governor Terry McAuliffe.

NIST Presentation. (2015). *Framework for improving critical infrastructure cybersecurity— implementation of executive order 13636*.

Rieger, C., Gertman, D., & McQueen, M. (2009). Resilient control systems: next generation design research. *International conference on human system interaction*.

The White House (WH). (2013). Executive order—improving critical infrastructure cybersecurity. Available from: https://obamawhitehouse.archives.gov/the-press-office/2013/02/12/executive-order-improving-critical-infrastructure-cybersecurity/.

US DOT. (2016). *V issues federal guidance to the automotive industry for improving motor vehicle security*. https://www.nhtsa.gov/press-releases/us-dot-issues-federal-guidance-automotive-industry-improving-motor-vehicle.

## FURTHER READING

Jones, R. A., & Horowitz, B. M. (2012). System-aware cyber security architecture. *Systems Engineering, 15*(2), 224–240.

# CHAPTER 6

# Trust and Human-Machine Teaming: A Qualitative Study

**Joseph B. Lyons\*, Kevin T. Wynne†, Sean Mahoney\*, Mark A. Roebke‡**
\*Air Force Research Laboratory, Dayton, OH, United States
†University of Baltimore, Baltimore, MD, United States
‡Air Force Institute of Technology, Dayton, OH, United States

## 6.1 BACKGROUND

Humans are surrounded by advanced technology on a regular basis. Technology is often a ubiquitous aspect of our daily routines, and for some, interactions with technology may overshadow interpersonal interactions. Due to the Internet of Things (IoT), technologies will be connected in a ubiquitous fashion enabling new interactions and novel forms of technology dependence. As the boundaries blur between the frequencies of human versus technology interactions, researchers have begun to examine the topic of human-machine teaming (Chen & Barnes, 2014; Groom & Nass, 2007). Whether one is working side-by-side in a factory with a collaborative robot (i.e., a co-bot), driving alongside an autonomous car or taxi, walking past a Knightscope robot patrolling a parking lot, working with a bomb-disposal robot in a military scenario, or trekking with a ground quadruped robot in the austere mountains of Afghanistan, humans are increasingly likely to interact with robotic systems. While in most of these extant interactions humans would likely characterize the robot as a "tool" versus a "teammate," teaming perceptions are increasingly warranted as technology advances in both capability and interactive capacity (Ososky, Schuster, Phillips, & Jentsch, 2013), notably driven by the omnipresent connectivity afforded by the IoT. Teaming with robots (versus teleoperation) is one of the emerging research domains within the military and society more broadly. The present chapter discusses the concepts of trust and teaming perceptions of advanced, yet contemporary, technology and this chapter is based, in part, on a proceedings paper from the 2018 AAAI Spring Symposium.

*Artificial Intelligence for the Internet of Everything*
https://doi.org/10.1016/B978-0-12-817636-8.00006-5

101

### 6.1.1 Human-Machine Trust

Technology is not only extending its breadth within society, but it is also increasing in its capacity for autonomous action. The combination of increased decision initiative and expanded decision authority is a recipe for potential disaster if and/or when the technology makes an error. A recent meta-analysis found that the consequences for automation errors are most severe when the systems exhibit the highest levels of automation (Onnasch, Wickens, Li, & Manzey, 2014). Thus researchers have for decades tried to understand the gamut of factors that shape trust in technologies such as automated systems (see Hoff & Bashir, 2015; Lee & See, 2004). Trust broadly refers to the belief that a technology will help an individual accomplish her/his goals in situations of high uncertainty and complexity (Lee & See, 2004). Trust captures one's willingness to be vulnerable to another entity—this vulnerability can be directed toward other people (Mayer, Davis, & Schoorman, 1995) or it could refer to vulnerability to machines (Lyons & Stokes, 2012). Trust researchers have predominantly examined these beliefs in lab contexts; however, researchers have begun to examine trust of actual fielded systems in applied contexts (see Lyons, Ho, et al., 2016a; Ho et al., 2017).

One of the key aspects of prior trust research is the identification of factors that influence the trust process—herein referred to as trust antecedents. The current study considers a number of trust antecedents each having support from previous research as a trust antecedent. The trust antecedents examined in this chapter include: reliability (Hancock et al., 2011), predictability (Lee & See, 2004), helping to solve a problem (i.e., supporting task accomplishment; Hoff & Bashir, 2015), proactively helping a person (similar to the notion of benevolence in the interpersonal trust literature; Ho et al., 2017), transparency of decision logic (Lyons, Koltai, et al., 2016b; Sadler et al., 2016), transparency of intent (Lyons, 2013; Lyons, Ho, et al., 2016a), transparency of state (Mercado et al., 2016), liking (Merritt, 2011), familiarity (Hoff & Bashir, 2015), and social interaction (Waytz, Heafner, & Epley, 2014).

### 6.1.2 Human-Machine Teaming

In addition to trust perceptions, the current chapter also examines perceptions of human-machine teaming. But what does it mean to be part of a "team"? Groom and Nass (2007) outline several components of effective teamwork, which include: shared goals, shared awareness (i.e., shared mental models), the desire for interdependence, motivation toward team versus individual objectives, action toward team objectives, and trust among team members. These factors are paramount to team effectiveness, and studies in the management domain have confirmed the importance of many of these team-performance characteristics (Cohen & Bailey, 1997; De Jong, Dirks, & Gillespie, 2016; Kozlowski & Bell, 2003; Salas, Cooke, & Rosen, 2008). Yet, which of these factors can/should apply toward machine partners? Wynne and Lyons (2018) define *autonomous agent teammate-likeness* as "the extent to which a human operator perceives and identifies an autonomous, intelligent agent partner as a highly altruistic, benevolent, interdependent, emotive, communicative and synchronized agent teammate, rather than simply an instrumental tool" (p. 355). The model posited by Wynne and Lyons is outlined further below. It should be noted that it is believed to be the interactive components of the dimensions below rather than a single dimension alone that influence teammate-likeness perceptions as a whole, thus teaming perceptions may include a combination of factors.

## 6.1.3 Perceived Agency

Robotic systems that have greater decision authority—and greater capability to execute that decision authority—should influence teammate perceptions. By definition, a teammate is an autonomous entity that can contribute to the team's goals, herein the notion of agency to execute those goals is key. Imagine playing soccer with a goalie who is not allowed to touch the ball. The goalie would probably not be viewed as a teammate since she/he couldn't actually participate in the game. Machine partners absent agency are mere programs that should be interpreted as more tool-like. Effective agents should be able to observe the environment, process relevant goal-oriented information, and act on the environment (Chen & Barnes, 2014)—hence exemplifying agency. A lack of perceived agency should infer lack of autonomy and increase perceptions that are tool-like versus teammate-like.

## 6.1.4 Perceived Benevolence

Like trust as discussed in the sections above, a core assumption of a teammate is that the teammate has one's best interests in mind. Teammates support one another and provide back-up where and when needed. The same should hold true of machine partners. As noted above, benevolence is a core trust antecedent (Mayer et al., 1995) and it has been discussed as a key factor in driving human-robot trust (Lyons, 2013). Understanding the intent of a robotic system is a key ingredient to acceptance of the technology (Lasota & Shah, 2015). In an experimental study, Lasota and Shah (2015) found that robots made better teammates with participants in a joint manual task when the robots were aware of the human's next action—thus adding predictability into the robot's future intent. Further, robots that convey empathy (attributed intent) are liked more by participants (Leite et al., 2013). Thus perceived benevolence from the technology should be an important factor in deciding whether the technology is a tool versus a teammate.

## 6.1.5 Perceived Task Interdependence

Mutual interdependence is a cornerstone of what it means to be part of a team. Interdependence presupposes some commonality in tasks and goals. When teaming with a machine partner, it is likely that the machine and human will work on separate aspects of the same task jointly. If structured appropriately, the task will be able to be divided into task components that are appropriate for the human and components that are appropriate for the machine to maximize the overall effectiveness of the human-machine team. In any case, interdependence with the machine will likely increase the perception of the technology as a teammate versus as a tool.

## 6.1.6 Relationship-Building

Imagine a world where teammates only discussed task-related information—what a boring relationship! True team members engage each other at a social level beyond the task. In fact, social engagement can often be an important precursor to effective task work. Ososky et al. (2013) suggests that for humans to view robotic systems as partners, the interactive affordances need to move from one-sided information-centric transmissions to more naturalistic and dynamic dialogue-based interactions. This will move the communication process from merely task-based to more relationship/team-building-focused. Research by Hamacher, Bianchi-Berthouze, Pipe, and Eder (2016) shows that when interacting with robots, humans prefer robots that are expressive and warm over robots that are just focused on the task. These team-focused communications can signal loyalty and help build rapport among team members, which are important team processes. As such, relationship-building communications will likely influence the perception of the technology as a teammate versus as a tool.

### 6.1.7 Communication Richness

Related to the above dimension, human–agent teams should be capable of rich dialogue to convey task and team-based information between each other (Chen & Barnes, 2014). Rich communicative and social cue affordances may make robots more effective when interacting with humans (Mutlu, 2011). The key distinction between this dimension and the above dimension is that the above dimension discusses nontask-oriented communications, which are geared toward team-building. The current dimension focuses on the richness of communication in general, which could include both task-oriented and nontask communications. Media richness is believed to facilitate team effectiveness due to the added social and task-based information that rich media can convey (Hanumantharao & Grabowski, 2006). The greater the richness of communication affordances between the human and the technology, the greater the likelihood of the human viewing the technology as a teammate versus a tool.

### 6.1.8 Synchrony

Effective teams are comprised of team members who have a shared awareness of the task, the team, and the context. Indeed, shared awareness and, more specifically, having synchronized mental models has been shown to enhance team effectiveness (Hinds & Mortensen, 2005). Shared mental models have also been hypothesized to be important for human–machine teams (Ososky et al., 2013). Having synchrony between team members allows the team to share a common perception of the team and its capabilities/limitations, the context, which facilitates joint adaptation, and the task, which enables the team members to anticipate the actions of others.

In summary, the current paper examines the antecedents of human–machine trust and the components of human–machine teaming using the Autonomous Agent Teammate-Likeness model (Wynne & Lyons, 2018) as a guiding rubric. It was expected that the trust antecedent themes of reliability, predictability, helping solve a problem, proactively helping, transparency (logic, intent, and state), liking, familiarity, and social interaction would be expressed in the open-ended rationale for why individuals report trust (or distrust) of the technology. It was expected that perceptions of agency, benevolence, interdependence, relationship-building, communication richness, and synchrony would be associated with more teammate (versus tool) perceptions.

## 6.2 METHOD

### 6.2.1 Participants

Six hundred and five US workers responded to an open call for participation on Amazon's Mechanical Turk (MTurk). The MTurk workers were all employed at least part-time and were at least 18 years of age. No other demographics were collected in this study. Participants were compensated for their participation.

### 6.2.2 Study Description and Items

As part of a study focused on trust in automated technologies, participants were asked to identify one "intelligent technology" that they use on a regular basis. The following definition and description was provided to participants:

> Intelligent technologies or autonomous systems are technologies that can decide how and when to interact with you during tasks, communicate and/or dialogue with you, and or technologies that can help you accomplish your goals. Examples might include things like autonomous cars, service robots, industrial robots, robotic assistants, navigation aids, Amazon Echo/Google Home, the Nest, Siri, etc.

Once a technology was identified, participants were asked to describe reasons why they trust or distrust the technology. No explicit definitions of trust were provided nor were any of the trust antecedents mentioned as possible reasons for trust/distrust. Participants were given an open text box to respond. Next, participants were asked to characterize the relationship they had with the technology as a teammate- or tool-like relationship. Then they were asked to discuss why they characterized the relationship as a teammate relationship or (if they earlier noted that the relationship was more tool-like) what it would take for the relationship to be viewed as one of a teammate. Thus in either characterization the present study sought to understand the components of human-machine teaming—either as perceived currently or as visualized for a future scenario involving this technology. These open-ended responses were, in turn, coded according to the scheme described later.

### 6.2.3 Coding Method

Four coders independently coded the open-ended items. Two raters coded the entire set and two others coded a portion of the data. All raters were first trained on the coding process and on the trust antecedents and human-machine teaming dimensions. Next, all four raters coded the first 70 participants and the coding team met to discuss their ratings. The next 30 participants were coded together as a team and consensus coding was used for the first set of participants (100 in total). For the remaining 505 responses, two raters coded for trust and two raters coded for teaming. The two rater pairs evidenced 90% agreement or higher for both sets of data. Approximately 5% of the data was not usable for the teaming item due to participants saying things like "there is no way a machine can be a teammate." The items were coded for the following dimensions.

## 6.2.4 Trust

The following trust antecedents were coded: reliability, predictability, helps solve a problem, proactively helped, evidenced transparency logic, evidenced transparent intent, evidenced transparent state, liking, familiarity, and social interaction. Examples of each rating category are below. It should be noted that the concepts of reliability and predictability are similar, and they were often both rated as present in the open-ended items. However, they were distinguished in the present study as reliability being more about "doing a task effectively or with high performance" whereas predictability was more about stability of some behavior over time (for instance, always failing at a certain task would be an example of predictability but not reliability, or always responding a certain way independent of performance). They were often used in conjunction with one another (e.g., "consistently works well"); however, not always. The "help solve a problem" and "proactively helps me" codes were distinguishable in the sense that in the latter, the technology actively supports the user without the user's constant inputs and monitoring.

*Reliability is the main thing. Once I get it set up I need to know it will stay working (reliability)*

*Dependability and consistency … (predictability)*

*This technology allows for an easier experience with less physical stress (helped solve a problem)*

*I gain trust in the device(s) as they show that they are becoming able to predict my preferences and behaviors from limited data points and when they demonstrate they can self-correct when their predictions are wrong—it makes me see them more like smart devices, like robots, than devices that simply react at a certain time, like an alarm clock (proactively helped me)*

*When it is pulling updated files from publishers nightly … (transparency—logic)*

*At first I was a little scared that anyone could make a purchase without my autho-rization (like a visiting friend or other family member) but there are verifications to go through that keep that from happening. This helped me to trust it a little better … (transparency—intent)*

*There is a constant and dynamic feedback loop that generates reports on system usage and efficiency ratings (transparency—state)*

*It is very intuitive and it just feels like there is an unspoken bond (liking)*

*Intuitive touch interface … (familiarity)*

*As far as 'behaviors,' I suppose the fact that it talks to you like a person is supposed to make you feel more comfortable. It does have a pleasant sounding voice (social interaction)*

## 6.2.5 Human-Machine Teaming

Next, items were coded as either teammate or tool according to the partic-ipants. There was 100% agreement among the raters on this dimension. Next, the open-ended item was coded using the teammate-likeness model as a guiding rubric. In addition to the six dimensions noted above, a seventh category of "humanness" was added based on initial coding training and consensus coding, which noted a high frequency of responses like, "it should act like a human" or "it should be like a human" or "it should have human qualities." The two raters averaged over 90% agreement across the seven dimensions. It was possible, and very common, for multiple dimensions to be coded in the same participant response. Example excerpts for each dimension are below.

*For it to be more of a teammate it would have to do things without me asking (Agency)*

*It is a teammate to me. We work together to achieve this great balance where I trust the technology and Nest achieves its goals in making sure my home's temperature is just the way I like it (Benevolence)*

*I think of the Nest as more of a teammate. This is because it is working with me to help me reach a goal of becoming more energy efficient and helping me save money by making changes together to make it work the best (Interdependence)*

*I see this completely as a tool. It's a functional item outside of me. A teammate would need to be more human, more personal, and more emotionally connected. I don't feel any emotional connection but rather a fully tool-like use (Relationship building)*

*I think for it to become more of a teammate, it would have to do far more than it does already. While it seems very personable, I know what kind of "data" it can tell me, and as far as that goes, it's not too personal. To be more of a teammate, it could recommend places to eat out of nowhere, randomly talk to me about things, chime in on conversations and just generally exhibit more human-like behavior (Communication richness)*

*… To be a teammate it would need to "understand" better. That is, instead of me anticipating it, it would need to anticipate my needs. It's smart, but still lacking sometimes (Synchrony)*

*I consider it more of a tool. It would have to become either an actual human being, or an AI that was so human like you couldn't tell it wasn't, in order for me to consider it a teammate (Humanness)*

## 6.3 RESULTS

Four-hundred and nine participants (68%) reported that they believed their technology was tool-like versus teammate-like. The remaining 32% reported the relationship as more teammate-like. Forty-one percent were home technologies, 31% mobile technologies, 15% navigation aids, 3% automotive, 3% robotic systems, and 7% were classified as "other." The technologies were further broken down based on brands. Twenty-two percent were Amazon products (Alexa, Echo), 15% were Apple products (Siri, iPhone), 11% were Google Maps, 6% were Androids or Google Assist, 5% were Google Home, 3% were Nest, and less than 1% for Tesla and iRobot each. An additional 36% was classified as "other." These classifications and brands were categorized a priori.

As shown in Fig. 6.1, reliability was the primary trust antecedent mentioned by participants. This was followed by predictability, helped solve a problem, and proactively helped, in order of frequency. The remaining trust antecedents were mentioned fewer than 50 times by the participants. There were no notable differences in trust antecedents based on whether the participants viewed the technology as a tool versus as a team member.

As shown in Fig. 6.2, humanness was the most noted reason for viewing a technology as a team member. This was followed by agency and communication richness.

However, given the imbalance between participants who noted a teammate relationship versus a tool-like perception, as opposed to reporting the absolute frequency of the dimensions by teammate versus tool perception, we also reported the percentage of the dimension reported by the participants.

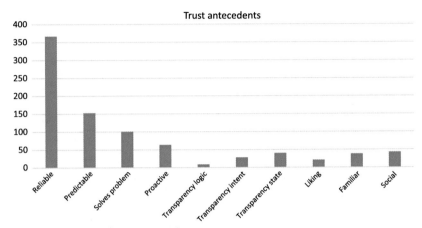

**Fig. 6.1** Frequency of trust antecedents.

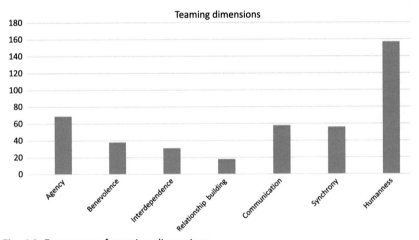

**Fig. 6.2** Frequency of teaming dimensions.

In other words, the percentage of the responses for that dimension were calculated for each of those who viewed the technology as a teammate and those who viewed the technology as a tool. As shown in Fig. 6.3, those who viewed the technology as a teammate reported a greater percentage of benevolence and interdependence comments relative to those who viewed the technology as a tool. In contrast, when participants viewed the technology as a tool, they reported a greater percentage of comments that it would take humanness and communication richness to view the technology as a teammate.

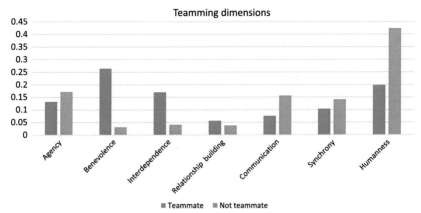

**Fig. 6.3** Percentage of teaming dimensions by teaming category (teammate versus not).

## 6.4 DISCUSSION

Advances in technology presence and capability are forcing research to examine social attitudes toward complex machines. Two variables of note include evaluations of *trust*—one's willingness to be vulnerable (and the associated antecedents of which)—and the construct of *human-machine teaming*, an elusive yet omnipresent term among contemporary researchers.

The current study examined the antecedents of trust and the dimensions of human-machine teaming using a qualitative sample and a broad cross-section of US workers. Participants were simply asked to list an intelligent technology that they use on a regular basis and then describe their use. The majority of these technologies were home-based technologies, such as the Amazon Echo, or mobile technologies, such as an iPhone equipped with Siri. First, the participants were asked to describe why they either trust or distrust the technology. Next, they were asked whether they viewed the technology as a tool or a teammate (and why). An emerging model of teammate-likeness was used to create a coding scheme for examining the qualitative data. The data largely confirm the extant trust antecedents and the utility of the teammate-likeness construct overall.

When considering trust antecedents, participants emphasized the constructs of reliability, predictability, and support (both task-oriented and proactive support). These results are consistent with prior literature on trust in automation. Several meta-analyses have confirmed the importance of reliability (i.e., high performance) on trust (Hancock et al., 2011; Schaefer, Chen, Szalma, & Hancock, 2016). Further, predictability is fundamental to trust perceptions (Hoff & Bashir, 2015; Lee & See, 2004). The combination of reliability and predictability allows users of automated systems to develop appropriate expectations of the technology in task contexts. Support in completing one's tasks (not merely the notion of high reliability) was found to be important, and this is logical as technology that makes people more effective at something (tasks or social functions) should be trusted more. The idea of proactive support was also relevant. This is consistent with the construct of benevolence. Despite the machine ontology of the systems considered by the humans, they appeared to value when the machine proactively monitors the environment and reacted on the behalf of the human without prompts by the humans. This behavior may be most relevant for systems that have both high competence and high decision authority (Lyons, 2013).

Interestingly, the facets of transparency involving understanding of the logic for decisions, state awareness, and intent did not play prominently in the participants' descriptions of trust rationale. There are a couple potential explanations for these findings. First, it is possible that transparency of intent overlapped with proactive support, as this is similar to benevolence, which is a form of transparency of intent. Second, it is possible that the technologies used as referents in the present study did not contain decision-making affordances. Prior research has found that transparency of decision logic has focused on complex automation, where an automated aid recommended a course of action in a highly complex situation (Lyons, Koltai, et al., 2016b). Further, recent research—which found benefits for added state awareness and projection—utilized highly complex automation and complex military scenarios (see Mercado et al., 2016). Thus it is plausible that greater emphasis would be placed on transparency in cases of highly complex systems that were being used in dynamic and multifaceted scenarios. Future research should examine this speculation, and future systems developed to exploit the IoT may enable these more complex scenarios.

There were also few mentions of the constructs of liking, familiarity, and social interaction. Again, it is possible that the types of technology considered by the participants influenced these findings. All of the technologies considered were systems that are currently in use (i.e., they were not notion, prototype, or futuristic systems), which could have created a ceiling effect for familiarity (i.e., it is unlikely that individuals referred to a technology that they were unfamiliar with). For this same reason it is possible that there was a ceiling effect for liking, as it is unlikely that participants used a technology referent for a system that was highly disliked. Future research can mitigate this limitation of the current study by using structured vignettes to manipulate features of technology to carefully investigate the nuances of various technologies. This will be particularly true for the social-interaction construct, as not all technologies considered by the participants had this feature.

The six dimensions of the teammate-likeness model were all invoked in the explanations for why the technology was (or could be) viewed as a teammate, though not equally. Among the a priori set of dimensions, agency was most common followed by communication richness and synchrony. This shows the importance of viewing the technology as possessing some level of decision authority for a human to view the technology as a teammate. Furthermore, the findings for interdependence correspond to the management literature in terms of the importance of interdependence among individuals on a team. These are clearly important features for humans when considering the teaming relationship with technology. While the current results are interesting from a research perspective, care should be taken so that decision authority and interdependence with automated systems is done only when it has been carefully considered along with the potential limitations of such technologies. Human–machine teams may prove to be more effective than either humans or technology alone; however, great care must be taken in the design and implementation of technology in the workplace to avoid overreliance on reliable technology, as such, overreliance can result in negative consequences if and when the technology (or the human) makes mistakes (see Onnasch et al., 2014 for a review).

Relationship-building was the least common explanation provided by participants. It is possible that the affordances provided by the existing technologies did not allow for relationship-building. While many of the technologies listed offer interactive features, many of these technologies lack the capacity to develop relationships. This dimension may be more relevant for more advanced future technologies. As noted above, this limitation could be addressed in future research by structuring the types of technologies considered (i.e., surveying participants with a wider gamut of technology affordances).

Interestingly, an unexpected dimension, *humanness*, was the most common response for what makes (or what should make) a technology be viewed as a teammate. The mere notion of a teammate may invoke anthropomorphic perceptions—engendering comparisons to a more traditional human partner. What remains unclear is whether or not the humanness dimension was a conglomeration of the other dimensions noted in the Autonomous Agent Teammate-Likeness Model (Wynne & Lyons, 2018).

For instance, agency, intent, rich communication affordances, and relationship-orientation may be facets of what people believe "humanness" consists. However, it was impossible to test this speculation with the current data given that many participants simply said the technology should be "like a human" without saying what that actually means. Future research should examine the dimensions of human–machine teaming to determine if humanness is unique from the other components of teammate-likeness.

Another interesting finding is that participants noted different dimensions of teaming depending on whether they viewed the technology as a teammate versus as a tool. For participants who perceived the technology as a teammate, they reported a higher percentage of comments relating to benevolence and interdependence. For these individuals the technology offered support and was believed to work interdependently with the humans. These factors are consistent with dimensions of team processes found in the literature on interpersonal teams (Cohen & Bailey, 1997; De Jong et al., 2016; Kozlowski & Bell, 2003). Human–machine teams appear to involve some of the similar team process variables. In contrast, when individuals viewed the technology as a tool, they believed that added communication richness and humanness would facilitate future teammate perceptions. It is interesting to note that these dimensions are what people might look for in prospective teammate relationships versus what they currently experience within teammate relationships.

A final notable finding in the current study is the fact that over 30% of the sample reported viewing the relationship with the technology as a teammate-based partnership. This suggests that human–machine teaming is a viable and fruitful topic of inquiry within the human factors and robotics literatures, because individuals do evidently establish very intimate connections with technologies. Future research is needed to validate the dimensions of human–machine teaming to better understand why and how humans make these connections with advanced technology.

## 6.5 CONCLUSION

The current study examined perceptions of current technology as described by a sample of US workers. Clearly, a significant portion of this sample viewed the technology as a partner, whereas the majority viewed them as tools. Several trust antecedents were revealed while questions remain why others were not as prominent. With regard to human–machine teaming, several dimensions were revealed and another robust factor emerged—humanness. However, additional research is needed to fully unpack the nomological network of human–machine teaming dimensions. The current study demonstrates that human–machine teaming is a promising and complex phenomenon for future research and practice.

## REFERENCES

Chen, J. Y. C., & Barnes, M. J. (2014). Human-agent teaming for multirobot control: a review of the human factors issues. *IEEE Transactions on Human-Machine Systems, 44* (1), 13–29.

Cohen, S. G., & Bailey, D. E. (1997). What makes teams work: group effectiveness research from the shop floor to the executive suite. *Journal of Management, 23,* 239–290.

De Jong, B. A., Dirks, K. T., & Gillespie, N. (2016). Trust and team performance: a meta-analysis of main effects, moderators, and covariates. *Journal of Applied Psychology, 101,* 1134–1150.

Groom, V., & Nass, C. (2007). Can robots be teammates? Benchmarks in human-robot teams. *Interaction Studies, 8,* 483–500.

Hamacher, A., Bianchi-Berthouze, N., Pipe, A. G., & Eder, K. (2016). Believing in BERT: using expressive communication to enhance trust and counteract operational error in physical human-robot interaction. *Proceedings of IEEE international symposium on robot and human interaction communication (RO-MAN),* New York: IEEE.

Hancock, P. A., Billings, D. R., Schaefer, K. E., Chen, J. Y. C., de Visser, E. J., & Parasuraman, R. (2011). A meta-analysis of factors affecting trust in human-robot interaction. *Human Factors, 53*(5), 517–527.

Hanumantharao, S., & Grabowski, M. (2006). Effects of introducing collaborative technology on communications in a distributed safety-critical system. *International Journal of Human-Computer Studies, 64,* 714–726.

Hinds, P. J., & Mortensen, M. (2005). Understanding conflict in geographically distributed teams: the moderating effects of shared identity, shared context, and spontaneous communication. *Organization Science, 16,* 290–307.

Ho, N. T., Sadler, G. G., Hoffmann, L. C., Lyons, J. B., Fergueson, W. E., & Wilkins, M. (2017). A longitudinal field study of auto-GCAS acceptance and trust: first year results and implications. *Journal of Cognitive Engineering and Decision Making, 11,* 239–251.

Hoff, K. A., & Bashir, M. (2015). Trust in automation: integrating empirical evidence on factors that influence trust. *Human Factors, 57,* 407–434.

Kozlowski, S. W. J., & Bell, B. S. (2003). Work groups and teams in organizations. W. Borman & D. Illgen (Eds.), *Handbook of psychology: Industrial and organizational psychology* (pp. 333–375). Vol. 12(pp. 333–375). New York, NY: John Wiley & Sons Inc.

Lasota, P. A., & Shah, J. A. (2015). Analyzing the effects of human-aware motion planning on close-proximity human-robot collaboration. *Human Factors, 57,* 21–33.

Lee, J. D., & See, K. A. (2004). Trust in automation: designing for appropriate reliance. *Human Factors, 46,* 50–80.

Leite, I., Pereira, A., Mascarenhas, S., Martinho, C., Prada, R., & Paiva, A. (2013). The influence of empathy in human-robot relations. *International Journal of Human-Computer Studies, 71,* 250–260.

Lyons, J. B. (2013). Being transparent about transparency: a model for human-robot interaction. In D. Sofge, G. J. Kruijff, & W. F. Lawless (Eds.), *Trust and autonomous systems: Papers from the AAAI spring symposium (Technical Report SS-13-07).* Menlo Park, CA: AAAI Press.

Lyons, J. B., Ho, N. T., Fergueson, E., Sadler, G., Cals, S., Richardson, C., et al. (2016a). Trust of an automatic ground collision avoidance technology: a fighter pilot perspective. *Military Psychology*, *28*(4), 271–277.

Lyons, J. B., Koltai, K. S., Ho, N. T., Johnson, W. B., Smith, D. E., & Shively, J. R. (2016b). Engineering trust in complex automated systems. *Ergonomics in Design*, *24*, 13–17.

Lyons, J. B., & Stokes, C. K. (2012). Human-human reliance in the context of automation. *Human Factors*, *54*(1), 111–120.

Mayer, R. C., Davis, J. H., & Schoorman, F. D. (1995). An integrated model of organizational trust. *Academy of Management Review*, *20*, 709–734.

Mercado, J. E., Rupp, M. A., Chen, J. Y. C., Barnes, M. J., Barber, D., & Procci, K. (2016). Intelligent agent transparency in human-agent teaming for multi-UxV management. *Human Factors*, *58*(3), 401–415.

Merritt, S. M. (2011). Affective processes in human-automation interactions. *Human Factors*, *53*(4), 356–370.

Mutlu, B. (2011). Designing embodied cues for dialogue with robots. *AI Magazine*, 17–30.

Onnasch, L., Wickens, C. D., Li, H., & Manzey, D. (2014). Human performance consequences of stages and levels of automation: an integrated meta-analysis. *Human Factors*, *56*, 476–488.

Ososky, S., Schuster, D., Phillips, E., & Jentsch, F. (2013). Building appropriate trust in human-robot teams. In *Proceedings of AAAI spring symposium on trust in autonomous systems* (pp. 60–65). Palo Alto, CA: AAAI.

Sadler, G., Battiste, H., Ho, N. T., Hoffmann, L., Johnson, W., Shively, R., et al. (2016). Effects of transparency on pilot trust and agreement in the autonomous constrained flight planner. In *Proceedings of digital avionics systems conference (DASC)* (pp. 1–9). IEEE/AIAA.

Salas, E., Cooke, N. J., & Rosen, M. A. (2008). On teams, teamwork, and team performance: discoveries and developments. *Human Factors*, *50*, 540–547.

Schaefer, K. E., Chen, J. Y. C., Szalma, J. L., & Hancock, P. A. (2016). A meta-analysis of factors influencing the development of trust in automation. *Human Factors*, *58*(3), 377–400.

Waytz, A., Heafner, J., & Epley, N. (2014). The mind in the machine: anthropomorphism increases trust in an autonomous vehicle. *Journal of Experimental Social Psychology*, *52*, 113–117.

Wynne, K. T., & Lyons, J. B. (2018). An integrative model of autonomous agent teammate-likeness. *Theoretical Issues in Ergonomics Science*, *19*, 353–374.

## FURTHER READING

Dzindolet, M. T., Peterson, S. A., Pomranky, R. A., Pierce, L. G., & Beck, H. P. (2003). The role of trust in automation reliance. *International Journal of Human-Computer Studies*, *58*, 697–718.

# CHAPTER 7

# The Web of Smart Entities—Aspects of a Theory of the Next Generation of the Internet of Things

**Michael Wollowski\*, John McDonald†**
*Rose-Hulman Institute of Technology, Terre Haute, IN, United States
†ClearObject, Fishers, IN, United States

## 7.1 INTRODUCTION

We argue that the next generation of the Internet of Things (IoT) is about a web of smart entities (WSE). We define smart entities as software applications that build real-time models that are informed by real-time data. Smart entities are authorized to act and will manage routine behavior. Software applications in WSE will interact with each other to regulate behavior so as to satisfy certain goals. This interaction will lead to as yet unforeseen levels of automation. We see smart entities as polite assistants, designed to make our lives more convenient; something that will gracefully bow out, when asked to do so. We will address several modes in which to interact with and control the resulting automation.

Gubbi, Buyya, Marusic, and Palaniswami (2013) present a vision of IoT in which they emphasize the importance of cloud computing; we agree with their assessment. On page 1646, the authors state that "This platform [i.e. cloud computing] acts as a receiver of data from ubiquitous sensors; as a computer to analyze and interpret the data; as well as providing the user with easy to understand web based visualization. The ubiquitous sensing and processing works in the background, *hidden* from the user." Again, we could not agree more and explain in detail what sort of processing may take place in the background.

*Artificial Intelligence for the Internet of Everything*
https://doi.org/10.1016/B978-0-12-817636-8.00007-7
**117**

Weiser, Gold, and Brown (1999) defines a smart environment as "the physical world that is richly and invisibly interwoven with sensors, actuators, displays, and computational elements, embedded seamlessly in the everyday objects of our lives, and connected through a continuous network." We will generalize this portrayal to emphasize real-time data that enables one to build real-time models. In this context, we will argue that there is real-time data that comes from sources other than sensors.

Stankovic (2014) sees a "… significant qualitative change in how we work and live." We will expose some of those changes and further refine his assessment. He continues by stating that "We will truly have systems-of-systems that synergistically interact to form totally new and unpredictable services." We agree with this assessment and shed light on the kinds of services we may expect.

This chapter continues to develop the themes of the book *The Internet of Things*, by Greengard (2015), *Precision*, by Chou (2016), and the paper "Network of 'Things'," by Voas (2016). From a perspective of analyzing the impact of IoT, this paper continues to refine the ideas presented in the book *How IoT Is Made* by McDonald, Pietrocarlo, and Goldman (2015).

Greengard (2015) is focused on a contemporary version of IoT. In particular he focuses on automation that results from real-time data. This automation is true even in his extended example entitled *2025: A Day in the Life*, pp. 180–186.

McDonald et al. (2015) argue that it is pertinent for companies to join the IoT space as it offers vast new opportunities for revenue streams and for optimizing operations. It furthermore exposes what the authors call the "democratization" of information. This book does not address the bigger picture that evolves when IoT devices act and interact. We go beyond this book with a nuanced discussion of how, where, and by whom data is generated, where it is stored, and who ought to own it.

Chou (2016), similar to McDonald et al. (2015), is focused on IoT for industry and makes a case for companies to join the IoT to develop new business models and revenue streams that take advantage of the data that is generated by smart devices. This book does not address the bigger picture that evolves when IoT devices act and interact.

Tucker (2014) and Siegel (2016) focus on big-data and predictive analysis. Predictive analysis can reveal things that may be shocking to individuals (see Duhigg, 2012). While predictive analysis will lead to automation, we focus on the automation that results when models that learn specifics about someone or something's behavior are empowered to act.

## 7.2 SMART THINGS

It has been argued that IoT has a PR problem (see Eberle, 2016). Eberle argues that rather than talking about IoT, we should be talking about smart things, such as smart cars or smart cities, which are powered by IoT. We agree with this assessment and so do others (Bassi et al., 2013; Willems, 2016). At the most basic, IoT is about connecting all sorts of things to the internet. Those things, whether washing machines, cars, our bodies, or our food, produce data, in particular real-time data (see Heikell, 2016). Often this data is useful on its own; however, we are interested in what we can do when those devices interact.

In addition to producing, processing, and reporting data from internal sensors, IoT devices may also receive input from entities external to them. Consider Google's "Nest" thermostat, which may receive weather information from a website in addition to data from internal sensors. As such people consider Nest to be a smart thermostat. Taking several devices inside the home and programming them so that they communicate with each other leads to a smart home.

While often data collected and processed by a smart device is useful on its own, and while connecting smart devices together is useful too, more value can be generated by building models of the data available to them. At the most basic, a model of a sensor may be used to interpolate missing data or determine whether data is out of an expected range and as such may be faulty. At a higher level, models of data can be used to produce considerable value. Cummins Engines, the largest independent manufactures of diesel engines, uses telematics, i.e., real-time engine data to build real-time models of how their engines actually perform. These models are then used by Cummins in several ways. By running live engine data against the model, they can ascertain the general health of a particular engine. By using predictive analysis, Cummins is able to predict various scenarios ruinous to an engine and as such is able to alert fleet operators, in real time, about fault-codes and their significance on the continued operation of the engine (see Cummins, 2016).

Moving a step further, one can authorize a model to act. While the model of a Cummins engine alerts an operator at Cummins, consider the Nest thermostat; it builds a model of the comfort preferences throughout a week and then enforces the preferences by turning on and off the air conditioner and heater.

We consider Google's Nest to be the state-of-the-art with regard to current practice for IoT, in the sense that robust and repeatable solutions in this mold exist. This state-of-the-art is captured in Fig. 7.1.

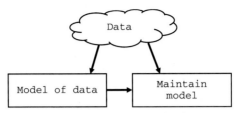

**Fig. 7.1** Current state-of-the-art in data processing for the Internet of Things.

## 7.3 A VISION OF THE NEXT GENERATION OF THE IOT

As mentioned in the prior section, the Google Nest thermostat represents the current state-of-the-art in advanced use of IoT technology: it uses data from several internal sensors and from the web and it plays well with other IoT devices, such as mobile phones and IoT devices found in the home. The Nest thermostat develops a model that is authorized to act: it learns the resident's temperature preferences and maintains the temperature according to those learned specifications. In many ways the Nest thermostat incorporates key properties we wish to formalize. We feel that it represents a glimpse into what the future might bring.

In this section, we paint a broader picture of a likely future in which smart entities in the form of software applications interact with each other. We show that those smart entities rely on data from sensors but also from data compiled and processed by each other. As such, some of the data is fairly far removed from sensors. We show that some of the data is produced and processed continuously and some is produced in an irregular fashion. In the next generation of IoT, we see many different systems interacting to produce data and information. They will be used to seamlessly manage many aspects of businesses and of people's lives.

Perhaps the best way to characterize the next generation is by describing a rich extended example. We pick the domain of personal health. We portray a future in which a person's health is maintained at an optimal level, expressing the sort of systems that we wish to formalize. While the next generation of IoT will impact all aspects of people's lives, this domain is sufficiently complex to expose pertinent aspects of WSE. We should point out that the future of IoT cannot be seen in isolation; it is imperative that advances in IoT be seen in the larger context of advances in technology, such as predictive analysis (see Siegel, 2016; Tucker, 2014) and automation, such as smart factories (see Wikipedia, 2018), an example of which is the Daimler's Factory 56 (see Daimler, 2018).

*Exercise.* IoT has made great strides in measuring physical exercise activities. Many wearables can synchronize exercise data to various websites. It is fair to state that a small set of wearables enables a typical user to record an accurate picture of their exercise activities. In this context, we would like to point out that in most people's lives, there are clearly identifiable periods when meaningful exercise takes place. As such, for large portions of the day, these sensors do not produce meaningful data.

*Diet.* In most people's lives there are identifiable events when food and drinks are consumed. Just as with exercise data, we are interested in developing a picture of when, how much, and what kind of nourishment a person consumes. Unlike exercise data, when it comes to entering diet information, much of the data entry is manual at this time. Similar to exercise data, diet information comes in bursts. Even if we were to read off data continuously, the data is meaningful only during certain times of the day, i.e., when people actually consume food.

Websites such as "myfitnesspal.com" take advantage of the fact that many people are creatures of habit. They simplify the data entry process by giving the user the ability to select from prior entries rather than having to re-enter detailed information about a food dish. Another way to automate the process of maintaining diet information is by tying a meal planner to a site that maintains information about a person's diet. Websites such as "yummly.com" offer diet information associated with a recipe. We imagine that restaurants, by way of an itemized bill augmented by nutrition information, will soon enable the automatic entering of diet information by uploading it to diet management software. For this to occur, think of augmenting "expensify.com" with diet information and a plug-in for your "myfitnesspal.com" account.

*Fitness.* Given diet and exercise data, one can now track whether a targeted balance of exercise and diet has been reached (Fig. 7.2). Websites such as "myfitnesspal.com" keep track of past exercise and diet activities and use various graphics to indicate the degree to which exercise and diet are balanced. While one can create a basic model of a person's physical fitness, these models are passive; they merely report fitness data.

We believe that in the future, we will see applications that, in addition to compiling an accurate real-time model of a person's fitness, are authorized to act to maintain it. For example, in an increasingly wired world, a fitness application could refuse to pre-approve a meal in a restaurant that is judged as not fulfilling set dietary goals. Alternatively, the fitness application may suggest a walk or bike ride instead of the use of either a car or public transportation.

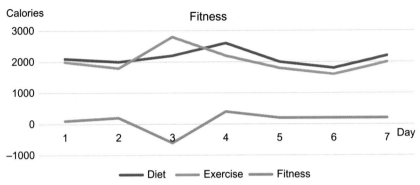

**Fig. 7.2** Measuring fitness through diet and exercise data.

For habitual offenders we imagine that such an app may schedule an appointment with a physician. Some insurance companies already tie their rates to their clients' fitness data; as such, insurance rates are, in some cases, already tied to fitness. In general, we imagine that many people wishing to lead healthy lives will appreciate an application that helps them maintain their fitness.

### 7.3.1 Interlude

So far, we have seen that meaningful data may be generated and uploaded continuously. However, we have also seen cases in which data is generated and uploaded sporadically. We consider both to be real-time data. Additionally, we have seen applications that model behavior and are authorized to act, while enforcing certain constraints. We will now continue to weave a larger web of interconnected applications that manage additional aspects of our lives. In this context we will move further away from sensor data. We will argue that data generated by applications are to be considered part of the next generation of IoT.

*Mental health.* Mental health is equally important to physical health. IoT and derived applications will enable us to monitor and gauge mental health as well. We know we will soon have mirrors that are equipped with cameras that can interpret a person's mood. Certainly, the same software can be installed on cameras of various computing devices that people use on a daily basis. We envision that someone will soon develop a working laugh-o-meter app for smartphones, providing useful information about a person's mental health. These are but two examples; we mention them to express our vision that some of the IoT data will require sophisticated processing to derive desirable information.

For those people who maintain precise calendars of most of their daily activities, one could determine the kinds and duration of their mental activities. By consulting a person's calendar, one could determine whether someone reads books, completes puzzles, engages in social activities, or has other creative pursuits. This kind of information, while not currently derived from sensors, provides useful information that we feel belongs in the space of smart entities and applications.

*Physical health.* We have already addressed fitness. While obtaining reliable and complete exercise data for healthy people seems fine, there are other aspects that also ought to be measured directly rather than inferred, especially for people with chronic illnesses. There are already medical devices that people use, such as pulse monitors, blood-pressure monitors, and wireless scales. If we included implanted devices, such as defibrillators, pace makers, and blood glucose monitors, a good picture of physical health emerges even for people with major illnesses.

An exciting future development will be the use of nano-bots (Akyildiz, Jornet, & Pierobon, 2017), which, when placed in the body, can provide more fine-grained monitoring of a person's health or can be used to treat diseases such as cancer (Gaudin, 2009).

*Automatic scheduling of doctor visits.* Combining a real-time accurate model of physical health with best practices in health care, we imagine that the model will be empowered to make appointments with various health-care professionals as necessary. There are several immediate benefits to such a system: it will likely reduce the number of frivolous office visits, it will likely provide health care for people who are unwilling to see their doctor, and it will provide for a fast response to an emerging illness. Some office visits will likely be eliminated entirely. For example, often when our children are ill we know that they need an antibiotic. Perhaps the systems and the regulations about prescribing medication will change so that some medication can be prescribed based on real-time data and best practices.

Another form of real-time data is input by a health-care provider. We imagine that visits with health-care providers will remain, except that the role of health-care providers will change. People are not often good diagnosticians of their own mental or physical states. We believe that it takes an independent expert to recognize and enter some health information. Notice that while the data provided by a health-care provider is not as frequent as that of, say, a wearable device, it nevertheless is real-time data. Another kind of data may come in the form of revised nutrition or exercise guidelines, such as those issued by the US Department of Health and Human Services.

An interesting side effect of this scenario is the effect it would have on how doctors and health-care professionals spend their time. According to the *New York Times,* doctors find it hard to spend more than 8 min per patient visit (Chen, 2013). With the ability to measure blood pressure and weight, run blood tests, and conduct other simple tests by connected devices, there will likely be a drop-off in patient visits. This reduction in office visits will allow doctors to spend more time with those patients who need it. More importantly it will change the role of a health-care professional. We believe that the role of health-care professionals will transform into that of a health coach or advocate.

With real-time data, emergency responses can be automated with great benefits; see Lange (2013) for an insightful use case. Consider a car crash; based on data from wearables as well as telematics of all of the involved parties, the severity of a crash can be assessed and the need for medical assistance evaluated. If emergency assistance is deemed necessary, controlling for privacy, pertinent information about the patient should be sent to the attending paramedics, and the person's physical health records should interact with the assigned hospital's scheduling system. Finally, if appropriate, the model could alert family members and coworkers. Notice that the data is sourced from wearable devices as well as from multiple devices external to us.

In today's healthcare world, patients and physicians are seen as partners. Many patients want to know more about their conditions or feel that they are in charge of their own health care. As such, we imagine that if a model determines a person has a certain illness, it may make information about that condition available to that person in a way that appeals to their background knowledge.

*Mens sana in corpore sano.* With an adequate model of a person's mental and physical health, one can now develop a more complete model of a person's overall health and automate the model to maintain overall health to specifications that will likely include competing parameters. This automation may be as simple as dynamically injecting physical or recreational mental exercises into a person's calendar, based on real-time data of a person's mental or physical state. Perhaps a system may decide to send an employee home at an earlier time or assign them different work so as to alleviate stress.

## 7.4 THE USE OF ARTIFICIAL INTELLIGENCE IN THE WEB OF SMART ENTITIES

Processing sensor data to elicit higher levels of information, such as might be seen in smart mirrors or laugh-o-meter applications, requires advanced artificial intelligence (AI) techniques. We imagine that when gathering data from different scenarios to form an overarching model there will be inconsistencies. Detecting and possibly resolving inconsistencies or conflicts can be accomplished with AI techniques such as proof checkers. The connected nature of WSE requires further, perhaps more mundane uses of AI techniques. In this section, we will highlight some of these, as they suggest additional benefits from WSE.

*Constraint satisfaction.* The most obvious use of constraint satisfaction is when more than one person occupies the same space. Consider temperature settings, light settings, or entertainment choices that need to be resolved. A more sophisticated example involves regulating sleep. With the creation of smart beds and wearables, it is possible to monitor people's sleeping patterns. A model of sleeping patterns informs whether one is getting enough sleep each night. The sleep model can interact with several systems in an attempt to regulate sleep. For example, it could be empowered to regulate the temperature in the bedroom. It could interact with the meal planner to detect foods or drinks that are not conducive to sleep. It could be empowered to remove or rescheduled these items to earlier in the day. The sleep model could interact with the calendar to reschedule certain kinds of physical exercises that are detrimental to sleep.

*Recommender system.* Given models of people's behavior, we are in a position to make recommendations. For example, the "yummly.com" website makes recommendations based on the preferences entered by a user. We imagine that in the future recommendations can be made based on matching a user's meal-time recipe usage to those of others. This matching would be similar to how Netflix and Amazon.com recommend movies and goods. Similarly, based on a user's exercise patterns, we imagine recommendations for modifications, additions, or substitutions of exercise regimes.

*Epidemics.* Automatic collection and consolidation of health data will enable public agencies to detect developing trends in real-time (Jalali, Olabode, & Bell, 2012). Since time is of the essence in formulating a response, the more real-time data that is available, the faster one can detect trends. On a more local scale, it will help health-care providers in a given community to determine what sort of illness is afflicting their patients, enabling them to act accordingly.

*Cognitive assistants.* Cognitive assistants, as proposed by IBM (Kelly, 2015), are aimed at digesting vetted data to provide additional information to health-care providers. IBM sees cognitive assistants as "wise counselors" (IBM Watson, 2012). As IBM sees it, "IBM Watson, through its use of information retrieval and natural language processing, draws from an impressive corpus of information, including MSK [Memorial Sloan-Kettering] curated literature and rationales, as well as over 290 medical journals, over 200 textbooks, and 12 million pages of text. Watson for Oncology also supplies for consideration supporting evidence in the form of administration information, as well as warnings and toxicities for each drug" (IBM Watson, 2016). In essence, cognitive assistants data-mine the results of research. In the context of this chapter we see cognitive assistants used to provide additional inputs to models.

## 7.5 TOWARDS A THEORY OF THE WEB OF SMART ENTITIES

In this section, we develop a theory of WSE. We use the examples described in the prior section to justify the components of the WSE theory. We show that this use of the web is about real-time data, real-time models that capture routine behavior, and models that are authorized to act. We show the effects of this automation. We will end this section by highlighting the changing roles of established stakeholders and practices.

### 7.5.1 Real-Time Data

Smart and not so smart devices already generate data. While data on IoT comes from "things," in the extended scenario we described earlier, we demonstrated that data originates not only from things, even if they are *everything*, but also from software applications that are not directly connected to things and, as a matter of fact, can be quite removed from the data produced by devices. We additionally exposed the applications to the readers that collect real-time data in a noncontinuous fashion.

**Definition 1.** *Real-time data* originates from different kinds of sources and is reported with different kinds of frequencies.

Let us consider some of the different kinds of data sources and frequencies under consideration.

*Sensor data.* Without a doubt, a key aspect of IoT and, by extension WSE, is real-time data obtained from sensors. Typically this data is reported continuously.

*Manually entered data.* If we look at how a person's diet data is entered into a system, it is currently not generated by sensors. If a meal planner is used, controlling for portion size, then some of the data is known and can be entered automatically. No matter how the data is entered, whether manually or automatically, it still is real-time data. It is just that most people do not eat continuously. While continued automation and perhaps video analysis will eventually enable the automatic generation of diet data, we believe that there will always be cases in which data will need to be entered manually. We would like to point out that, in the case of video recognition, the data, while technically coming from a sensor, requires sophisticated image processing.

*Aggregated data.* If we look at how "Google maps" ascertains traffic data, it is simply the aggregate of data from cell phones in cars. There is certainly a good amount of processing necessary to produce useful data about the movement of phones in vehicles. Notice that "Google maps" uses this data to eventually produce a model of congestion. However, before doing so, "Google maps" does produce aggregate data.

*Other models.* We have seen several examples in which data from models feed into other models and, as such, generate useful data for these other models. For example, a model that is designed to balance fitness will need access to the data from a model capturing diet data as well as a model capturing exercise data. We imagine that a model that balances fitness would furthermore interact with other models, such as calendars, vehicles, public transportation and restaurants.

*Aggregate models.* Just as Google aggregates data from individual phones in cars to construct a model of traffic flow, we can imagine cases in which we wish to aggregate models. Consider models of exercise data. If we were interested in simply ascertaining the overall exercise activities of a firm's employees, we would only need to gather a single data point from each employee. However, if we wish to ascertain exercise patterns, perhaps in the context of scheduling gym hours or to determine how big of a gym to build, then models of exercise patterns are necessary.

*Feedback loop.* A feedback loop of a model to itself enables monitoring and reflection on the workings of the model. Suppose a model of a person's food preferences is matched to someone else's model. A recipe may be returned that is deemed to match a person's preferences. In case the person does not like the recipe, or perhaps the matching parameters are insufficient or were weighted improperly, we would like to adjust the model. We then think of how case-based reasoning matches new cases to an existing case-base (see Wikipedia, 2016).

## 7.5.2 Real-Time Models

A good number of smart devices already maintain real-time models. Consider a Nest thermostat; it builds a model of a user's heating and cooling preferences. In particular it builds a real-time model as it constantly learns from real-time data. Similarly a Cummins Engine is processing sensor data from an engine to produce a model that reflects the performance and health of an engine, another prime example of a real-time model.

**Definition 2.** *Real-time models* represent aspects of the world that are continuously updated by real-time data.

We use the term "model" as shorthand for applications that maintain an underlying model of the data available to them. Fig. 7.3 captures the discussion so far to show potential inputs to a model.

### 7.5.3 Automation

If we look at the Nest thermostat, in addition to building a model it acts on data by turning on and off the air-conditioner or the heater. Cummins Engines analytics at this point in time notifies an operator who will then act on the information provided to them. A key effect of automation is that smart entities will learn routine behavior and automate it. In many instances, such routine behavior is not very exciting, but is rather considered a "nuisance" activity.

**Definition 3.** *Automation* results from real-time models that are authorized to act.

Automation takes on several forms and we list some of them in the following section.

*Managing learned behavior.* Suppose a model learned that every Tuesday evening is pizza night. Suppose it also learned that a given family always orders the same pizza. In that case the model can order the same pizza to arrive at the usual time. To look at a more complex case, suppose that the model also learned that the given family never orders pizza twice in a row and that this family had pizza the night before. In that case the model could ask for input, or perhaps act on some other learned behavior. Notice that in this case the model acts on learned behavior as well as real-time data.

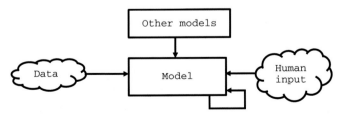

**Fig. 7.3** A model and its potential inputs.

*Smart substitutions.* The use of AI technologies and the use of ontologies such as used in the context of the semantic web enable smart substitutions. We see examples of this substitution when, based on dietary restrictions, alternate meals may be suggested, or when certain kinds of exercises are recommended based on availability or opportunity.

## 7.5.4 Web of Smart Entities

Consider Google's Nest thermostat; in addition to processing data from its internal sensors, it can process data about the weather communicated to it by a weather app. We see Google's Nest as highlighting the beginnings of a richly interwoven fabric of applications that are directly or indirectly informed by sensor data.

**Definition 4.** WSE consists of a highly connected web of software applications that manage and automate routine behavior.

A few representative tasks for these smart applications are listed in the following section.

*Balancing.* If an application that manages a person's exercise activities interacts with an application that manages a person's dietary intake, physical fitness can be balanced to specifications. If we empower the fitness model to make the relevant decisions, we can dynamically adjust a person's fitness. For example, the fitness model may encourage a walk or bike ride rather than the use of a car or public transportation. Perhaps together they recommend a dish that lowers a person's caloric intake at a restaurant within walking distance.

*Seamlessness.* Given the proliferation of data, it is likely that models will gather data about particular activities in different contexts. For example, food preferences will likely be gathered not just from meals prepared at home, but also from meals ordered at restaurants or consumed in other settings. This way an overarching and more informed model can be built. Seamlessness comes about when an overarching model is applied in different contexts. If the model learned that someone likes their coffee black, then this is how it should be prepared, whether at home, at work, or by a coffee shop.

*Recommendations.* Models of a person's behavior can be used to make recommendations based on matching to like models. For example, diet preferences, just as preferences that Netflix and Amazon gather about their customers, can be used to match to similar models and, based on those matches, recommendations may be made.

## 7.5.5 Changing Roles of Stakeholders

We expect that the large-scale automation described in this chapter will have a significant impact on the participants of WSE.

**Prediction 1.** The *web of smart entities* will have a transformative effect on its stakeholders.

Consider an application that manages a person's health. It ensures that we live our lives within scientifically based parameters. One may wish to call such an application the "guardian angel" app. Knowing that such an application provides a kind of safety net, it is not unreasonable to assume that many people will live their lives to the fullest; i.e., they will "die with their boots on." At the very least, automating the management of health will enable people to live longer, more productive and, hopefully, happier lives. In this context, such health management applications would be able to make the necessary health-care appointments for those people who are reluctant to visit doctors, and as such may bring about a situation in which illnesses are diagnosed early, before they become terminal. Equally beneficial, such applications may be able to identify mentally disturbed people and offer or make them seek help long before they become a danger to themselves or society.

Health-care providers, such as general practitioners, will likely see their roles transform from a service provider that patients seek to individuals who will manage and fine-tune a patient's health. Similarly, people will likely have personal trainers who fine-tune their exercise regimens and personal dietitians who fine-tune their diets beyond what big-data might do for them. On the subject of diets, we imagine that cook-book authors may transform from writers who cook to consultants for people who like to cook. In order to better manage mental health, we see life coaches as becoming a staple in people's lives, someone who will not just give advice on living life to the fullest, but who may fine-tune personal calendars to eliminate stresses and replace them by leisure activities.

We can see insurance companies as transforming into businesses that ultimately manage and determine what people can and cannot do for some cost. Perhaps it is not a black-and-white decision, rather a spectrum of choices that people may make. Perhaps it depends on agreed-upon standards of care or even agreed-upon risk a person wishes to assume.

In this context, we hope that we have outlined scenarios that either change people's jobs for the better or generate additional forms of employment.

## 7.6 INTERACTING WITH AUTOMATION

We described a highly automated world that is built on and derived from real-time data and a world in which models of routine behavior are authorized to act for the benefits of their users. It might be daunting to know that various computing systems record our every activity and build various models about us, constructing a kind of a virtual alter ego. It is not unreasonable to assume that various computing systems know aspects of a person's live better than the person knows him of herself. To some, this may be exciting, but to others, this scenario may be frightening. How will this affect the way people conduct their lives? Will it be liberating, as our own personal systems watch over us? Will people live more vicarious lives as they know the system will intervene when necessary? Will people feel watched? Will they feel "verklemmt"? Will people hide things from the model or purposefully engage in activities to deceive it, as described in Orwell (1950)? Will people get used to "big brother" watching them? Will the automation limit what we can do, a point made by Agamben (2010), or will it liberate us to live life to the fullest?

We attempted to give a reasonable view of the future, which we see as largely positive. We see the WSE as inhabited by polite assistants, designed to make our lives more convenient. We envision automated assistants that gracefully bow out, when asked to do so. As such, we envision, perhaps too hopefully, a future in which people can choose and change, at a moment's notice, the level of interaction with the WSE. In particular we would argue that the ability to choose the degree of automation should be a design feature, something that the user can explicitly manage and, to a certain degree, something that the model anticipates. In the same context, users should be able to control what information is gathered about them and who has access to it.

We now describe three points across a spectrum of interactions with automation: autonomous, semiautonomous, and manual interaction. Among others, a model authorized to act will seamlessly switch between modes, or, better yet, move across the spectrum of automation. A smart system will learn when to bow out, when to step in and at what level to take over.

### 7.6.1 Fully Autonomous

In this mode of interacting with automation the system makes all of the decisions. For example, as already mentioned, some people eat the same dish on specific days of the week. This stability is behavior that can be quickly learned.

The meal planner can be authorized to order dishes or the ingredients for them and arrange for delivery at desired times (another learned behavior). Similarly, some people always order the same dish at a particular restaurant. This behavior, too, can be quickly learned and applied appropriately. There are many other components of our lives that have little to no variation. Many people order the same toiletries, clothes, cars, take the same route to drive to work, have the same weekly work schedule, and engage in the same sort of recreational activities on a weekly basis. It is not unreasonable to assume that large swatches of our lives can be automated. The benefit of this mode is that it would take care of routine activities.

On a side note, we recall a time when people first attempted to "live off" the world-wide web for a given period of time. In the same vein, it might be asked whether people would be able to live in a fully autonomous mode. Many people are creatures of habit. We believe that people can live in fully autonomous mode. Whether such a life is interesting is another question.

## 7.6.2 Semiautonomous

In this mode the user gives some input to the model. In some cases information will be requested, in other's the user will simply override certain inputs or parameters. The override may be as innocuous as not following the directions of a navigation system. For a more concrete example, suppose a cook heard about substituting riced cauliflower for rice in stir-fry dishes. The cook may simply ask the recipe manager to use the new ingredient. If there is a recipe in some user-permitted or accessible data base that already accounts for the new ingredient, then it can be consulted. The automated pantry would be authorized to purchase the new ingredient, if necessary. If the system is sufficiently knowledgeable, it may inform the cook that they may first have to obtain an appropriate device to turn cauliflower into riced cauliflower.

When operating in this mode, we imagine that the input range will be limited to acceptable operating parameters. Examples of this are Airbus airplanes; they are designed not to be placed in a stall situation, no matter what input a pilot gives.

## 7.6.3 Manual

In this mode, the user acts without the assistance of automation, but the system will likely continue to record information. In this mode, the system will enforce certain boundary conditions. For example, for a logger, a square donut burger with bacon may be fine. For someone who spends most of their time in an office, a burger may still be fine if consumed within reason. For people with high cholesterol, a burger may not be an option at all and they may not be authorized to purchase it.

This brings up the issue of abilities. This system would disable some of the choices available to users and as such there will be certain things users cannot do, a concern raised by Agamben (2010). While such a system would take choice away from us, on the flipside, it may encourage us to live life to the fullest. Just as technologies like engine rev-limiters take choices away from us, there certainly are people who take advantage of technology to push their cars to the limit without reproach.

### 7.6.4 Extent of Automation

Shall there be limits to the hyper-automation we have described? Consider the following example. Suppose someone is in a car accident. Certainly emergency response should be scheduled immediately. With real-time data and models, a system may select a hospital based on distance, the availability of medical personnel with the necessary skills to treat the given injuries once known, especially in the context of a given health history. Obviously pertinent health data will be made available to approved providers to ensure proper and expedited care. In addition, the health insurance company, loved ones, colleagues, and superiors will be informed.

However, the automation does not have to stop there. After a car accident, in addition to the health insurance company and the car insurance company, advanced telematics will likely have been informed of the crash too. It could then arrange for a rental car to be delivered to the customer at a time when the injured person is expected to be released from the hospital, or for an autonomous car if the client is impaired. In the same context, the car insurance company can and will likely arrange for the damaged car to be repaired. If the car is considered a total loss, something that, based on telematics, additional sensors, and big data, can likely be determined automatically, should the car insurance company purchase a new car? To many, purchasing a car is not a pleasant experience. This experience is not made more pleasant when conducted from a hospital bed. So anticipated, the automation described in this example may be much appreciated.

Suppose the injury requires a longer-lasting recuperation period. We can imagine that short-term disability insurance will be activated automatically. However, what sort of response should an employer automate? An employer could automatically reassign others to cover the duties of the injured colleague or they could automatically hire a temporary employee. If the disability is judged to be longer lasting or permanent, would the employee be automatically terminated? Would some system automatically find the ex-employee a new job, based on skills and disability? What if the new job pays less? Would some system automatically sell the house and purchase a cheaper one? All of this automation can be seen as useful. However, at what point are we just along for the ride?

## 7.7 DEPTH OF WSE

We argued that the WSE will consist of many applications generating and processing data; applications that will interact with each other to produce an unseen level of automation.

Some people have expressed concern about designing applications for trillions of devices (Sangiovanni-Vincentelli, 2015). We submit that based on our analysis this problem may be quite manageable. In particular it is unlikely that any application will directly interact with three trillion devices. Based on our theory, the WSE will be compartmentalized so that many applications will process fairly local data. If we look at the dependencies of the models from our extended example about a person's health, we see a fairly low depth, where depth is measured by the number of applications that depend on crucial data from those applications that report to them.

Consider Fig. 7.4, in which we portray this scenario. It should be noted that we only included a small subset of the applications that were mentioned in the health scenario. The figure suggests that the complexity of the WSE, as judged by the depth of it, might grow approximately in a logarithmic fashion in relationship to the number of linked IoT devices. To be clear, while we believe that there will be an exponential growth in the number of applications, we think that the WSE will be wide rather than deep, with depth as defined above and where width is measured by applications that loosely depend on data from other applications.

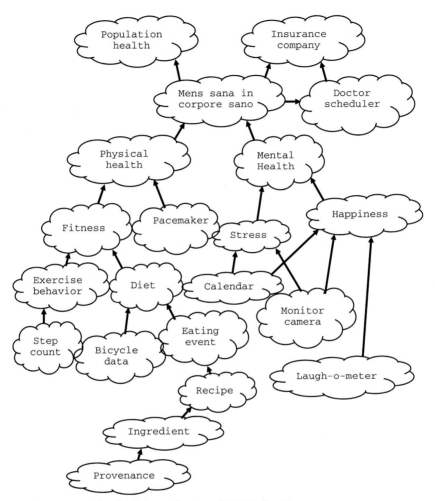

**Fig. 7.4** Notional depth of dependencies of WSE in health.

## 7.8 CONCLUSIONS

In this chapter we described a likely future scenario in which IoT maintains people's health. It is a fascinating world in which software applications manage health based on real-time data and to scientific specifications.

We defined the next generation of IoT as a WSE. We argued that this web is about real-time data that originates from many sources at varying frequency, but where only some of the sources are sensors. We argued that a defining characteristic of the WSE is the development of accurate real-time models that capture and model the data. We argued that when models are empowered to act, an unprecedented level of automation will result. We depicted a world in which this automation will manage and arrange many routine activities.

We discussed the effects of this automation on several stakeholders. We believe that the hyper-automation described in this chapter will enable people to live life to the fullest. We portrayed three principle ways of interacting with models: fully autonomous, semiautonomous, and manual.

We believe that IoT is an exponential technology and that it is crucial that we consider and debate its likely future developments so that we can create an environment that brings to fruition a positive future. We believe that developers of this technology, stakeholders, customers, and regulatory agencies need to work together to define standards, best practices, and a legal framework for the vision to become a reality.

## ACKNOWLEDGMENTS

This work was completed while the first author was on sabbatical at Clear Object. The authors would like to thank Ben Chodroff and Vishal Kapashi who provided input on an earlier version of this chapter.

## REFERENCES

Agamben, G. (2010). On what we can not do. In G. Agamben (Ed.), *Nudities*. Stanford, CA: Stanford University Press.

Akyildiz, I. F., Jornet, J. M., & Pierobon, M. (2017). Nanonetworks: a new frontier in communications. *Communications of the ACM, 54*, 84–89.

Bassi, A., Bauer, M., Fiedler, M., Kramp, T., van Kranenburg, R., Lange, S., et al. (2013). *Enabling things to talk—Designing IoT solutions with the IoT architectural reference model*. Cham, Switzerland: Springer Verlag.

Chen, P. (2013). For new doctors, 8 minutes per patient. Retrieved from http://well.blogs.nytimes.com/2013/05/30/for-new-doctors-8-minutes-per-patient/?\_r=0.

Chou, T. (2016). *Precision: Principles, practices and solutions for the internet of things*. CrowdStory Publishing.

Cummins (2016). *Connected diagnostics—the lifeline for your engine*. Retrieved from https://cumminsengines.com/connected-diagnostics.

Daimler (2018). *Factory 56: the inventor of the car re-invents production*. Retrieved from https://blog.daimler.com/2018/02/20/factory-56/.

Duhigg, C. (2012). How companies learn your secrets. The New York Times, February 19. Retrieved from http://www.nytimes.com/2012/02/19/magazine/shopping-habits.html?pagewanted=6\&\_r=2\&hp.

Eberle, R. (2016). The internet of things has a vision problem. Retrieved from http://www.cio.com/article/3028054/internet-of-things/the-internet-of-things-has-a-vision-problem.html.

Gaudin, S. (2009). Nanotech could make humans immortal by 2040. Retrieved from http://www.computerworld.com/article/2528330/app-development/nanotech-could-make-humans-immortal-by-2040–futurist-says.html.

Greengard, S. (2015). *The internet of things*. Cambridge, MA: The MIT Press.

Gubbi, J., Buyya, R., Marusic, S., & Palaniswami, M. (2013). Internet of Things (IoT): a vision, architectural elements, and future directions. *Future Generation Computer Systems, 29*, 1645–1660.

Heikell, L. (2016). Connected cows help farms keep up with the herd. Retrieved from https://news.microsoft.com/features/connected-cows-help-farms-keep-up-with-the-herd/\#sm.001npdttm13z6dn2spb2ce2sm2jay.

IBM Watson (2012). Assisting oncologists with evidence-based diagnosis and treatment. Retrieved from https://www.ibm.com/developerworks/community/blogs/efc1d8f5-72e5-4c4f-99df-e74fccea10ca/resource/Case\%20Studies/IBMWatsonCaseStudy-MemorialSloan-KettingCancerCenter.pdf?lang=en.

IBM Watson (2016). *IBM Watson platform helps fight cancer with evidence-based diagnosis and treatment suggestions*. Retrieved from http://www.ibm.com/watson/watson-oncology.html.

Jalali, A., Olabode, O. A., & Bell, C. M. (2012). Leveraging cloud computing to address public health disparities: an analysis of the SPHPS. *Online Journal of Public Health Informatics, 4*(3).

Kelly III, J. (2015). Computing, cognition and the future of knowing. Retrieved from http://www.research.ibm.com/software/IBMResearch/multimedia/Computing\_Cognition\_WhitePaper.pdf.

Lange, S. (2013). *The internet of things architecture, IoT-A*. Retrieved from https://www.youtube.com/watch?v=nEVatZruJ7k.

McDonald, J., Pietrocarlo, J., & Goldman, J. (2015). *How IoT is made*. (n.p.): Author.

Orwell, G. (1950). *1984*. New York, NY: Signet Classics.

Sangiovanni-Vincentelli, A. (2015). *Design tools for the trillion-device future*. Retrieved from https://www.youtube.com/watch?v=ViJ3SH5t4Ys&feature=youtu.be.

Siegel, E. (2016). *Predictive analytics: The power to predict who will click, buy, lie, or die* (2nd ed.). Hoboken, NJ: Wiley.

Stankovic, J. (2014). Research directions for the Internet of Things. *IEEE Internet of Things Journal, 1*(1), 3–9.

Tucker, P. (2014). *The naked future—What happens in a world that anticipates your every move*. New York, NY: Current Publishers.

Voas, J. (2016). Networks of 'Things'. NIST Special Publication 800-183. Retrieved from https://doi.org/10.6028/NIST.SP.800-183.

Weiser, M., Gold, R., & Brown, J. (1999). The origins of ubiquitous computing research at PARC in the late 1980s. *IBM Systems Journal, 38*(4).

Wikipedia (2016). Case-based reasoning. Retrieved from https://en.wikipedia.org/wiki/Case-based\_reasoning.

Wikipedia (2018). *Industry 4.0*. Retrieved from https://en.wikipedia.org/wiki/Industry_4.0.

Willems, C. (2016). Cruising to safer, smarter street. Retrieved from https://blogs.cisco.com/government/cruising-to-safer-smarter-streets.

# CHAPTER 8

# Raising Them Right: AI and the Internet of Big Things

**Alec Shuldiner**
Autodesk, Inc, San Francisco, CA, United States

## 8.1 INTRODUCTION

Nature displays phantasmagorical complexity in all its parts: it may be grokked, but it resists analysis. The made world, our intuition tells us, works differently. While research and experience alike turn up exceptions, deep down we hold these beliefs to be self-evident: that actors in the marketplace are rational; that someone, somewhere, knows how a thing works; that there is a little man behind the curtain, and that we could catch him, if we were only quick enough.

Artificial intelligence (AI) is employed to boost human mental capacity, thereby facilitating our understanding of nature, our own society, the global economy, and like complexities. Yet AI, akin to natural systems in its complexity, its interactivity, and, increasingly, its autonomy, itself likewise resists analysis. Despite this, we are working hard to realize a vision of the Internet of Everything that requires us to embed AI in our software, our private and public operations, and our (smart) things. We may come to understand old problems better than we have in the past, and we are undoubtedly creating important new capabilities, but we are working at least as quickly to obscure the chain of intention in this new world we are building.

## 8.2 "THINGS ARE ABOUT TO GET WEIRD"

A couple of years ago my employer, the software house Autodesk, began training IBM's Watson system to understand and to respond helpfully to the questions asked by our customers in online forums. The goal was to eliminate a significant portion of the customer interactions handled by human employees, and in this Watson has been successful. The path to get there, though, turned out to be different from the one we usually follow when creating business capabilities, and much harder to understand both as a

*Artificial Intelligence for the Internet of Everything*
https://doi.org/10.1016/B978-0-12-817636-8.00008-9
**139**

process and as an outcome. I characterized these differences as a set of directional changes:

Deterministic ➔ Probabilistic

Mechanism ➔ Organism

System ➔ Ecosystem

Outcomes ➔ Tendencies

Predefined ➔ Emergent

A colleague, reading this list, responded: "so things are about to get weird," and, indeed, they have.

The current Autodesk Virtual Agent is a reasonably helpful bot. It isn't weird.[1] But more expansive implementations of its type have displayed odd behavior, most recently Amazon's Alexa, which developed a habit of laughing at customers at unpredictable and irregularly repeated intervals from the Echo home speakers it haunts. Amazon rushed a "fix" into production, explaining only that the behavior was a result of "false positives."[2] What is truly weird—aside from the customers' decidedly creepy experiences—is that Amazon's machine-learning experts probably cannot deliver a complete explanation of the phenomenon. Contrast this with other "big data" systems, which process comparable volumes of data but that do so via fully deterministic channels, rather than via the recursively nested weightings that characterize the "natural language processing" that makes Alexa go. For a computer scientist this is a new model. For an Amazon executive, no doubt likewise.

## 8.3 RAISE THEM RIGHT

Though a novelty in the office, the experience of developing a capable operator by encouragement rather than command was by no means new to me. Indeed, many people of a certain age have deep experience training massively complex, opaque-thinking systems from a blank slate to a state of sophistication. We call it parenting.

As parents we come to recognize the impossibility of knowing how much of either the credit or blame we deserve for our children's makeup. This is in part due to the complexity of the system we are training, but also in part because we are not the only ones doing the training. There are

---

[1] Try it yourself: https://ava.autodesk.com/.

[2] https://www.pcmag.com/news/359719/alexa-is-randomly-laughing-but-nobodys-in-on-the-joke is the best titled of the many articles on the topic.

**Fig. 8.1** The MX3D bridge, not well understood in engineering terms but still lovely to look at. *Photo March 2018, courtesy of the author.*

teachers, relatives, nannies, friends, and, increasingly, strangers on the Internet. This, too, is relevant as we consider the degree to which we will, or will not, be able to understand and to control AI actors. Microsoft provided one notorious example when "Tay," their chatbot intended to model teen behavior, transformed into a "neo-Nazi sexbot" within days of being given a Twitter account.[3]

To learn more about parenting AI, I proposed a project to endow a bridge with awareness and reactivity. The project began with a Dutch company that undertook to use robots to 3D print in stainless steel a pedestrian bridge. This form of 3D printing, in which a robot wields a welding device to lay down layers of metal that accrete to form a monolithic structure, is groundbreaking, and the resulting objects are poorly understood in engineering terms (Fig. 8.1). I suggested we use sensors to monitor the bridge's

---

[3] https://www.technologyreview.com/s/601111/why-microsoft-accidentally-unleashed-a-neo-nazi-sexbot/. See also https://arstechnica.com/information-technology/2016/03/tay-the-neo-nazi-millennial-chatbot-gets-autopsied/ for a comparison with Xiaoice, a similar Chinese chatbot that did not encounter these problems.

performance and that we feed the resulting data streams to machine-learning algorithms designed to make the bridge "smart."[4]

To realize this vision, I and my colleagues built a simple prototype using an existing bridge in our workshop in San Francisco. We applied sensors to that structure, channeled the data output through the cloud, and brought to bear a variety of computer vision and other advanced capabilities. The result is a bridge that reports on its own use, publishing the number and, in an upcoming v. 2, the position of its occupants, moment to moment.

Heroically assuming we overcome the many additional technical challenges entailed in applying the same approach to a vastly more heavily trafficked bridge placed in an exposed, uncontrolled, outdoors setting largely populated by roistering tourists, we will soon have a similarly capable bridge live in Amsterdam. That city of bridges will then have unprecedented insight into how one of those bridges is used; the beginning, we propose, of a system of data capture and analysis to be operated at city scale. We envision this "Internet of Big Things" as a network of smart bridges generating status reports—$n$ occupants at a point in time $t$ for bridge #1, bridge #2, bridge #3, and so on—to be interpolated into static and longitudinal views showing changes in patterns of usage for individual bridges and for entire neighborhoods or collections of neighborhoods. We anticipate an enthusiastic response from traffic engineers[5] and city planners, as well as private sector actors such as real estate investors.

This is a classic "smart cities" narrative, and like all such narratives there is, or should be, an accompanying story of unintended consequences. We are concerned about the possibility of this system being used for the ubiquitous social and commercial surveillance of individuals: a high density of sensors and suitable AI might be able to identify not just that people are using a piece of infrastructure but also who those people are, what they are doing and when, and even something about their physical attributes or personal character, for example, using their gait data to determine if they have Parkinson's disease, or analyzing tagged selfie capture to flag tourists versus local users. These unintended consequences could scale to entire cities. Furthermore, our growing ability to squeeze more data out of systems of this sort, for example, by oversampling the sensors or combining data streams, means it is impossible to predict at what point precisely a system could be misused. For an "open" project such as ours—by mandate and design, our bridge will

---

[4] For a quick background on the project see https://mx3d.com/smart-bridge/.

[5] I wrote on the topic of data sources for transportation demand modeling in 2013 (Shuldiner, A.T., & Shuldiner, P.W. (2013). *Transportation, 40*: 1117. https://doi.org/10.1007/s11116-013-9490-5).

share its data streams publicly—this possibility poses a real challenge. How to generate enough data to make the bridge useful but not so much that it becomes the infrastructure equivalent of a neo-Nazi sexbot?

## 8.4 LEARNING TO LIVE WITH IT

One of my colleagues on the bridge project suggests that since the structure will have been built by robots we should expect it to be altered by robots too. He imagines them tweaking the design in response to the usage patterns revealed in the sensor data, and then coming out at night to add metal here, take it away there: a virtual update followed by a physical one, both driven by robot intelligence free of human decision making. The idea may seem far-fetched, but only in its application to the direct amendment of physical objects.

There is reason to believe that Amsterdam as an experience is already being significantly reshaped by AI. Consider the city's massive tourist flows: they are directed to their dinners by Yelp's AI-powered search and to their beds by Booking.com's.[6] My colleagues and I are trying to understand these flows by using smart infrastructure to observe them in motion. We may succeed, but, in a kind of intellectual arms race, the subtlety of AI influence will probably continue to outstrip our ability to understand that influence overall, despite our own use of AI tools to do so. Amsterdam will continue to change but, beyond a certain point, we may not be able to explain those changes or influence them with precision.

I am not one of those losing sleep worrying about AI running amok, but being unable to figure out why something good happened can keep you awake at night too. I propose again the analogy of parenting. There you begin by training, progress to teaching, fall back on influencing, and finally learn yourself to live with your grownup child as best you can. Hopefully with pride, but perhaps with horror, you eventually get to see that child's impact on the wider world.

---

[6] Yelp uses AI for much more than just search. Yelp recommendations, for example, begin with AI interpreting the multitude of photos diners take in the city's many restaurants. (See https://www.fastcompany.com/3060884/your-photo-of-a-burrito-is-now-worth-a-thousand-words. This use of AI was pioneered by an acquaintance of mine who after much thought realized that his hyper-local recommendation engine was identifying "hipster" bars in part by the disproportionate amount of facial hair seen in photos of male patrons. His startup was, predictably, purchased by Google.) Booking.com, which happens to be based in Amsterdam, matches travelers to rooms thousands of times daily across the city—https://www.booking.com/content/about.html states that "Every day, more than 1,550,000 room nights are reserved on our platform"; the Amsterdam-specific number was provided to me by an internal source.

# CHAPTER 9

# The Value of Information and the Internet of Things[a]

**Ira S. Moskowitz\*, Stephen Russell[†], Niranjan Suri[†]**
\*Information Management and Decision Architectures Branch, Code 5580, Naval Research Laboratory, Washington, DC, United States
[†]Battlefield Information Processing Branch, Computational Information Sciences Directorate, Army Research Laboratory, Adelphi, MD, United States

## 9.1 INTRODUCTION

Shannon (1948) laid the groundwork for information theory in his seminal work. However, Shannon's theory is a quantitative theory, not a qualitative theory. Shannon's theory tells you how much "stuff" you are sending through a channel, but it does not care if it is a cookie recipe or the plans for a time machine. The quality of "stuff" is irrelevant to Shannon theory. This focus on sending messages, exclusive of understanding or context, is in contrast to Value of Information (VoI) theory, which concerns what, and not necessarily how much, "stuff" we are considering. That is, Shannon is a purely quantitative theory, whereas any theory of information value must include a qualitative aspect that is equal in relevance as any quantitative measures.

This qualitative characteristic finds it way into many information-centric areas, particularly when humans or artificial intelligence (AI) is involved in a decision-making process. For example in Russell, Moskowitz, and Raglin (2017), the authors, not surprisingly, state "We note that a purely quantitative approach to information is far from satisfactory." They then back this statement with discussions on Paul Revere, the Small Message Criteria (Moskowitz & Kang, 1994), and steganography. This is also discussed in Allwein (2004) where that research merged the work of Barwise and Seligman (1997) and Shannon's theory using channel theory tools from the logic discipline. However, these types of approaches in the literature do not offer

---

[a] This is an invited, revised, and expanded version of a paper of the titled "Valuable Information and the Internet of Things" by the first two authors that was presented at the 2018 AAAI Spring Symposium on the Internet of Everything.

immediate help with pragmatic concerns that exist in the Internet of Things (IoT) where information is plentiful and can also be excessive.

The nature of the IoT is one of pervasive data, continuously gathered and acted on by fully or semiautonomous devices and systems. This nature creates an interesting paradox in the context of VoI. If the IoT ushers in unimaginable volumes of information and one considers value as an economic construct, should not the "value" of information decrease? Perhaps in the average sense, for example, *all information's* overall value may decrease, but certain information would still retain a value higher than most. This notion calls into question how applicable existing VoI theory would be in the context of IoT information and related decision making. Moreover, the implications of an intelligent IoT system of systems, which the IoT is, in implementation and operation, introduce another complicating factor toward a generalized theory of VoI. The intelligence in the IoT itself necessarily makes VoI determinations in its autonomous operation on behalf of human decision makers. In this manner, the IoT itself is imbued with its own AI, that manifests as self-star (self-*) behaviors. Self-* behaviors are (Babaoglu et al., 2005) autonomic behaviors (such as self-management, self-awareness, self-protecting, etc.) that provide a device or system with an understanding of its contribution (or value) to global, greater, or external objectives/goals. The concept of the IoT's AI brings additional constraints to understanding VoI, given such a pervasive information system. Like the limitations of Shannon's information theory (Shannon, 1956), these considerations also create a fundamental issue for a solely quantitative theory of information's applicability to IoT decision making.

We attempt to address this issue by examining a *VoI theory* in the context of information provided by the IoT. Our thinking is grounded in the work of Ponssard (1975) and especially Howard (1966). These works discuss how VoI is part of decision analysis. We attempt to make an optimal decision, based upon expected utility/value. Howard (1966) discusses how a company decides how much to bid on a contract based upon the a priori information it has available. In this situation, the company attempts to maximize its expected profit. We note though that we disagree with how Howard obtained his "clairvoyant" results in the situation when additional information is available to the decision maker. AI plays a major role in any consideration of the VoI because techniques, such as machine learning, can distill additional information from the IoT, which can be used by a decision maker.

## 9.2 THE INTERNET OF THINGS AND ARTIFICIAL INTELLIGENCE

IoT is touted as the next wave in the era of computing (Gubbi, Buyya, Marusic, & Palaniswami, 2013) and has quickly been relabeled the Internet of Everything (Roy & Chowdhury, 2017). While the definition of the IoT may take many forms, there is little debate about the enormous amount of information it will make available (Barnaghi, Sheth, & Henson, 2013; Papadokostaki et al., 2017; Taherkordi, Eliassen, & Horn, 2017) for decision-related activities. Quoting from Moskowitz, Russell, and Jalaian (2018):

> The Internet of Things (IoT) is the realization of interconnected and ubiquitous computing, pervasive sensing, and autonomous systems that can affect the physical world. … The "things" that exist in the IoT can be generally thought of as physical or computational objects that label, sense, communicate, process, or actuate thereby bridging the physical and virtual worlds (Oriwoh & Conrad, 2015; Pande & Padwalkar, 2014). While there is no universally accepted definition of the IoT, the International Telecommunication Union Telecommunication Standardization Sector (ITU-T) defines the IoT as "a global infrastructure for the information society, enabling advanced services by interconnecting (physical and virtual) things …"

In Moskowitz et al. (2018), beyond providing a definition of the IoT, the authors showed how side channels in the IoT architecture can cause information to be covertly/steganographically transmitted from one place in the IoT to another. They argue that IoT will make so much information available that new threats will emerge from hiding in (information's) plain sight. We posit that the amount of available information in the IoT will change the supply and demand dynamic, resulting in a need for a new understanding of information's value. This relationship will likely follow an econometric view of value, where scarcity increases perceived and/or real value (Hansen & Serin, 1997; Rymaszewska, Helo, & Gunasekaran, 2017; Worchel, 1992). What makes the IoT such an interesting arena for VoI research is that even where the number of bits is the same everywhere in the IoT, the value of those bits can differ depending upon where and when you are in a certain location in the IoT. For example, if my smart refrigerator sends a message that I only have one egg left (extrapolating from Borgonovo, 2017), that information is only valuable to my cook, and it depends upon what my cook is planning on preparing before going to the market again. Since I do not cook, that information is of no value to me. However, if my alarm system sends a message to my smart phone that there is someone in my house when no one is supposed to be home, that information may be of some value to my cook, but it is extremely valuable information to me.

The IoT changes a user's normal perspective on how valuable information is obtained. We have many, many sources potentially sending information to a decision maker. This number of sources and amount of information can be both good and bad. It can be good by enabling us to reduce the uncertainty of some random variables. That is, one may be able to replace a continuous random variable with a large region of support, ideally with a Dirac delta distribution, where we would precisely know the information. That would be the ideal case and is discussed in the later sections of Howard (1966). However, in the following section we will illustrate some mathematical differences in what Howard did, and discuss our findings with regard to perfect information (clairvoyance), which are also different.

The IoT can also have negative effects; particularly when it comes to varied sources of potentially valuable decision-relevant information. Since the IoT is a huge conglomeration of processing and sensing devices, it is possible, and perhaps even likely, that contradictory information is obtained. Furthermore, the IoT will also be artificially intelligent itself (Elvy, 2017; Etzion, 2015). Machine learning algorithms are currently employed in the IoT at the local device and global usage levels (Ren & Gu, 2015). Much of the machine-learning approaches are implemented to provide the IoT with decision-making autonomy. In the next dimension of system intelligence, the IoT has already begun incorporating technologies to add increasing/improving autonomic or self-star (self-*) behaviors. Self-* behaviors are those characteristics that form self-awareness and include self-organization, self-adaptation, and self-protection. The dependence on AI in IoT, in this context, is apparent. However, the implications for AI-enabled self-* behaviors to impact information value are less clear. Nonetheless, there is ample documentation in the literature about how AI can and will be employed as a gatekeeper for information (Camerer, 2017; Conitzer, Sinnott-Armstrong, Borg, Deng, & Kramer, 2017; Naseem & Ahmed, 2017).

The overwhelming number of devices and data that they provide has already necessitated a need for machine learning (Witten, Frank, Hall, & Pal, 2016). The IoT easily interconnects devices and the information between them and with other objects and humans, facilitating the ability to transfer data to them without human-to-computer or human-to-human interaction. Reasoning capabilities stemming from machine learning and also from exploiting other (potentially centralized) resources brings beneficial effects in terms of system efficiency and dependability and adaptive physical and behavioral human–system interactions and collaborations for users

(Vermesan et al., 2017). Moreover, the machine learning and intelligence in the IoT provides systems with user, ambient, and social awareness, and enables a wide range of innovative applications (Guo et al., 2013). Beyond the volumes of information the IoT provides, the collective intelligence it manifest represents a new form of information-driven value (de Castro Neto & Santo, 2012).

The elicitation of value through the use of machine learning is not a new phenomenon (Dean, 2014). However, the IoT is transformative because it combines embedded machine learning, and thus collective intelligence, with an exponential ubiquity of devices, vast amounts and variety of data, and an ability to provide virtual interfaces to physical objects that can act on the real world. In this manner, advances in machine learning and AI will complement the technological capability of IoT and significantly impact of many facets of the traditional value chain (Kaplan, 1984). Contrast modern organizations' exploitation of the intelligent IoT with the historical perspective of 1997 research (Plant & Murrell, 1997) that casts AI as:

> The ultimate enabler of [organizational] agility through technology is the artificial intelligent component. AI demands greater organizational internal understanding of technology and thus is only applicable to mature organizations that have internally streamlined processes and a high degree of connectivity.

This view of the future from 1997 speaks to the sophistication of most modern organizations and the impact that more timely and accurate information sharing has on increasing interest in the VoI. Moreover, in narrow domains specific AI techniques that target the predictability of information insights necessary for profit generation, for example, the supply-chain, have proven quantitative measures of value and its relationship to the insights delivered (Lumsden & Mirzabeiki, 2008).

It is interesting to consider how AI itself will have to make VoI determinations relative to tasked goals and objectives. This is because the AI will be responsible for ensuring the automation of a variety of tasks and execution of services. Particularly in a collectively intelligent IoT setting, AI necessarily must make decisions that adapt local behaviors to accommodate global missions and dynamics. From this perspective, the decisions that both humans and AI make utilizing IoT information and processes must do so by focusing on the information itself rather than on technology, as the real carrier of value (Glazer, 1993). Glazer's research both (1) reiterates our earlier point that information itself is difficult and contextual to define in a value context, and (2) offers a transactional basis for VoI that involves decision making in a consumer–supplier process:

> A completely satisfactory definition of what constitutes information is problematic. The idea of information is context-dependent and multidimensional. Analogous to the level at which modern physics describes the entire universe in terms of the equivalence between matter and energy is the level at which communications theory provides a procedure for specifying anything (including matter and energy) in terms of its formal information content. The formal or quantitative definition and measure of information is that which reduces uncertainty or changes an individual's degree of belief about the world. However, except for the utility of this construct in purely engineering contexts, it has not provided the foundation for a practical information-measurement system in most general applications.

Glazer's work uses a case study to illustrate the relationship between information value and transactions and thus does little toward as theoretic approach to quantifying VoI. Further, while Glazer illustrates processes that may be automated by AI, his treatment does little to support the detailed decision-making process. Within a complex intelligent system such as the IoT, local AI as a decision maker will have to make microdecisions that enable scalability, given the decentralized nature of the IoT network (Ge, Yang, & Han, 2017). This raises the question, how can value be determined quantitatively in an application agnostic or generalizable sense? It is through this merged lens of IoT and AI that we examine a theory of VoI. To provide grounding and leverage the literature that examines value from a transactional basis, we start with the work of Howard.

## 9.3 REWORKING HOWARD'S INITIAL EXAMPLE

Howard's work (Howard, 1966) takes a business approach to defining information value. In this section we borrow freely from Howard. We do not quote phrases for the sake of readability. We do not make any claims to this work and just we rework Howard's; the only novel thing in this section is our choice of notation and exposition.

We begin with Howard's very practical problem of how much a company should bid to win a contract. If the bid is too high, it loses the contract. If the bid is too low, it gets the contract, but loses money on the deal. Therefore the company attempts to place the bid that will get it the contract while maximizing its profit. The *information* that the company uses to decide its bid is therefore of extreme importance and this range of information is considered to make up the sample space in question.

We assign a random variable $\mathcal{C}$ to be the cost of performing on the contract. Unfortunately, this cost is a probabilistic guess. We let the random variable $\mathcal{L}$ be the random variable representing the lowest bid of the competitors. The company's bid is given by the random variable $\mathcal{B}$. The company's profit is the random variable $\mathcal{V}$.

If $b > l$, the company loses the contract, and it is profit is $0$. If $b < l$ the company wins the contract and performs the work at a cost of $c$. Therefore the profit is $v = b - c$. Hence, similarly to Eq. (9.3) (Howard, 1966), the company gets the contract in case of a tie ($b = l$). In terms of the random variables:

$$\mathcal{V} = \begin{cases} \mathcal{B} - \mathcal{C}, & \text{if } \mathcal{B} \leq \mathcal{L} \\ 0, & \text{if } \mathcal{B} > \mathcal{L} \end{cases} \tag{9.1}$$

In Fig. 9.1 we see the plot of Eq. (9.1) when $c = 3$, $l = 8$. There is no upper bound on what $b$ may be, but $v$ is always $0$ for large enough $b$. Let us consider the density functions following Howard (1966) but with a modified[1] notation of Ross (2002). We have:

$$f(v|b) = \int\int_{\mathbb{R}^2} f(v|b,c,l) \cdot f(c,l|b) \, dc \, dl \tag{9.2}$$

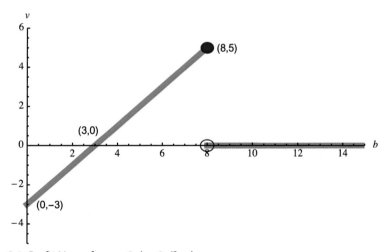

**Fig. 9.1** Profit $\mathcal{V} = v$, for $c = 3$, $l = 8$, $\mathcal{B} = b$.

[1] For typographical simplicity, we do not include the subindex of the density function when the context is clear. That is, for example, we write $f(x)$ instead of $f_X(x)$; however, the complete notation is taken as being understood.

Eq. (9.2) only makes sense when $0 \leq b$. The company never places a negative amount bid, so any event involving $b < 0$ has zero probability. Thus the conditional probability is not defined in that range.

We are interested in the expected value of profit conditioned on the bid. That is, we wish to determine $E(\mathcal{V}|b)$:

$$
\begin{aligned}
E(\mathcal{V}|b) &= \int_{-\infty}^{\infty} v \cdot f(v|b) \, dv \\
&= \iiint_{\mathbb{R}^3} v \cdot f(v|b,c,l) \cdot f(c,l|b) \, dc \, dl \, dv \\
&= \iint_{\mathbb{R}^2} f(c,l|b) \left( \int_{-\infty}^{\infty} v \cdot f(v|b,c,l) \, dv \right) dc \, dl \\
&= \iint_{\mathbb{R}^2} E(\mathcal{V}|b,c,l) \cdot f(c,l|b) \, dc \, dl
\end{aligned}
\tag{9.3}
$$

Now, Howard makes two assumptions (Eqs. 9.6, 9.7) Howard (1966) to simplify the problem.

Assumption 9.1 The joint distribution of cost and lowest bid $\mathcal{C}$, $\mathcal{L}$ is independent of our company's bid $\mathcal{B}$. That is:

$$
f(c,l|b) = f(c,l)
$$

Assumption 9.2 The company's cost $\mathcal{C}$ is independent of the lowest bid $\mathcal{L}$. That is:

$$
f(c,l) = f(c)f(l)
$$

We realize that one could certainly argue the reality of these assumptions in all cases. Using Assumptions 9.1 and 9.2 we now have that:

$$
E(\mathcal{V}|b) = \iint_{\mathbb{R}^2} E(\mathcal{V}|b,c,l) \cdot f(c)f(l) \, dc \, dl
\tag{9.4}
$$

From Eq. (9.1) we see that once we set the values of $\mathcal{B}$, $\mathcal{C}$, $\mathcal{L}$ at $b$, $c$, $l$, respectively, the density function of $\mathcal{V}$ becomes deterministic. That is:

Theorem 9.1
$$
f(v|b,c,l) = \begin{cases} \delta(v-(b-c)), & \text{if } b \leq l \\ \delta(v), & \text{if } b > l \end{cases}
$$

and therefore:

$$
E(\mathcal{V}|b,c,l) = \begin{cases} b-c, & \text{if } b \leq l \\ 0, & \text{if } b > l \end{cases}
$$

The following theorem follows from Eq. (9.4).

Theorem 9.2 Using Assumptions 9.1 and 9.2, we have:

$$E(\mathcal{V}|b) = \int\int_{\mathbb{R}^2} E(\mathcal{V}|b,c,l) \cdot f(c)f(l)\,dc\,dl \text{ (as above)}$$

$$= \int_{-\infty}^{\infty} (b-c)\left(\int_{b}^{\infty} f(l)\,dl\right) f(c)\,dc \tag{9.5}$$

$$= P(\mathcal{L} > b) \cdot \int_{-\infty}^{\infty} (b-c)f(c)\,dc \tag{9.6}$$

$$= [b - E(\mathcal{C})] \cdot P(\mathcal{L} > b) \tag{9.7}$$

The above corresponds to Eq. (9.10) (Howard, 1966). After our above assumptions, to obtain $E(\mathcal{V}|b)$, we only need the distribution of $\mathcal{L}$ and $E(\mathcal{C})$. Howard (1966) models $\mathcal{C}$ as a uniform distribution on $[0, 1]$, which implies $E(\mathcal{C}) = \frac{1}{2}$.

Next we relax what Howard did, and model the distribution of $\mathcal{C}$ such that $E(\mathcal{C}) = \frac{1}{2}$. We also follow Howard and model $\mathcal{L}$ as a uniform distribution on $[0, 2]$.

We say that the *base Howard example* is $\mathcal{L} = U[0,2]$ and $E(\mathcal{C}) = \frac{1}{2}$.

The above gives us $P(\mathcal{L} > b) = \frac{1}{2}(2-b)$, $b \leq 2$ (0 for $b > 2$). Of course, we do not consider $b < 0$ as discussed earlier. And so, we arrive at:

$$E(\mathcal{V}|b) = \frac{1}{2}(2-b)\left(b - \frac{1}{2}\right), \quad 0 \leq b \leq 2 \tag{9.8}$$

We see that $E(\mathcal{V}|b) = -\frac{1}{2}\left[b^2 - \frac{5}{2}b + 1\right]$ is a simple quadratic and that $\frac{d}{db}E(\mathcal{V}|b) = -b + \frac{5}{4}$, so $E(\mathcal{V}|b)$ obtains a maximum of 9/32 when $b = 5/4$ (Fig. 9.2).

We define:

$$\lceil\langle\mathcal{V}\rangle\rceil_b \triangleq \max_b E(\mathcal{V}|b)$$

From this definition, we see that when $E(\mathcal{C}) = 0.5$ and $\mathcal{L} = U[0,1]$:

$$\lceil\langle\mathcal{V}\rangle\rceil_b = 9/32$$

We are in agreement with everything that Howard has done to this point. What we do not agree with is how he used the concept of clairvoyance for additional information that may be learned. We note that the concept of clairvoyance is also discussed in (Borgonovo, 2017, Chapter 11). We return to this later in the chapter.

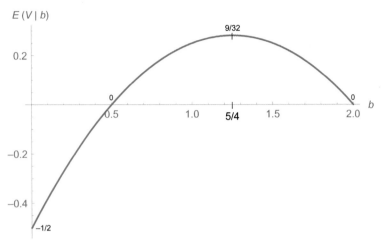

**Fig. 9.2** $E(\mathcal{V}|b)$.

## 9.4 VALUE DISCUSSION

We see from the above that the expected value of a random variable is very important to a decision maker; the information that is used has value. This notion of value is important in the IoT because it can/will be the source of information, moderated by AI that provides it, modifies it, or protects it. From this perspective, the IoT may provide all of the information, too much information, or a limited amount of the information. We see in the above example, that we do not need the entire cost, given Howard's assumptions, only the mean of the cost. Therefore, it need not require many bits of valuable information. Extending Howard's notion at this point, what is the information we have and what is its value?

1. Eq. (9.1): Modeling equation
2. Eq. (9.2): Standard probability theory
3. Assumption 9.1: Independence of the company's bid
4. Assumption 9.2: Cost and lowest bid independence
5. Behavior of $\mathcal{C}$
6. Behavior of $\mathcal{L}$

Let us just concentrate on the last two items for now. What we have actually used to this point is only the mean of $\mathcal{C}$, and for simplicity, we set:

$$\mu \triangleq E(\mathcal{C})$$

The distribution of $\mathcal{L}$ is given by its density function $f_L(l)$. Modifying *this* information changes the quantity we care about, that is:

*What is the "value" of the information in items 5 and 6 of the previous list in how it affects $\lceil \langle \mathcal{V} \rangle \rceil_b$? Does the shape of the graph change, does the maximum behavior change, etc.?*

We return to Eq. (9.4) to see the impact of changes in the information for items 5 and 6. First, let us change the distribution of $\mathcal{L}$ so that it is uniformly distributed on $[0, L]$, $L > 0$, instead of $[0, 2]$.

We see that $P(\mathcal{L} > b) = \frac{1}{L}(L - b)$, $b \leq L$ (0 for $b > L$). We see that, in general, for and arbitrary positive $\mu$ we have:

$$E(\mathcal{V}|b) = \frac{1}{L}(L - b)(b - \mu), \quad 0 \leq b \leq L \tag{9.9}$$

$$= -\frac{1}{L}\left(b^2 - [L + \mu]b + L\mu\right) \tag{9.10}$$

Simple calculus shows that the value $b_o$ that maximizes $E(\mathcal{V}|b)$ is either the critical point $b_c = \frac{L+\mu}{2}$, if $b_c \leq L$, or the boundary point $L$ if $\mu > L$. Thus,

$$\lceil \langle \mathcal{V} \rangle \rceil_b = \begin{cases} \dfrac{(L - \mu)^2}{4L}, \text{ with } b_o = \dfrac{L + \mu}{2}, & \text{if } 0 \leq \mu < L \\ 0, \text{ with } b_o = L, & \text{if } \mu \geq L \end{cases} \tag{9.11}$$

We see that the only interesting case is when $0 < \mu < L$, which makes logical sense. We call this case the nontrivial region and denote the function defined on that region as $\langle\!\langle \mathcal{V} \rangle\!\rangle$ (Fig. 9.3).

Note that we also have:

$$\frac{\partial \lceil \langle \mathcal{V} \rangle \rceil_b}{\partial L} = \begin{cases} \dfrac{1}{4}\left(1 - \left(\dfrac{\mu}{L}\right)^2\right) > 0, & \text{if } 0 \leq \mu < L \\ 0, & \text{if } \mu \geq L \end{cases} \tag{9.12}$$

and

$$\frac{\partial \langle\!\langle \mathcal{V} \rangle\!\rangle}{\partial \mu} = \frac{1}{2}\left(\frac{\mu}{L} - 1\right) < 0 \tag{9.13}$$

In the nontrivial region, increasing $L$ increases $\lceil \langle \mathcal{V} \rangle \rceil_b$, and decreasing $\mu$ decreases $\lceil \langle \mathcal{V} \rangle \rceil_b$.

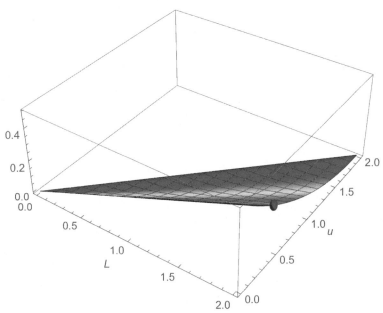

**Fig. 9.3** Surface plot of nontrivial values, for $L \in [0, 2]$, $\mu \in [0, 2]$, of $\lceil \langle\!\langle \mathcal{V} \rangle\!\rangle \rceil_b$, with point $(L = 2, \mu = 0.5, \lceil \langle\!\langle \mathcal{V} \rangle\!\rangle \rceil_b = 9/32)$ highlighted.

Let us pause and think about VoI. Is there any additional value in learning more about $\mathcal{C}$ other than its mean? No! This realization is an important understanding.

Also, if we are at a point in the nontrivial region, what is more important to learn with respect to $\langle\!\langle \mathcal{V} \rangle\!\rangle$, a change in $L$ or a change in $E(\mathcal{C})$? That is, if we have to prioritize the information that is sent to a decision maker and we can only send one "fact" at a time, which one would we send first, information about a change in $L$ or $E(\mathcal{C})$? Consider the total differential:

$$d\langle\!\langle \mathcal{V} \rangle\!\rangle = \frac{\partial \langle\!\langle \mathcal{V} \rangle\!\rangle}{\partial L} dL + \frac{\partial \langle\!\langle \mathcal{V} \rangle\!\rangle}{\partial \mu} d\mu \qquad (9.14)$$

$$= \frac{1}{4}\left(1 - \left(\frac{\mu}{L}\right)^2\right) dL - \frac{1}{2}\left(1 - \frac{\mu}{L}\right) d\mu \qquad (9.15)$$

Then, using $1 - x^2 = (1 - x)(1 + x)$, we see that:

$$\left|\frac{\partial \langle\!\langle \mathcal{V} \rangle\!\rangle}{\partial L}\right| < \left|\frac{\partial \langle\!\langle \mathcal{V} \rangle\!\rangle}{\partial \mu}\right| < 2\left|\frac{\partial \langle\!\langle \mathcal{V} \rangle\!\rangle}{\partial L}\right| \qquad (9.16)$$

In the infinitesimal sense, the value of $E(\mathcal{C})$ is more important than the value of $L$, but not by much. Therefore, if we have to prioritize information sent to a decision maker, it should be $E(\mathcal{C})$, then $L$.

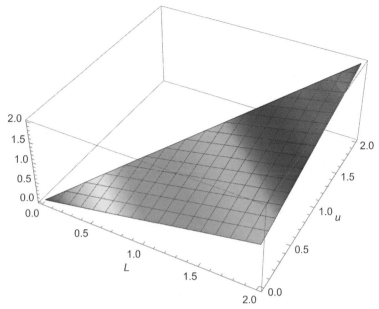

**Fig. 9.4** Surface plot of $b_o$ in the nontrivial region for $L \in [0, 2]$, $\mu \in [0, 2]$.

Of course, all of the above is based upon the fact that we know the optimal $b_o = \frac{L+\mu}{2}$, which we learned from our above assumptions and calculations (Fig. 9.4).

### 9.4.1 Generalization

Let us summarize the above as a generality.

**1.** We are given distributions on $\mathcal{L}$ and $\mathcal{C}$.

**2.**
$$\mathcal{V} = \begin{cases} \mathcal{B} - \mathcal{C}, & \text{if } \mathcal{B} < \mathcal{L} \\ 0, & \text{if } \mathcal{B} > \mathcal{L} \end{cases}$$

**3.** $\mathcal{L}$ and $\mathcal{C}$ are independent of the company's bid $\mathcal{B}$.

**4.** The company's cost $\mathcal{C}$ is independent of the lowest bid $\mathcal{L}$.

Given this summary:

$$E(\mathcal{V}|b) = [b - E(\mathcal{C})] \cdot P(\mathcal{L} > b) \text{ and now, in general}$$
$$\lceil \langle \mathcal{V} \rangle \rceil_b \triangleq \max_b E(\mathcal{V}|b)$$

Assuming that $\frac{d}{db}E(\mathcal{C}) = \frac{d}{db}f(l) = 0$ (which is not a far stretch from the statistical independence we have assumed for the underlying random variables), we have $\frac{d}{db}E(\mathcal{V}|b) = P(\mathcal{L} > b) - [b - E(\mathcal{C})] \cdot f_{\mathcal{L}}(b)$, where the term $f_{\mathcal{L}}(b)$ is the density function $f(l)$ of $\mathcal{L}$ evaluated at $l = b$. The optimal $b_o$ in the non-trivial region solves the integral equation:

$$b = E(\mathcal{C}) + \frac{P(\mathcal{L} > b)}{f_{\mathcal{L}}(b)} = E(\mathcal{C}) + \frac{1}{f_{\mathcal{L}}(b)} \int_b^\infty f_{\mathcal{L}}(l) dl$$

and in the nontrivial region $[\langle \mathcal{V} \rangle]_b = \dfrac{(P(\mathcal{L} > b_o))^2}{f_{\mathcal{L}}(b_o)}$

## 9.5 CLAIRVOYANCE ABOUT $\mathcal{C}$

Let us go back to Eq. (9.4), but now let us assume that the company knows the cost $\mathcal{C}$. In this case the company will never bid less than the cost or it will lose money! Note that our results in this section differ from Howard's results on clairvoyance.

Assumption 9.3 The company has knowledge of the cost.

We must modify Theorem 9.1 so that:

$$E(\mathcal{V}|b,c,l) = \begin{cases} b - c, & \text{if } c \le b \le l \\ 0, & \text{otherwise} \end{cases} \tag{9.17}$$

We have that:

$$\begin{aligned} E(\mathcal{V}|b) &= \int\int_{\mathbb{R}^2} E(\mathcal{V}|b,c,l) \cdot f(c) f(l) dc\, dl \text{ (as above)} \\ &= \int_{-\infty}^b (b-c) \left( \int_b^\infty f(l) dl \right) f(c) dc \end{aligned} \tag{9.18}$$

$$= P(\mathcal{L} > b) \cdot \int_{-\infty}^b (b-c) f(c) dc \tag{9.19}$$

$$= \left[ b \cdot P(\mathcal{C} \le b) - \int_{-\infty}^b cf(c) dc \right] \cdot P(\mathcal{L} > b) \tag{9.20}$$

We will go through an example similar to what we did before. Previously, we followed Howard and modeled $\mathcal{C}$ so that $E(\mathcal{C}) = 1/2$ and $\mathcal{L} = U[0,2]$. Note that, as before, the distribution of $\mathcal{C}$ did not matter, only its mean. We see from the above that this is no longer true. Let us try some examples.

Example 9.1 [$\mathcal{L} = U[0,2]$ and $P(\mathcal{C} = 1/2) = 1$] So we have that $f(c) = \delta(c - 1/2)$, and Eq. (9.20) becomes (Fig. 9.5):

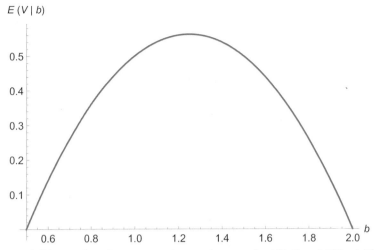

**Fig. 9.5** $E(\mathcal{V}|b) \geq 0$ when the company knows the cost, $\mathcal{L} = U[0,2]$ and $P(\mathcal{C} = 1/2) = 1$.

$$E(\mathcal{V}|b) = \begin{cases} [b - 1/2] \cdot P(\mathcal{L} > b), & \text{if } 1/2 < b \leq 2 \\ 0, & \text{otherwise} \end{cases} \quad (9.21)$$

Eq. (9.21) simplifies to:

$$E(\mathcal{V}|b) = \begin{cases} (b - 1/2)\left(\dfrac{2-b}{2}\right), & \text{if } 1/2 < b \leq 2 \\ 0, & \text{otherwise} \end{cases} \quad (9.22)$$

In Example 9.1, $E(\mathcal{V}|b)$ has a maximum value of 18/32, when $b = 5/4$.
Example 9.2 $[\mathcal{L} = U[0,2]$ and $\mathcal{C} = U[0,1]]$ Eq. (9.20) now becomes:

$$E(\mathcal{V}|b) = \begin{cases} \left[b \cdot \left(\dfrac{b-0}{1-0}\right) - \displaystyle\int_0^b c \cdot \dfrac{1}{1} dc\right] \cdot \left(\dfrac{2-b}{2}\right), & \text{if } 0 \leq b \leq 1 \\ \left[b \cdot P(\mathcal{C} \leq 1) - \displaystyle\int_{-\infty}^1 c\, dc\right] \cdot \left(\dfrac{2-b}{2}\right), & \text{if } 1 < b \leq 2 \\ 0, & \text{otherwise} \end{cases} \quad (9.23)$$

Eq. (9.23) simplifies to:

$$E(\mathcal{V}|b) = \begin{cases} \dfrac{b^2}{4}(2-b), & b \in [0,1] \\ [b - E(\mathcal{C})] \cdot \left(\dfrac{2-b}{2}\right) = \dfrac{1}{2}(2-b)\left(b - \dfrac{1}{2}\right), & b \in (1,2] \\ 0, & \text{otherwise} \end{cases}$$

$$(9.24)$$

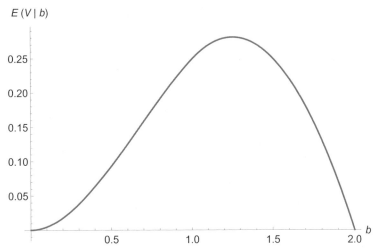

**Fig. 9.6** $E(\mathcal{V}|b) \geq 0$ when the company knows the cost, $\mathcal{L} = U[0,2]$ and $\mathcal{C} = U[0,1]$.

We note with interest that $E(\mathcal{V}|b)$ is a (once) differentiable function on $[0, 2]$ (Fig. 9.6).

In Example 9.2, $E(\mathcal{V}|b)$ has a maximum value of $9/32$ when $b = 5/4$, which is the same as Howard's base example.

We see that when the company knows the cost $\mathcal{C}$, the distribution and not just the mean, it affects the behavior of $E(\mathcal{V}|b)$. We also see that knowledge of $\mathcal{C}$ guarantees that $E(\mathcal{V}|b) \geq 0$. That is, the company never loses money.

## 9.6 CLAIRVOYANCE ABOUT $\mathcal{L}$

Now we are in the situation where the company knows the competitor's lowest bid, which is represented by $\mathcal{L}$. As before we assume that if the company's bid $b$ ties with the competition's lowest bid $l$ that the company wins the contract. If we know $l$ we bid $l$; this bid is placed to win the contract *and* maximize profit. Note, if one finds this result disturbing, we can always make the bid $b$ a tiny amount less than $l$. Nonetheless, we therefore see that $\mathcal{B}$ and $\mathcal{L}$ must be the same. The company will always win the bidding, but it may lose money depending on the value of $c$. Therefore,

$$E(\mathcal{V}|b) = E(\mathcal{V}|l) \tag{9.25}$$

Modifying Eq. (9.1), now differently than Eq. (9.17), we have:

$$E(\mathcal{V}|b,c,l) = \begin{cases} l-c, & l \in \text{support of } \mathcal{L} \\ 0, & \text{otherwise} \end{cases} \tag{9.26}$$

We have that ($\mathcal{C}$ and $\mathcal{L}$ still independent):

$$E(\mathcal{V}|l) = \int_{\mathbb{R}} E(\mathcal{V}|c,l) \cdot f(c)\, dc \tag{9.27}$$

$$= \int_{\mathbb{R}} (l-c) \cdot f(c)\, dc \tag{9.28}$$

$$= l\int_{\mathbb{R}} f(c)\, dc - \int_{\mathbb{R}} c \cdot f(c)\, dc \tag{9.29}$$

$$= l - E(\mathcal{C}) \tag{9.30}$$

when $l \in$ support of $\mathcal{L}$.

Example 9.3 [$\mathcal{L} = U[0,L]$ and $E(\mathcal{C}) = 1/2$] Below we show a plot of $E(\mathcal{V}|l) = l - 0.5$ against $l$ for $\mathcal{L} = U[0,2]$ and $E(\mathcal{C}) = 1/2$ (Fig. 9.7).

For Example 9.3, $\lceil \langle \mathcal{V} \rangle \rceil_b = 1.5$, achieved when $b = 2$.

Note that $E(\mathcal{V}|b)$ is a linear function of $b = l$ and that it can be negative, zero (once), or positive depending on the support of $\mathcal{L}$. Furthermore, the maximum of $E(\mathcal{V}|b)$ is achieved when $b$ is the largest value of $l$ in the support of $\mathcal{L}$. Heuristically, another way of saying this is that the maximum is achieved for the largest value of $l$ such that $P(L \in (l - dx, l)) \neq 0$.

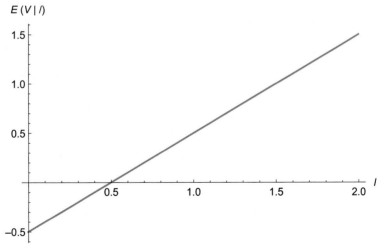

**Fig. 9.7** $E(\mathcal{V}|b)$ such that $E(\mathcal{C}) = 1/2$, and the company knows the lowest bid, distributed as $\mathcal{L} = U[0,2]$.

Unlike with the clairvoyant knowledge of $C$, with knowledge of $\mathcal{L}$, $E(\mathcal{V}|b)$ may be negative, but the profit may be much larger. Knowledge of $C$ gives the company nonnegative profit, whereas knowledge of $\mathcal{L}$ gives it a larger potential profit. This result is in-line with the results Howard obtained.

## 9.7 CLAIRVOYANCE ABOUT $C$ AND $\mathcal{L}$

After we combine both pieces of information, the bid $b$ will never be less than $c$, and it will always match $l$, meaning that we must modify Eq. (9.1) again, now different from Eq. (9.25) because $\mathcal{L}$ is more restricted, resulting in:

$$E(\mathcal{V}|b,c,l) = \begin{cases} l-c, & \text{if } c \le l, \text{ and } l \in \text{support of } \mathcal{L} \\ 0, & \text{otherwise} \end{cases} \tag{9.31}$$

So we have an assumption of independence between $C$ and $\mathcal{L}$:

$$E(\mathcal{V}|l) = \int_{\mathbb{R}} E(\mathcal{V}|c,l) \cdot f(c)\,dc \tag{9.32}$$

$$= \int_{-\infty}^{l} (l-c) \cdot f(c)\,dc \tag{9.33}$$

$$= l \cdot P(C < l) - \int_{-\infty}^{l} c \cdot f(c)\,dc \tag{9.34}$$

when $l \in$ support of $\mathcal{L}$.

Example 9.4 [$\mathcal{L} = U[0,2]$ and $C = U[0,1]$]

$$E(\mathcal{V}|b) = \begin{cases} l \cdot \int_0^l dc - \int_0^l c\,dc & \text{if } 0 \le l < 1 \\ l \cdot \int_0^1 dc - \int_0^1 c\,dc, & \text{if } 1 \le l \le 2, \\ 0, & \text{otherwise} \end{cases} \tag{9.35}$$

The results:

$$E(\mathcal{V}|b) = \begin{cases} \dfrac{l^2}{2}, & \text{if } 0 \le l < 1 \\ l - .5, & \text{if } 1 \le l \le 2, \\ 0, & \text{otherwise} \end{cases} \tag{9.36}$$

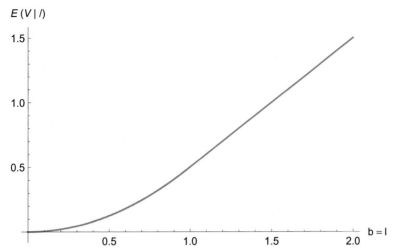

E (V | I)

**Fig. 9.8** $E(\mathcal{V}|b)$ for when $\mathcal{C} = U[0,1]$ and the company knows the lowest bid has distribution $\mathcal{L} = U[0,2]$.

Below we plot $E(\mathcal{V}|b) = E(\mathcal{V}|l)$ against $b$ for $\mathcal{L} = U[0,2]$ and $\mathcal{C} = U[0,1]$ (Fig. 9.8).

For Example 9.4, $\lceil \langle \mathcal{V} \rangle \rceil_b = 1.5$, achieved when $b = 2$. Note that the behavior of Examples 9.3 and 9.4 is identical for $b > 1$. The difference is that if the company know $\mathcal{C}$, it may never place a bid that will lose money.

## 9.8 DISCUSSION

What does Howard's model teach us from a business perspective? How companies capture value remains largely the same, a function of competitive position and competitive advantage. Companies that control the flow of information in the value creation process enjoy competitive positions that are likelier to afford better opportunities to capture value from other participants in their ecosystem. In other words, they know where to play. Companies that differentiate the way in which they control the flow of information from other companies with similar positions enjoy a competitive advantage. In other words, they know how to win.

This leads to the conclusion that information creates value only when it is used to modify future action in beneficial ways. Ideally, this modified action gives rise to new information, allowing the learning process to continue. Information, then, creates value not in a linear value chain of process steps but, rather, in a never-ending value loop. Whether information is viewed discretely or from a continuous variable perspective the question remains: what is the probability that new value can be derived?

From a systems standpoint, as well as a system-augmented human decision-making perspective, machine learning and AI is implied in the never-ending value-loop. This notion is consistent with and supported by the decision science literature, which generally views decision making as an ongoing process (Simon, 1960). If value, derived from plentiful IoT information is created in a nonlinear loop (Baker, Song, & Jones, 2017), then information's relationship to the decision is inseparable. Further, given an abundance of supply-side information, VoI would decrease proportionally to its decision relevance. This is logical, because if everyone has perfect information in a bidding situation, VoI would correlate highly with its perceived potential for modification (Sánchez-Fernández & Iniesta-Bonillo, 2007). The decision-transactional basis of Howard's on theoretical VoI and thereby our own extension, may introduce contextual bias in this sense, so we provide some discussion here on the nature of sensed information and VoI from the sensor network literature.

Bisdikian, Kaplan, and Srivastava (2013) have conducted a significant amount of research in quality of information (QoI), VoI, and the relationship between them. Their findings are relevant here because their work helps define the differences between quantitative and qualitative characteristics of information. Moreover, they provide these definitions from the perspective of sensor networks making the application to IoT direct, if on a somewhat smaller scale. The work of Bisdikian et al. is a departure from the information theoretic perspective taken in our work and instead provide a descriptive characterization of QoI and VoI. Their definition casts VoI as a function of QoI, where QoI is use-independent facts about information (e.g., percentage of error, age, resolution) and VoI is use-dependent qualitative judgments (e.g., trustworthiness, completeness, readability). Figs. 9.9 and 9.10 show the semantic taxonomy from Bisdikian et al., where it is evident that our treatment of VoI is consistent with the qualitative judgment.

The semantic descriptions of QoI and VoI suggest that AI's use of the IoT would concentrate primarily on QoI because VoI characteristics are

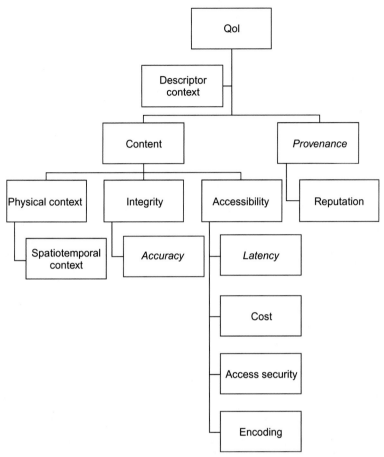

**Fig. 9.9** Quality of Information attribute taxonomy. *(Adapted from Bisdikian, C., Kaplan, L. M., & Srivastava, M. B. (2013). On the quality and value of information in sensor networks.* ACM Transactions on Sensor Networks (TOSN), 9(4), 48.)

essentially human characteristics that are difficult to capture computationally in open-domain problems. However, QoI characteristics may provide a basis for deriving a probabilistic VoI to be used in transactional (nonclairvoyant) estimates. Further, it may be feasible to learn over QoI values to bound a purely computational VoI. Future research, building on our work, may warrant additional consideration about how machine-learned QoI could translate to a functional VoI.

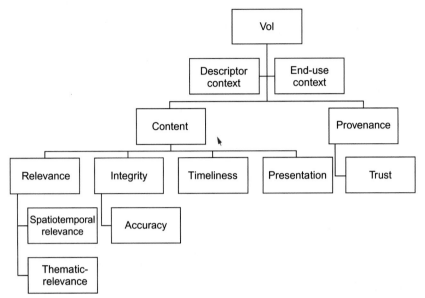

**Fig. 9.10** Volume of Information attribute taxonomy. *(Adapted from Bisdikian, C., Kaplan, L. M., & Srivastava, M. B. (2013). On the quality and value of information in sensor networks.* ACM Transactions on Sensor Networks (TOSN), 9(4), 48.)

## 9.9 CONCLUSION

IoT will provide a rich environment, supplying VOIs for nearly every aspect of humans' activities and environments. The IoT will gain ever increasing amounts of AI that will only provide greater degrees of autonomic capabilities and self-star behaviors. This AI-enriched IoT environment will change the fundamental notions of information value for decision making by producing huge quantities of information that are managed by AI functionality. Like Shannon's information theories, our understanding of VoI theory will implicitly go beyond just a quantitative concept to include qualitative notions. However, there is surprisingly little literature that examines VoI in the context of the IoT. In this chapter, we have extended Howard's (1966) VoI theory to examine a generalization of that notion toward a guarantee of a minimal value.

We presented a rework of Howard's theoretical problem and solution identifying some limitations in his treatment of a random variable, relative to VoI. Howard's idea of *clairvoyance*, or insight into future information (and its value) treats the value of the random variable deterministically rather than probabilistically. By giving the random variable a probabilistic context, such as would be the case of the information provided by AI-enabled IoT, the theoretical handling of clairvoyance changes. We see, as did Howard, that knowledge about $\mathcal{L}$ is more important than knowledge about $\mathcal{C}$ when it comes to maximizing $E(\mathcal{V}|b)$. But we have shown that a knowledge of $\mathcal{C}$ in a bid guarantees that a bidder will never have a negative expected profit. Therefore, the VoI depends on what one is trying to do, or the contextual objective. This qualitative consideration must be kept in mind for future research on VoI. Existing work from the sensor network domain, specifically on QoI, and VoI may provide quantitative measures that can form a probabilistic derivative VoI.

We explained the relevance of our approach in this chapter's section on IoT and AI. We have taken the opportunity to adjust Howard's seminal theory to provide an extended foundation for the VoI theory in the IoT. One must keep in mind that AI techniques, such as machine learning and artificial reasoning, when employed in the IoT for self-star system behaviors, will require additional consideration for managing information provided to a human or machine decision maker. While we continued with Howard's "market" context in this chapter for its explainability and theoretic continuity, our future work will examine the implications of our theoretical VoI guarantee, described herein, in an IoT-specific experimental simulation or empirical study, that incorporates semantic notions of QoI.

## ACKNOWLEDGMENTS

The authors acknowledge the assistance of Swmbo Heilizer. The authors also thank William F. Lawless for his careful reading of the draft version of this chapter and his helpful suggestions.

## REFERENCES

Allwein, G. (2004). A qualitative framework for Shannon information theories. In: *Proceedings of the 2004 workshop on new security paradigms* (pp. 23–31). ACM.

Babaoglu, O., Jelasity, M., Montresor, A., Fetzer, C., Leonardi, S., van Moorsel, A., & van Steen, M. (2005). The self-star vision. In: *In Self-star properties in complex information systems* (p. 397).

Baker, J., Song, J., & Jones, D. R. (2017). Closing the loop: Empirical evidence for a positive feedback model of IT business value creation. *The Journal of Strategic Information Systems*, *26*(2), 142–160.

Barnaghi, P., Sheth, A., & Henson, C. (2013). From data to actionable knowledge: Big Data challenges in the web of things [Guest Editors' Introduction]. *IEEE Intelligent Systems*, *28*(6), 6–11.

Barwise, J., & Seligman, J. (1997). *Information flow: The logic of distributed systems: Vol. 44.* Cambridge: Cambridge University Press.

Bisdikian, C., Kaplan, L. M., & Srivastava, M. B. (2013). On the quality and value of information in sensor networks. *ACM Transactions on Sensor Networks (TOSN)*, *9*(4), 48.

Borgonovo, E. (2017). Global sensitivity analysis with value of information. In *Sensitivity analysis* (pp. 201–210). New York: Springer.

Camerer, C. F. (2017). *Artificial intelligence and behavioral economics. In Economics of artificial intelligence.* Chicago: University of Chicago Press.

Conitzer, V., Sinnott-Armstrong, W., Borg, J. S., Deng, Y., & Kramer, M. (2017). Moral decision making frameworks for artificial intelligence. In: *In AAAI* (pp. 4831–4835).

de Castro Neto, M., & Santo, A. E. (2012). Emerging collective intelligence business models. *MCIS Proceedings 14.*

Dean, J. (2014). *Big data, data mining, and machine learning: Value creation for business leaders and practitioners.* New York: John Wiley & Sons.

Elvy, S. -A. (2017). *The artificially intelligent internet of things and Article 2 of the Uniform Commercial Code. Forthcoming, Research Handbook on the Law of Artificial Intelligence.* Edward Elgar Press, NYLS Legal Studies. Research Paper No. 3046558. Available at: *https://doi.org/10.2139/ssrn.3046558.*

Etzion, O. (2015). When artificial intelligence meets the internet of things. In: *Proceedings of the 9th ACM international conference on distributed event-based systems* (p.246). Oslo, Norway: ACM246.

Ge, X., Yang, F., & Han, Q. -L. (2017). Distributed networked control systems: A brief overview. *Information Sciences*, *380*, 117–131.

Glazer, R. (1993). Measuring the value of information: The information-intensive organization. *IBM Systems Journal*, *32*(1), 99–110.

Gubbi, J., Buyya, R., Marusic, S., & Palaniswami, M. (2013). Internet of things (IoT): A vision, architectural elements, and future directions. *Future generation computer systems*, *29*(7), 1645–1660.

Guo, B., Zhang, D., Yu, Z., Liang, Y., Wang, Z., & Zhou, X. (2013). From the internet of things to embedded intelligence. *World Wide Web*, *16*(4), 399–420.

Hansen, P. A., & Serin, G. (1997). Will low technology products disappear?: The hidden innovation processes in low technology industries. *Technological Forecasting and Social Change*, *55*(2), 179–191.

Howard, R. A. (1966). Information value theory. *IEEE Transactions on Systems Science and Cybernetics*, *2*(1), 22–26.

Kaplan, J. (1984). The industrialization of artificial intelligence_ From by-line to bottom line. *AI Magazine*, *5*(2), 51.

Lumsden, K., & Mirzabeiki, V. (2008). Determining the value of information for different partners in the supply chain. *International Journal of Physical Distribution & Logistics Management*, *38*(9), 659–673.

Moskowitz, I. S., & Kang, M. H. (1994). Covert channels-here to stay? In Computer assurance, 1994. COMPASS'94 safety, reliability, fault tolerance, concurrency and real time, security. *Proceedings of the ninth annual conference on* (pp. 235–243): IEEE.

Moskowitz, I. S., Russell, S., & Jalaian, B. (2018). *Steganographic Internet of Things: Graph topology timing channels. Workshops at the Thirty-Second AAAI Conference on Artificial Intelligence.* New Orleans: AAAI Publications, LA.

Naseem, S., & Ahmed, K. (2017). Information protection in cognitive science. *International Journal of Computer Science and Network Security (IJCSNS)*, *17*(3), 1.

Oriwoh, E., & Conrad, M. (2015). 'Things' in the Internet of Things: Towards a definition. *International Journal of Internet of Things*, *4*(1), 1–5.

Pande, P., & Padwalkar, A. R. (2014). Internet of things—A future of internet: A survey. *International Journal*, *2*(2), 832–839.

Papadokostaki, K., Mastorakis, G., Panagiotakis, S., Mavromoustakis, C. X., Dobre, C., & Batalla, J. M. (2017). Handling Big Data in the era of internet of things (IoT). In *Advances in mobile cloud computing and Big Data in the 5G Era* (pp. 3–22). New York: Springer.

Plant, R., & Murrell, S. (1997). The agile organisation: Technology and innovation. In: *In AAAI-97 workshop on using AI in electronic commerce* (pp. 26–32).

Ponssard, J. -P. (1975). A value theory for experiments defined extensive form. *Management Science, 22*(4), 449–454.

Ren, F., & Gu, Y. (2015). Using artificial intelligence in the Internet of Things. *ZTE Communications, 1.*

Ross, S. M. (2002). *A first course in probability* (6th ed.). Upper Saddle River: Prentice Hall.

Roy, S., & Chowdhury, C. (2017). Integration of Internet of everything (IoE) with cloud. In *Beyond the internet of things* (pp. 199–222). New York: Springer.

Russell, S., Moskowitz, I. S., & Raglin, A. (2017). Human information interaction, artificial intelligence, and errors. In *Autonomy and artificial intelligence_ A threat or savior?* (pp. 71–101). Cham: Springer. https://doi.org/10.1007/978-3-319-59719-5_4.

Rymaszewska, A., Helo, P., & Gunasekaran, A. (2017). IoT powered servitization of manufacturing: An exploratory case study. *International Journal of Production Economics, 192*, 92–105.

Sánchez-Fernández, R., & Iniesta-Bonillo, M. A. (2007). The concept of perceived value: A systematic review of the research. *Marketing Theory, 7*(4), 427–451.

Shannon, C. E. (1948). A mathematical theory of communication. *Bell Systems Technical Journal, 27*(379–423), 623–656.

Shannon, C. E. (1956). The bandwagon. *IRE Transactions on Information Theory, 2*(1), 3.

Simon, H. A. (1960). *The new science of management decision.* Prentice-Hall

Taherkordi, A., Eliassen, F., & Horn, G. (2017). From IoT Big Data to IoT big services. In: *Proceedings of the symposium on applied computing* (pp. 485–491): ACM.

Vermesan, O., Bröring, A., Tragos, E., Serrano, M., Bacciu, D., Chessa, S., et al. (2017). Internet of robotic things: Converging sensing/actuating, hypoconnectivity, artificial intelligence and IoT platforms. In O. Vermesan & J. Bacquet (Eds.), *Cognitive hyperconnected digital transformation: Internet of things intelligence evolution* (pp. 97–155). River Publishers

Witten, I. H., Frank, E., Hall, M. A., & Pal, C. J. (2016). *Data mining: Practical machine learning tools and techniques.* Morgan Kaufmann

Worchel, S. (1992). Beyond a commodity theory analysis of censorship: When abundance and personalism enhance scarcity effects. *Basic and Applied Social Psychology, 13*(1), 79–92.

# CHAPTER 10

# Would IOET Make Economics More Neoclassical or More Behavioral? Richard Thaler's Prediction, a Revisit

**Shu-Heng Chen**
AI-ECON Research Center, Department of Economics, National Chengchi University, Taipei, Taiwan

*It was the best of times, it was the worst of times, it was the age of wisdom, it was the age of foolishness, it was the epoch of belief, it was the epoch of incredulity, it was the season of Light, it was the season of Darkness, it was the spring of hope, it was the winter of despair, we had everything before us, we had nothing before us, we were all going direct to Heaven, we were all going direct the other way …*
**(Charles Dickens, 1859, A Tale of Two Cities, Book the First, Chapter I.)**

## 10.1 MOTIVATION AND INTRODUCTION

What would be an "effective characterization" of the current era with its great advances in artificial intelligence (AI)? Although we could refer to everything around us as "smart"[1] and these smart things could now be further connected together as a smart universe, called the Internet of Everything (IoE), this universe seems to be having difficulty pulling itself out

---

[1] A quick glossary of the vocabularies in the current conversation reveals smart phones, smart belts, smart mirrors, smart mirrors, smart homes, smart factories, smart cities, smart health, smart governance and nudging, smart nations, and even a smart planet.

*Artificial Intelligence for the Internet of Everything*
https://doi.org/10.1016/B978-0-12-817636-8.00010-7
**171**

of the mud that has trapped the *old universe* for so long.[2] There are alarms and alarmists everywhere in our "smart" surroundings. It seems that every single timely issue that has already troubled us for long may also be "upgraded" with the advent of modern AI. A long but nonexhaustive list includes human intelligence and civilization, economic instability, employment, income inequality, dishonesty, discrimination, populism, polarization, social exclusion, privacy and security, democracy, etc. Celebrities such as Elon Musk (Tesla Motors), Bill Gates (Microsoft), Steve Wozniak (Apple), and Stephen Hawking (1942–2018) have all voiced their alarms in one way or another.

Given this conundrum, maybe Charles Dickens' (1812–1870) magnum opus, *A Tale of Two Cities*, and his leading message, as we quoted above at the beginning of the chapter, stands as the most powerful illumination of what the era of AI can mean for us. In this chapter, we shall embark on a research project on the potential economic implications of IoE. As we shall argue, this research project, if placed in the history of economic analysis is not new (Section 10.2); however, IoE can be regarded as the advancement in technology from *ubiquitous computing* to *ubiquitous networking*, and its impact is unprecedented and overwhelming. Therefore the framework required to address this issue will be more comprehensive and extensive than the ones we have used before. This revisit will bring in new challenges associated with new concepts for economists.

As the first attempt to address this issue, our strategy is twofold. At the macro level, we shall examine the possibility of the *unmanned markets* as a continuation of the earlier socialist calculation debate (Section 10.2), whereas at the micro level we shall examine the rationality of individuals in economic theory in light of the long-standing debate between homo eco-nomicus and homo sapiens (Section 10.3). It may be worthwhile noticing that the earlier socialist calculation debate did not explicitly involve the

---

[2] The web of smart things or the smart universe brings in a new idea that is very different from the conventional "pride" pursued by economists under the title *the Hayek Hypothesis*. The Hayek hypothesis is a statement of collective intelligence, which can emerge from a society made up of many individuals whose intelligence is constrained (Hayek, 1945). This concept has been very powerful and influential in the development of economics over the last two decades. The spirit of the Hayek hypothesis has been manifested in the economic theory of zero-intelligence agents (entropy-maximizing agents) and has been incorporated into part of the foundation for Econophysics (Chen, 2012). To economists, IoE evokes the following curiosity: would a web of smart agents outperform a web of "dumb" agents? Would institutions, such as the market mechanism, play a less important role than before?

micro (individual) part, while assumptions regarding individuals were made somewhat opaquely. In this chapter, as we shall see, the concept of individuals as *cyborgs* or *extended minds* enable this debate to have a bottom-up version. In other words, the modern version of the socialist calculation debate needs to begin with the issue of the rationality of individuals.

The rest of this chapter is organized as follows. Section 10.2 provides a review of the socialist calculation debate. Section 10.3 first presents the idea of cyborgs, and then assesses the impact of IoE on the rationality of individuals in economic theory. Concluding remarks follow in Section 10.4.

## 10.2 WALRASIAN AUCTIONEER AND UNMANNED MARKETS

We have been through various episodes of industrial revolutions or, if expressed in a less overwhelming way, technological innovations. They each have their "dark side," echoing well with what Joseph Schumpeter (1883–1950) referred to as "creative destruction" (Schumpeter, 1942). Hence, from the viewpoint of the history of economic analysis, if we wish to sympathize with some of the critics, pessimists, or skeptics, we need to ask why *this time is different.*[3]

This time is different because, unlike the past "industrial revolutions" or "technological shocks," the current AI revolution driven by the advance in information and communication technology (ICT) is fundamental *in the Walrasian sense* (Walras, 1874). Interestingly enough as Dickens worked on one side of the Channel on his "Tale" his French counterpart in the other city (Paris), Leon Walras (1834–1910), an economist, had just started his academic career and 15 years later published his own magnum opus, *Elements of Pure Economics* (Walras, 1874). While this book has constantly been viewed as a groundbreaking step in economic analysis (specifically, the use of mathematical analysis in economics), the society for which the mathematics in his book operated has generally been ignored by those working in modern ICT

---

[3] Here we use the title of the book by Reinhart and Rogoff (2009). In their review of the financial follies over more than eight centuries, we often encountered what Reinhart and Rogoff referred to as the *this-time-is-different* syndrome. "The essence of the this-time-is-different syndrome is simple. It is rooted in the firmly held belief that financial crises are things that happen to other people in other countries at other times; crises do not happen to us, here and now. We are doing things better, we are smarter, we have learned from past mistakes. The old rules of valuation no longer apply. The current boom, unlike the many booms that preceded catastrophic collapses in the past (even in our country), is built on sound fundamentals, structural reforms, technological innovation, and good policy. Or so the story goes" (Ibid, p. 15).

and data scientists. In his book, Walras introduced an ideal type of economic society in which buyers and sellers not only have full information about the prices in the market, but could also participate in market transactions in an unrestricted (frictionless) manner. Markets are characterized by a high degree of organization and transactions, such as auctions, are centralized, and the terms of trade are made known openly to all market participants who, in turn, are given the opportunity to react to the prevailing prices.

Since both Charles Dickens and Leon Walras had experienced the political and economic upheavals after the Industrial Revolution, their work, especially that of the latter, regardless of how distant it may be from us in time, could still be useful as we experience the digital revolution, which, undoubtedly, is more significant in its impacts than previous industrial revolutions.

For the purpose of this chapter the significance of Walras' *Elements of Pure Economics* is twofold. First, it can be read as the first book in economics that portrays the economy in the era of ICT and big data, and, second, based on that portrait, the entire market can be *unmanned*, with all the trading media replaced by machines. Of course Walras did not mention anything explicitly about ICT in *Elements*, but the entirety of his thought experiments regarding general equilibrium analysis cannot be taken seriously without some proper assumptions related to the availability of ICT. In fact, the *Walrasian auctioneer*, his brilliant intellectual invention, can be interpreted as a platform (network of supercomputers) employing a large number of robot traders or software agents to perform cloud trading. In this sense, one may treat his perception of markets as IoE, which came to the mind of this genius way ahead of his time.

This idea of an unmanned market (the Walrasian auctioneer) was then further developed by socialist economists, notably, Oscar Lange (1904–1965) (Lange & Taylor, 1938) and Abba Lerner (1903–1982) (Lerner, 1944), becoming the foundation of the socialist economy and economic planning. Along this intellectual line, the idea of *cybernetics*, which originated from the earlier servo-mechanism (automation) and was popularized by Norbert Wiener (1894–1964), was introduced into economics by Oscar Lange, who also authored his posthumous publication *Introduction to Economic Cybernetics* (Lange, 1970). In the 1970s and 1980s, economic cybernetics was further pursued by Western economists under a new subject title, referred to as *optimal control theory* (Kendrick, 1981).

Despite its long burgeoning period of development, the idea of an unmanned market, that is, economic planning as a substitute for the market economy, has been constantly questioned and challenged, and constitutes what is known as the socialist calculation debate (Boettke, 2000). Ludwig von Mises (1881–1973) and Friedrich Hayek (1899–1992) led the charge against socialism; this debate, while alien to most computer scientists and AI researchers, can be considered to be the longest and the largest-scale debate on the possibility and desirability (consequences) of AI.[4] Alongside this debate, Hayek published his pathbreaking book, *The Road to Serfdom* (Hayek, 1944), which is probably the earliest penetrating and thought-provoking warning against unlimited exposure to AI. Notice that Hayek did not object to the use of machines or chess games with robot players; he raised objections to the use of AI to institutionalize the market mechanism.

So, *is this time different?* Even though ICT in the last century was insufficient to make the Walrasian auctioneer "smart enough" to support a centralized unmanned market, the current ICT revolution is in a better position to exhibit that function. Therefore what concerns us this time is not the usual job-loss alarm, which does not make this time different, but rather the market-annihilation alarm, which does. Insofar as Hayek's warning is valid, Helbing et al. (2017) can then be read as a refreshing message of Hayek (1944): instead of empowering the state over individuals, technology can now empower the platform over individuals. In any case, we could be under the shadow of Thomas Hobbes' (1588–1679) *Leviathan* (Hobbes, 1977).

## 10.3 HOMO ECONOMICUS VS. HOMO SAPIENS

Economics deals with the causes and consequences of human decision (choice) making in resource allocation subject to various physical constraints and desires. Mainstream economics has long established a standard representation for the rationality of this decision-making agent, which is normally known as *homo economicus* or the von Neumann-Morgenstern *expected-utility maximizing agent* (Von Neumann & Morgenstern, 1944). These agents can learn from experiences and hence can cope with the future without making systematic errors. They can also solve various trade-offs in their lives: consumption and saving, portfolio returns and risk, education and employment, work and leisure, diet and health, residential location and commute flexibility, numbers of kids, etc. Apart from the accidents, incidents and natural disasters that are beyond their control, their rationality implies that they have

---

[4] It is only very recently that the computational-theoretic nature of the debate was realized when this issue was visited by computer scientists (Cockshott & Cottrell, 1997; Cottrell & Cockshott, 1993).

self-control to carry out the choices made above so that their lives can be as happy as possible, probably even better than what is archived in George Vaillant's *Aging Well* (Vaillant, 2008). The chaos depicted in Charles Mackay's classic *Extraordinary Popular Delusions and the Madness of Crowds* (MacKay, 1841) may never occur in their "real" lives.

Obviously not everyone enjoys this self-portrait,[5] and efforts made to search for the alternatives contributed to the formation of a new kind of homo, known as *homo sapiens*, that has become the statue of behavioral economists. The 2017 Nobel Laureate in Economics, Richard Thaler, predicts that models of individuals in economic theory will be characterized by a paradigm shift from homo economicus to homo sapiens (Thaler, 2000). His prediction was made almost two decades ago, when the current ICT revolution was not yet fully developed. If humans can be empowered with intelligent wearable devices, bionic chips, and IoE, will the evolving *cyborgs* eventually reverse this trend and revive homo economicus?

## 10.3.1 Cyborgs

It seems to be a good place to detour slightly to involve the term "cyborg" (short for *cybernetic organisms*) here when one is addressing the economic consequences of IoE. If placed in a proper historical context, IoE may be regarded as the further implementation of cyborg science. The term cyborg was coined in 1960 by Manfred Clynes and Nathan Kline (Clynes & Kline, 1960). As Manfred Clynes recalled in an interview, "I thought it would be good to have a new concept, a concept of persons who can free themselves from the constraints of the environment to the extent that they wished. And I coined this word cyborg" (Gray, 1995, p. 47). Is not the statement also the pursuit for those who are so enthusiastically devoted to IoE? Despite this being the case, IoE differs from the idea of cyborgs by placing its focus, not on individuals, but on societies. Hence the picture is not just one of a man "travelling" through different "spaces" freely in the sense of communication and control, but more about the novel prototypes of interaction and coordination that can emerge with the availability of these extending "spaces."

The relationship between cyborg science and economics has been splendidly reviewed by the economic historian, Philip Mirowski. Mirowski

---

[5] This self-portrait of economists, homo economicus, contributed not only to the establishment of *economic imperialism* (Hodgeson, 2001; Chapter 13), but also to the enlargement of the intellectual gap between economists and other social scientists.

(2002) suggested that ideas pertaining to machines can be regarded as a thread connecting a myriad of branches of economics developing side by side with neoclassical economics after World War II that include computational economics, artificial economies, autonomous agents, and experimental economics; hence, cyborg science is closely associated with the history of economic analysis. Earlier we discussed the socialist calculation debate and the idea of the unmanned market, already pointing to cybernetics. Our revisit here will enable us to more clearly see why IoE will inevitably get involved in the continuation of this debate, while in different forms and with different rhetoric, primarily because its "formal body" has already been placed in the very heart of economics.

Indeed, if one reflects upon the history of behavioral economics and is sufficiently open-minded to include those great novels that deal with the complexity (or perplexity) and uncertainty of human nature, the core issue remains human decision making under limited intelligence, cognitive capability or bounded rationality, and, very recently, emotional influences (Wälde & Moors, 2017). With the advancement in AI and the ubiquitous IoE, it is feasible now to enhance the human's cognitive functionality with various cyborg-like extensions, using not just external (wearable) devices, such as smart phones or Google glasses, but also internal (implant) devices, such as the *extended mind* (Clark & Chalmers, 1998; Rosenfeld & Wong, 2017) and also the shared (networked) powerful "mind" (IoE). It then seems relevant to ask whether the increasingly enhanced cyborgs will become more like homo economicus.

In the following, we propose two contrasting possibilities in response to Thaler's prediction in light of IoE, which will be distinguished by different names: one is called *trend reversal* (Section 10.3.2) and the other *trend sustaining* (Section 10.3.3). As for the former, Thaler's prediction will be overthrown, whereas for the latter it will be fulfilled.

## 10.3.2 Trend Reversal

The main argument that IoE could support trend reversal lies in the possibility that IoE can facilitate human decision making or even automate it. However, that enhancement or automation has already existed for a long while. What is new is that, through IoE, this decision-supporting function can be further enhanced not just at the individual level (optimization), but further up to a social level (interaction and coordination) by means of ubiquitous networking.[6] A *frictionless economy*, as well presented by the neo-classical economy, will then be just around the corner.[7]

To elaborate on the above point, we first recognize that various intelligence tools (robots, software agents) have been extensively applied to "learn" and to "know" humans using the big data collected from IoE. These intelligent artificial agents can discover the repertoire of each decision maker in terms of preferences, moral judgments, beliefs, risk preferences, and routines or habitual behavior; hence, not only can IoE predict what individuals will choose, but, moreover, in their best interests, what they *ought to* choose; furthermore, if authorized, they will execute the choices for them as their incarnations. Since machines have little difficulty in exercising self-control, they can execute the choice with little hesitation.[8]

If these artificial agents are further applied to automate human decisions to a rather extensive extent, instead of merely driving an automobile, they can "routinize" many nontrivial decisions for humans. In this way, through IoE, networks of human agents are essentially mapped to networks of their cyborg equivalents. The entire (dual) economy is then run with enhanced rationality and coordination; the coordination scale is much more extensive than the idea of a city having only driverless cars or programmed drivers (Sasaki & Flann, 2005). In this manner, humans through their incarnations will behave as if they are homo economicus. This in turn helps with the formation of a frictionless economy.

Now, let us leave the unmanned vehicles behind, and focus on unmanned markets. With the information availability supported by IoE, the market mechanism as manifested by its *automated matching mechanism* can match couples or crowds to form partners, teams, firms, or various organizations. Matching per se is a highly complex issue, but good matches can

---

[6] One may use the term *dense everywhere* from topology to think of ubiquitous networking. In the vein of topology, if we take the closure of each individual or entity, their union should be the entire universe. Here, closure means the space reachable through networkings.

[7] The frictionless economy can be considered as an economic *Utopia*. It reflects a highly smooth operation of the economy, specifically, where information required for decisions is easily available, or, alternatively put, search is not costly. In this economy, prices of the homogeneous good are identical, the so-called *law of one price*. The degree of information asymmetry is low, and the distinction between informed traders and uninformed traders is negligible. Also see Hamel (2000).

[8] From behavioral economics, we know that agents may act according to a will that is not their own. Sometimes people get swept up and do what they would not otherwise do and what they may wonder about later. Self-control, as analyzed by behavioral economists, is treated as an exhaustible human resource (Muraven & Baumeister, 2000); when it is depleted, a human may lose his/her persistence in resisting temptation. This economic analysis of self-control has many policy implications (Shafir, 2013).

enhance human well-being dramatically.[9] Thanks to IoE, when the whole life span of humans can fundamentally be copied (mapped) into a cyber space, which is "topologically equivalent" to our real world, its digital landscape will be very "machine-friendly" for the artificial agents who are designed and dispatched to this space to search for and explore all possible opportunities.

As an illustration, consider the following example concerning the labor market. A college student upon his/her graduation has his/her resume automatically generated, which is then automatically sent to a matching pool where vacancies are matched with talents, followed by the provision of the most favorable deals for both (employer/employee) sides. A sequence of information processing, preference discovering, and skill endorsing, skill matching wage bargaining problems is automatically handled by artificial agents (robots) in cyberspace. When this happens, a collection of artificial agents takes over the labor market, which was for a long time run by humans, and the labor market as we understand it in the conventional sphere is gone and becomes unmanned.

One side effect associated with the advancement in matching technology carried out by the artificial agents in the IoE space is the development of the *customization-oriented economy*. The advancement in matching technology also facilitates the emergence of new production models, such as peer production, sharing and a pro-social economy. We can add more to extend this list, but what will happen if something we say is not correct?

### 10.3.3 Trend Sustaining

The above argument is built upon the key assumption that we have artificial agents smart enough to learn from humans, to "nudge" them,[10] and even

---

[9] Matching is a subject in *cooperative game theory*. Lloyd Shapley (1923–2016), the 2012 Nobel Laureate in economics, is acknowledged for his prominent work in cooperative game theory. One of his masterpieces is the solution of the stable matching problem, which he proposed jointly with David Gale (1921–2008), known as the *Gale–Shapley algorithm* (Gale & Shapley, 1962). This algorithm provides a foundation for the study of the two-sided matching mechanism, and has many far-reaching implications, including its application to the New York public school systems in assigning students to schools (Abdulkadiroglu & Sonmez, 2003; Roth, 2002).

[10] Here we borrow the term from Richard Thaler and Cass Sunstein (Thaler & Sunstein, 2008). Nudging can be considered as a kind of soft paternalism. Nudges are there because decision makers are simply not fully rational. Hence nudges are a kind of decision support. While Thaler and Sunstein authored the book before the advent of the era of IoE, they refer to many kinds of nudges, such as the design of choice architectures, which can benefit from using ubiquitous networking technology. Hence, it is not surprising to see that nudges will be incorporated into the IoE economy. Doing so may also evoke some ethical concerns, which are beyond the scope of this chapter. The interested reader is, however, referred to Standing (2011).

replace them. However, in each of these aggressive steps, there are not only promises, but also pitfalls, which, if outweighed, can together paralyze the design of autonomous agents as human incarnations. In what follows we shall provide a short, but not exhaustive, list of impediments. The three points that we shall raise below are all concerned with the *economics of attention* (Lanham, 2006).

First, IoE has endowed us with a degree of information richness to an unprecedented level. Now, within the IoE environment, information is constantly flowing around us. Some of our idle time, such as waiting for the bus, the traffic light, the elevator, or the waiter, is now recruited to processing the constant inflow of information. We then gradually lose these idle moments, and certainly cannot entertain them with our conventional styles of dazing, dreaming, pondering, reflecting, or run-away thinking. A neologism, the *smartphone zombie*, has been invented to describe this unparalleled phenomenon. While the effect of IoE on our brains and minds is unclear at this point, it may be fair to say that it has shaped or defined what *thinking* can mean for us. Now the conventional way of thinking by "staring at the wall" or *offline thinking* is being dramatically replaced by *online thinking*, i.e., thinking with constant interruptions. Comparing these two different styles of thinking is not that straightforward, and while the familiar *dual-task* or *multiple-task* psychological experiments may help shed some light on this comparative study, further work needs to be done (Damos, 1991). However, when decision makers are often required to make their decisions online and spontaneously, the deliberation efforts normally required by homo economicus may be severely curtailed.

Second, a related point is that our attention capacity is a scarce resource and the information richness brought by IoE can make attention scarcity even more strained. In the literature this tension is known as *information overload* (Sutcliffe & Weick, 2008). Information overload can adversely affect our decision-making capability, which has already been well studied in psychology and behavioral economics (Iyengar, 2010). In fact, Herbert Simon (1916–2001) had long noticed such a tension (Simon, 1971). Although he did not immediately exclude the possibility that the advances in ICT may compound the information overload problem rather than solve or mitigate it, he did provide the condition required for avoiding the appearance of the downside.

"Whether a computer will contribute to the solution of an information-overload problem or instead compound it depends on the distribution of its own attention among four classes of activities: listening, storing, thinking and speaking. A general design principle can be put as follows: An information processing subsystem (a computer or new organization unit) will reduce the net demand on the rest of the organization's attention only if it absorbs more information previously received by others than it produces—that is, *if it listens and thinks more than it speaks.*" (Ibid, p. 42; italics added). Briefly put, IoE has to make us feel quieter rather than noisier.

So far there is no clear evidence to show that our IoE environment can satisfy the *Simon condition*, and it is not entirely implausible to say that it tends to speak more than it can effectively listen and think (Chen, Chie, & Tai, 2016; Chen & Venkatachalam, 2017). If so, while a myriad of interconnections and interactions provided by IoE allow us to surf over a huge space of opportunities, it also exposes us to a potentially large number of decision problems, each with many alternatives. The latter is notoriously known as the *choice overload problem* or the *paradox of choice* (Iyengar & Lepper, 2000; Schwartz, 2004). Time and attention allowed for each of these choice problems is, therefore, severely diluted. Under such circumstances, to facilitate decision making, the attention-lacking agents may rely more on their fast track of information processing (i.e., the *reflexive system*), and less on their slow or deliberate track, the *reflective system* (Kahneman, 2011). In addition to emotion and gut feeling, various *fast and frugal heuristics*, such as following the herd, choice reinforcement, or using rules of thumb, will play a more contributory role in decision making (Gigerenzer & Gaissmaier, 2011), which may again make decision makers more like homo sapiens instead of homo economicus.

Finally, if information overload and choice overload have driven decision makers to behave more like homo sapiens, then even though machine learning can effectively extract and learn the behavioral patterns of these decision makers, the artificial agents that have been built may be, at best, another homo sapiens, since what was learned by artificial agents is what they actually did, but not what they ought to do for the sake of their own best interest. If one employs these artificial agents as the incarnation of their human counterparts and automates the decisions for them, then the well-known GIGO (garbage in, garbage out) principle may be applied (Stephens-Davidowitz & Pabon, 2017), and the things that are in action are again homo sapiens and not homo economicus.

The above three cases, while not exhaustive, justify why Thaler's prediction remains valid, and is independent of the IoE technology.

## 10.4 CONCLUDING REMARKS

Unlike the usual articles on IoE, which deal with a specific application of IoE, this chapter provides a panoramic view of IoE in economic theory, specifically, across the history of economic analysis. Reviewing the history of economic analysis in the light of developments in mathematics, physics, and machines has become a unique approach in economics. In that direction, this chapter can be regarded as a continuation of the intellectual inquiry initiated by Philip Mirowski (Mirowski, 2002, 2007).

Our inquiry has been carried out at both the macro and micro level. At the macro level, we explored the possibility of the unmanned markets as the continuation of the socialist calculation debate, while in the context of IoE, and at the micro level, we address the rationality or irrationality of individuals in economics under IoE. The two inquiries are closely related because the unmanned markets are largely built upon the automated decisions for individuals. Hence, these automated decisions, to some extent, determine the performance of the unmanned markets.[11] When automated decisions take place on a large scale, the individuals' decisions are facilitated not just by pens and pencils, abacuses, decision-support systems, or high-performance computing, but also by ubiquitous networking (IoE). With this "extended (augmented) mind," would these individuals (cyborgs) behave more like homo economicus? Or, alternatively, would the prediction of Richard Thaler be affected by the presence of IoE?

In this chapter, we addressed the plausible models of individuals in economic theory, when these individuals become part of the IoE economy. This issue seems to be particularly relevant since in neoclassical economics decision makers have long been treated as *information-processing units*. This notion was already formalized when decision sciences and economics were fully integrated in von Neumann and Morgenstern's collaborative magnum opus, *Theory of Games and Economic Behavior* (Von Neumann & Morgenstern, 1944), and was further strengthened when statistics also adopted a decision-making ontology and a game-theoretic methodology (Savage, 1954). The later *rational expectations revolution* in the 1970s and 1980s had pushed the concept of the information-processing unit to unprecedentedly high ground, probably achieving the golden age of homo economicus. However, this portrait has long worried psychologists and

---

[11] This issue has already triggered a very active research area, at least in the domain of financial markets (Lewis, 2014; Patterson, 2012).

behavioral economists, and there seems to be a turn to homo sapiens (Zou & Chen, 2018).

In this chapter we provided supporting arguments on both sides. We first use the idea of *economics as a cyborg science* (Mirowski, 2002) and enriched that idea with ubiquitous networking to form an "optimistic" expectation that the fading-away homo economicus will be recruited back to the center of the IoE economy. If this happens, the high time of behavioral economics will come to a stop, and the "mainstream" (neoclassical economics) will once again triumph. We then used Simon's *economic theory of attention* to indicate that the reverse expectation can also be plausible. According to Simon (1971), attention is a scarce resource. Simon warned us that the persistent deficiency in attention may not mitigate the problem of information overload, and as long as information overload remains, humans need to cope with these cognitive burdens with various heuristics and hence they are not immune to various biases and errors.[12]

If homo sapiens remains the major species in IoE times, what could the ecology of the IoE economy look like? What else will happen if machines do not make men smarter? This question is probably more philosophical than scientific, and some judgment needs to be exercised for questions like this. Earlier, Bauerlein (2008) and Carr (2011) argued how "things" can make humans "dumber"; interestingly, in a reverse direction, O'Neil (2017) and Stephens-Davidowitz and Pabon (2017) also enabled us to see how vice versa humans can make "things" dumber. Altogether, an ecological cycle of these foolish reciprocities can be self-constructing. While this proposition could run the risk of being an over-exaggeration, this saying recurs through history. "The road to serfdom" as "paved" by Friedrich Hayek (Hayek, 1944) has not become a relic; that "road," once in a while is still filled with "pilgrims"; recently the road has been renovated (Helbing et al., 2017).

## ACKNOWLEDGMENTS

An earlier version of the chapter was presented at the *AAAI, 2018 Spring Symposium on Artificial Intelligence for the Internet of Everything* at Stanford University, March 26–28, 2018. The author is grateful to the organizer of the symposium, Professor William Lawless, specifically

---

[12] An assumption underlying this thesis is that even though attention capacity may also grow with the availability of mind-extension technology, the arrival of information may grow even faster with the same generation of technology, say, one with an exponential rate, and one with a polynomial rate. A fundamental cause of this persistent gap is not just technology, but the use of technology by humans, whose wants are unlimited. Hence, just like speed is never fast enough, bandwidth is never wide enough, and storage is never roomy enough, our attention is never sufficiently focused.

for the invitation generously extended. The author is also grateful for the support for this research received from the Ministry of Science and Technology (MOST) [grant number MOST 106-240-2410-H-004-006-MY2].

## REFERENCES

Abdulkadiroglu, A., & Sonmez, T. (2003). School choice: a mechanism design approach. *The American Economic Review, 93*(3), 729–747.

Bauerlein, M. (2008). *The dumbest generation: How the digital age stupefies young Americans and jeopardizes our future (or, don't trust anyone under 30)*. Penguin.

Boettke, P. J. (Ed.), (2000). *Socialism and the market: The socialist calculation debate revisited*: Psychology Press.

Carr, N. (2011). *The shallows: What the Internet is doing to our brains*. WW Norton & Company.

Chen, S. -H. (2012). Varieties of agents in agent-based computational economics: a historical and an interdisciplinary perspective. *Journal of Economic Dynamics and Control, 36*(1), 1–25.

Chen, S. -H., Chie, B. -T., & Tai, C. -C. (2016). Smart societies. In F. Roger, S. -H. Chen, K. Dopher, F. Heukelom, & S. Mousavi (Eds.), *Routledge handbook of behavioral economics* (pp. 250–285). Routledge (Chapter 18).

Chen, S. -H., & Venkatachalam, R. (2017). Information aggregation and computational intelligence. *Evolutionary and Institutional Economics Review, 14*(1), 231–252.

Clark, A., & Chalmers, D. (1998). The extended mind. *Analysis, 58*(1), 7–19.

Clynes, M., & Kline, N. (1960). Cyborgs and space. *Astronautics, Astronautics, 5*(9), 26–27. 74–76.

Cockshott, W. P., & Cottrell, A. F. (1997). Information and economics: a critique of Hayek. *Research in Political Economy, 18*(1), 177–202.

Cottrell, A., & Cockshott, W. P. (1993). Calculation, complexity and planning: the socialist calculation debate once again. *Review of Political Economy, 5*(1), 73–112.

Damos, D. (Ed.), (1991). *Multiple task performance* (pp. 250–285). Routledge: CRC Press Economics.

Gale, D., & Shapley, L. S. (1962). College admissions and the stability of marriage. *The American Mathematical Monthly, 69*(1), 9–15.

Gigerenzer, G., & Gaissmaier, W. (2011). Heuristic decision making. *Annual Review of Psychology, 62*, 451–482.

Gray, C. H. (1995). An interview with Manfred Clynes. In C. H. Gray, H. J. Figueroa-Sarriera, & S. Mentor (Eds.), *The cyborg handbook* (pp. 43–53). New York: Routledge.

Hamel, G. (2000). Will the 'frictionless' economy slip you up? *Wall Street Journal, 6*.

Hayek, F. A. (1944). *The road to Serfdom*. Dymock's Book Arcade.

Hayek, F. A. (1945). The use of knowledge in society. *The American Economic Review, 35*(4), 519–530.

Helbing, D., Frey, B., Gigerenzer, G., Hafen, E., Hagner, M., Hofstetter, Y., et al. (2017). Will democracy survive big data and artificial intelligence? *Scientific American, 25*, Available from: https://www.scientificamerican.com/article/will-democracy-survive-big-data-and-artificial-intelligence/.

Hobbes, T. (1977). Leviathan or the matter, form, and power of a commonwealth ecclesiastical and civil, c. 1651. *The English works of Thomas Hobbes*. Vol.3. The British Library.

Hodgeson, G. (2001). *How economics forgot history: The problem of historical specificity in social science*. London and New York: Routledge.

Iyengar, S. (2010). *The art of choosing*. Twelve.

Iyengar, S. S., & Lepper, M. R. (2000). When choice is demotivating: can one desire too much of a good thing? *Journal of Personality and Social Psychology, 79*(6), 995.

Kahneman, D. (2011). *Thinking, fast and slow*. Macmillan.

Kendrick, D. A. (1981). *Stochastic control for economic models.* McGraw-Hill Companies.

Lange, O. (1970). *Introduction to economic cybernetics: Prepared With the collaboration of Antoni Banasiński on the basis of lectures delivered at the University of Warsaw.* Pergamon Press.

Lange, O., & Taylor, F. (1938). *On the economic theory of socialism.* University of Minnesota Press.

Lanham, R. A. (2006). *The economics of attention: Style and substance in the age of information.* University of Chicago Press.

Lerner, A. P. (1944). *The economics of control: Principles of welfare economics.* New York: Macmillan.

Lewis, M. (2014). *Flash boys: A wall street Revolt.* New York: WW Norton & Company. Inc.

MacKay, C. (1841). *Extraordinary popular delusions and the madness of crowds.* New York: Farrar, Straus and Giroux (original ed.).

Mirowski, P. (2002). *Machine dreams: Economics becomes a cyborg science.* Cambridge University Press.

Mirowski, P. (2007). Markets come to bits: evolution, computation and markomata in economic science. *Journal of Economic Behavior & Organization, 63*(2), 209–242.

Muraven, M., & Baumeister, R. F. (2000). Self-regulation and depletion of limited resources: does self-control resemble a muscle? *Psychological Bulletin, 126*(2), 247.

O'Neil, C. (2017). *Weapons of math destruction: How big data increases inequality and threatens democracy.* Broadway Books.

Patterson, S. (2012). *Dark Pools: The rise of the machine traders and the rigging of the US stock market.* Crown Business.

Reinhart, C. M., & Rogoff, K. S. (2009). *This time is different: Eight centuries of financial folly.* Princeton University Press.

Rosenfeld, J. V., & Wong, Y. T. (2017). Neurobionics and the brain-computer interface: current applications and future horizons. *The Medical Journal of Australia, 206*(8), 363–368.

Roth, A. E. (2002). The economist as engineer: game theory, experimentation, and computation as tools for design economics. *Econometrica, 70*(4), 1341–1378. https://doi.org/10.1111/1468-0262.00335.

Sasaki, Y., & Flann, N. S. (2005). Multi-agent evolutionary dynamics and reinforcement learning applied to online optimization for the traffic policy. In S. H. Chen (Ed.), *Computational economics: A perspective from computational intelligence* (pp. 161–177). IGI Global.

Savage, L. (1954). *The foundations of statistics.* New York: Wiley & Sons.

Schumpeter, J. A. (1942). *Socialism, capitalism and democracy.* Harper and Brothers.

Schwartz, B. (2004). *The paradox of choice: Why more is less.* (Vol. 6). New York: HarperCollins.

Shafir, E. (Ed.), (2013). *The behavioral foundations of public policy:* Princeton University Press.

Simon, H. (1971). Designing organizations for an information-rich world. In M. Greenberger (Ed.), *Computers, communications and the public interest* (pp. 37–72): *Johns Hopkins University Press.*

Standing, G. (2011). Behavioural conditionality: why the nudges must be stopped—an opinion piece. *Journal of Poverty and Social Justice, 19*(1), 27.

Stephens-Davidowitz, S., & Pabon, A. (2017). *Everybody lies: Big data, new data, and what the internet can tell us about who we really are.* HarperLuxe.

Sutcliffe, K. M., & Weick, K. E. (2008). Information overload revisited. In G. P. Hodgkinson & W. H. Starbuck (Eds.), *The Oxford handbook of organizational decision making* (pp. 56–75). Oxford: Oxford University Press (Chapter 3).

Thaler, R. H. (2000). From homo economicus to homo sapiens. *Journal of Economic Perspectives, 14*(1), 133–141.

Thaler, R. H., & Sunstein, C. R. (2008). *Nudge: Improving decisions about health, wealth, and happiness.* New Haven, CT: Yale University Press.

Vaillant, G. E. (2008). *Aging well: Surprising guideposts to a happier life from the landmark study of adult development*. Little, Brown.

Von Neumann, J., & Morgenstern, O. (1944). *Theory of games and economic behavior*. Princeton: Princeton University Press.

Wälde, K., & Moors, A. (2017). Current emotion research in economics. *Emotion Review, 9* (3), 271–278.

Walras, L. (1874). *Elements d'economie politique pure, ou theorie de la richesse sociale, first instalment, Lausanne: L. Corbaz*. Paris: Guillaumin. Basel: H. Georg.

Zou, Y., & Chen, S. H. (2018). Has Homo economicus evolved into Homo sapiens from 1992 to 2014? What does corpus linguistics say? In S. H. Chen (Ed.), *Big data in computational social science and humanities*: Springer.

# CHAPTER 11

# Accessing Validity of Argumentation of Agents of the Internet of Everything

**Boris Galitsky\*, Anna Parnis†**
\*Oracle Corporation, Redwood Shores, CA, United States
†Department of Biology, Technion-Israel Institute of Technology, Haifa, Israel

## 11.1 INTRODUCTION

One of the key features of the Internet of Everything (IoE) is communication in a complex system that includes people, robots, and machines. According to Chambers (2014), IoE connects humans, data, processes, and entities to enhance business communication and facilitate employment, well-being, education, and health care between various communities of people. As billions of people are anticipated to be connected the validity, truthfulness, and authenticity of the textual messages being delivered have become essential requirements. To make decisions based, in particular, on textual messages, the claims and their argumentation need to be validated in a domain-independent manner. The validation of claims in IoE messages needs to be done based on argumentation patterns rather than on costly domain-dependent ontologies, which are hard to scale.

Intentional or unintentional untruthful claims and/or their faulty argumentation can lead to accidents, and machines should be able to recognize such claims and their arguments as a part of tackling human errors (Galitsky, 2015; Lawless, Mittu, Sofge, & Russell, 2017). Frequently human errors are associated with extreme emotions, so we aim at detecting and validating both affective and logical argumentation patterns. Intentional disinformation in a message can also be associated with a security breach (Munro, 2017).

When domain knowledge is available and formalized, truthfulness of a claim can be validated directly. However, in most environments such knowledge is unavailable and other implicit means need to come into play, such as writing style and writing logic (which are domain independent).

*Artificial Intelligence for the Internet of Everything*
https://doi.org/10.1016/B978-0-12-817636-8.00011-9
**187**

Hence we employ the discourse analysis in our message validation pipeline and explore which discourse features can be leveraged for argumentation validity analysis.

When an author attempts to provide a logical or affective argument for something, a number of argumentation patterns can be employed. The basic points of argumentation are reflected in the rhetorical structure of text where an argument is presented. A text without argument, with an affective argument and with a logical one would have different rhetoric structures (Moens, Boiy, Palau, & Reed, 2007). When an author uses an affective argument instead of logical arguments it does not necessarily mean that his argument is invalid.

We select customer relationship management (CRM) as an important domain of IoE. One of the trickiest areas of CRM, involving a number of conflicting agents, is handling customer complaints (Galitsky & de la Rosa, 2011). In customer complaints the authors are upset with the products or services they received, as well as how customer support communicated with them. Complainants frequently write complaints in very strong, emotional language, which may distort the logic of argumentation, therefore making a judgment on complaint validity difficult. Both affective and logical argumentation is heavily used.

Banking is one of the industries one would expect to pioneer Internet of Things (IoT) technologies. In the personal finance domain, customers would expect a fully automated CRM environment that would solve 100% of their issues. In banking's customer complaints, customers usually explain what was promised and advertised, and what they ended up receiving. Therefore a typical complaint arises when a customer attempts to communicate this discrepancy with the bank and does not receive an adequate response. Most complaint authors mention misinformation provided by company agents, a reluctance to accept responsibility, and a denial of a refund or compensation to a customer. At the same time, frequently, customers write complaints attempting to get compensation for allegedly problematic service.

Judging by complaints, most complainants are in genuine distress due to a strong deviation between what they expected from a service, what they received, and how it was communicated. Most complaint authors report incompetence, flawed policies, ignorance, indifference to customer needs, and misrepresentation from the customer service personnel. The authors have frequently exhausted the communicative means available to them; confused, they may seek recommendations from other users. They often advise other customers to avoid particular financial services. Multiple affective argumentation patterns are used in complaints; the most frequent is an intense description by a complainant of a deviation from what was expected, according to common sense, to what actually happened. This pattern covers both valid and invalid argumentation.

We select rhetoric structure theory (RST) (Mann & Thompson, 1988) as a means to represent discourse features associated with logical and affective argumentation. Nowadays, the performance of both rhetoric parsers and argumentation reasoners has dramatically improved (Feng & Hirst, 2014). Taking into account the discourse structure of conflicting dialogs, one can judge the authenticity and validity of these dialogs in terms of its affective argumentation. In this work we will evaluate the *combined* argument validity assessment system that includes both the *discourse structure extraction* and *reasoning about it* with the purpose of the validation of a complainant's claim. Either approach on argument detection from text or on reasoning about formalized arguments has been undertaken (Galitsky & Pampapathi, 2003; Symeonidis, Chatzidimitriou, Athanasiadis, & Mitkas, 2007), but not the whole text assessment pipeline required for IoT systems.

Most of the modern techniques treat computational argumentation as specific discourse structures and perform detection of arguments of various sorts in text, such as classifying a text paragraph as argumentative or nonargumentative (Moens et al., 2007). A number of systems recognize components and structures of logical arguments (Sardianos, Katakis, Petasis, & Karkaletsis, 2015; Stab & Gurevych, 2014). However, these systems do not rely on discourse trees (DTs); they only extract arguments and do not apply logical means to evaluate them. A broad corpus of research deals with logical arguments irrespectively of how they may occur in natural language (Bondarenko, Dung, Kowalski, & Toni, 1997). A number of studies addressed argument quality in logic and argumentation theory (Damer, 2009; van Eemeren, Grootendorst, & Henkemans, 1996); however, the number of systems that assess the validity of arguments in text is very limited (Cabrio & Villata, 2012). This number is especially low for studies concerning affective argumentation. Most argument mining systems are either classifiers that recognize certain forms of logical arguments in text, or reasoners over the logical representation of arguments (Amgoud, Besnard, & Hunter, 2015). Conversely, in this project we intend to build the *whole argumentation pipeline*, augmenting an argument extraction from text with its logical analysis (Fig. 11.1). This pipeline is necessary to deploy an argumentation analysis in a practical decision support system.

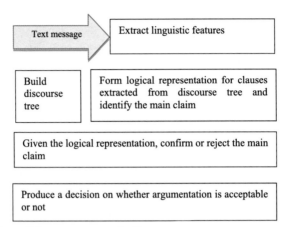

**Fig. 11.1** Claim validity assessment pipeline.

The concept of automatically identifying argumentation schemes was first discussed by Walton, Reed, and Macagno (2008). Ghosh, Muresan, Wacholder, Aakhus, and Mitsui (2014)) investigate argumentation discourse structure of a specific type of communication—online interaction threads. Identifying argumentation in text is connected to the problem of identifying truth, misinformation, and disinformation on the web (Galitsky, 2015; Pendyala & Figueira, 2015; Pisarevskaya, Litvinova, & Litvinova, 2017). Lawrence and Reed (2015) combined three types of argument structure identification: linguistic features, topic changes, and machine learning.

To represent the linguistic features of text, we use the following sources:

**(1)** *Rhetoric relations* between the parts of the sentences, obtained as a *DT*, and

**(2)** *Speech acts and communicative actions*, obtained as verbs from the Verb-Net resource.

To assess the logical validity of an extracted argument, we apply the Defeasible Logic Program (DeLP) (Garcia & Simari, 2004), part of which is built on the fly from facts and clauses extracted from these sources. We integrate argumentation detection and validation components into a decision support system that can be deployed, for example, in the CRM domain. To evaluate our approach to extraction and reasoning for argumentation, we chose the dispute resolution/customer complaint validation task because affective argumentation analysis plays an essential role in it.

## 11.2 REPRESENTING ARGUMENTATIVE DISCOURSE

We start with a political domain and give an example of conflicting agents providing their interpretation of certain events. These agents provide argumentation for their claims; we will observe how formed rhetoric structures correlate with their argumentation patterns. We focus on the Malaysia Airlines Flight 17 example with the agents exchanging affective arguments: *Dutch investigators, The Investigative Committee of the Russian Federation,* and *the self-proclaimed Donetsk People's Republic.* It is a controversial conflict where each agent attempts to blame its opponent. Keywords indicating sentiments are underlined. To sound more convincing, each agent does not just formulate its claim, but postulates it in a way to attack the claims of its opponents. To do that, each agent does its best to match the argumentation style of opponents, defeat their claims, and apply negative sentiments to them.

> Dutch accident investigators say that *strong* evidence points to pro-Russian rebels as being *fully responsible* for shooting down plane. The report indicates where the missile was fired from and identifies who was in control of the territory and *pins* the downing of MH17 on the pro-Russian rebels (Fig. 11.2A).
>
> The Investigative Committee of the Russian Federation believes that the plane was hit by a missile, *which could not be produced* in Russia. The committee cites an investigation that established the type of the missile and *disagrees* with Dutch accident investigators (Fig. 11.2B).
>
> Rebels, the self-proclaimed Donetsk People's Republic, *deny* that they controlled the territory from which the missile was *allegedly* fired. They confirm that it became possible only after three months after the tragedy to say if rebels controlled one or another town and the claim of Dutch accident investigators is *flawed* (Fig. 11.2C).

To show the structure of arguments one needs to merge discourse relations with information from speech acts. We need to know the discourse structure of interactions between agents, and what kinds of interactions they are. For argument identification we do not need to know the domain of interaction (here, aviation), the subjects of these interaction, what are the entities, but we need to take into account the mental, domain-independent relations between them. We accomplish this by introducing the concept of communicative discourse tree (CDT).

CDT is a DT with labels for edges that are the VerbNet expressions for verbs (which are communicative actions or CA; Galitsky & Kuznetsov, 2008). Arguments of verbs are substituted from text according to VerbNet frames (Kipper, Korhonen, Ryant, & Palmer, 2008). The first and possibly second argument is instantiated by agents. The consecutive arguments are instantiated by noun or verb phrases, which are the subjects of CA. For example, the nucleus node for *elaboration* relation (on the left of

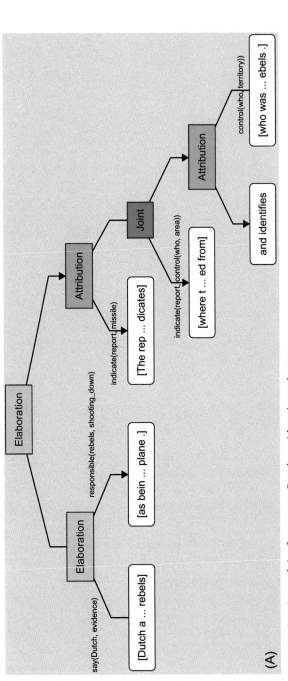

**Fig. 11.2** (A) The claim of the first agent, Dutch accident investigators;

*(Continued)*

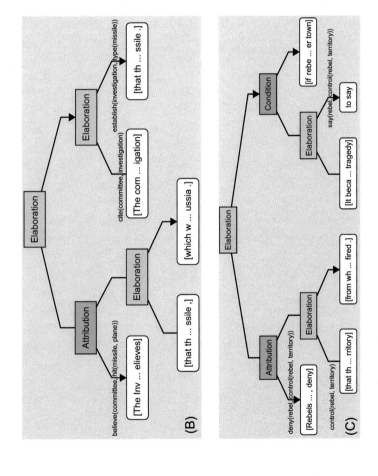

**Fig. 2, cont'd**
(B) the claim of the second agent, the Committee; (C) the claim of the third agent, the rebels.

Fig. 11.2A) is labeled with *say(Dutch, evidence)*, and the satellite is labeled with *responsible(rebels, shooting_down)*. These labels are not intended to express that the subjects of elementary discourse units (EDUs) are *evidence* and *shooting_down* but instead are intended for matching this CDT with others for the purpose of finding similarity between them.

Notice that in the CDTs for three paragraphs expressing the views of conflicting parties (Fig. 11.2A–C), communicative actions with their subjects contain the main claims of the respective party, and the DTs without these labels contain information on how these claims are logically packaged. To summarize, a typical CDT for a text with argumentation includes rhetoric relations other than "elaboration" and "join," and a substantial number of communicative actions. However, these rules are complex enough so that the structure of CDT matters and tree-specific learning is required (Galitsky, Ilvovsky, & Kuznetsov, 2015).

## 11.3 DETECTING INVALID ARGUMENTATION PATTERNS

Starting from the autumn of 2015, we became interested in the controversy about Theranos, the health-care company that hoped to make a revolution in blood tests. Some sources including the *Wall Street Journal* started claiming that the company's conduct was fraudulent. The claims were made based on the whistleblowing of employees who left Theranos. At some point the US Food and Drug Administration got involved, and as the case developed, we were improving our argumentation mining and reasoning techniques (Galitsky, 2016; Galitsky, Ilvovsky, & Kuznetsov, 2018) while keeping an eye on Theranos' story. As we scraped from the websites the discussions about Theranos back in 2016, the audience believed that the case was initiated by Theranos' competitors who felt jealous about the proposed efficiency of the blood test technique promised by Theranos. However, our argumentation analysis technique was showing that Theranos' argumentation patterns mined at their website were faulty and our finding confirmed the case, which led to the massive fraud verdict. SEC (2018) says that Theranos' CEO Elizabeth Holmes raised more than $700 million from investors "through an elaborate, years-long fraud" in which she exaggerated or made false statements about the company's technology and finances.

Let us imagine that we need to index the content about Theranos for answering questions about it. If a user leans towards Theranos and not its opponents, then we want to provide answers favoring Theranos' position. Good arguments of its proponents, or bad arguments of its opponents would also be good. Table 11.1 shows the flags for various combinations of agency,

**Table 11.1** The flags for various combinations of agency, sentiments and argumentation for tailoring search results for a given user with certain preferences

**Request from user**

| Answer type | Positive sentiment for A | Negative sentiment for B | Proper argumentation that A is right | Improper argumentation that A is wrong | Proper argumentation by a proponent of A | Improper argumentation by a opponent of A | … |
|---|---|---|---|---|---|---|---|
| Favoring A rather than B | + | + | + | + | + | + | − ⋮ / + ⋮ |
| Favoring B rather than A | | | + | | + | | |
| Equal treatment of A and B | + | | | | | | |

sentiments, and argumentation for tailoring search results for a given user with certain preferences of entity A versus entity B. The far right grayed side of the column in the table has opposite flags for the second and third row. For the fourth row, only the cases with generally accepted opinion-sharing merits are flagged to be shown.

In a product recommendation domain, texts with positive sentiments are used to encourage a potential buyer to make a purchase. In a domain such as politics, the logical structure of sentiment vs. argument vs. agency is much more complex.

We build an RST representation of the arguments and observe if a DT is capable of indicating whether a paragraph communicates both a claim and possesses argumentation that backs it up. We will then explore what needs to be added to a DT so that it is possible to judge if it expresses an argumentation pattern or not.

This is the beginning of Theranos' story, according to Carreyrou (2016):

> Since October [2015], the Wall Street Journal has published a series of anonymously sourced accusations that inaccurately portray Theranos. Now, in its latest story ("U.S. Probes Theranos Complaints," Dec. 20), the Journal once again is relying on anonymous sources, this time reporting two undisclosed and unconfirmed complaints that allegedly were filed with the Centers for Medicare and Medicaid Services (CMS) and U.S. Food and Drug Administration (FDA).

Fig. 11.3A shows the communicative discourse tree (CDT) for the following paragraph (Carreyrou, 2016):

> But Theranos has struggled behind the scenes to turn the excitement over its technology into reality. At the end of 2014, the lab instrument developed as the linchpin of its strategy, handled just a small fraction of the tests then sold to consumers, according to four former employees.

Please notice the labels for communicative actions are attached to the edges of DTs (on the left and in the middle-bottom).

In the following paragraph Theranos attempts to rebuke the claim of *WSJ*, but without communicative actions it is unclear from the DT (see Fig. 11.3B):

> Theranos remains actively engaged with its regulators, including CMS and the FDA, and no one, including the Wall Street Journal, has provided Theranos a copy of the alleged complaints to those agencies. Because Theranos has not seen these alleged complaints, it has no basis on which to evaluate the purported complaints.

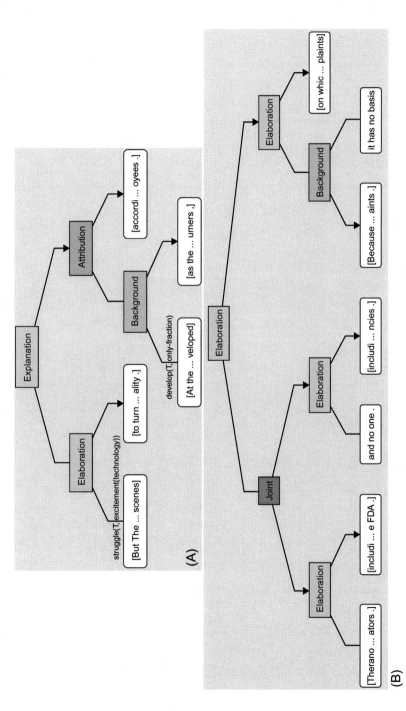

**Fig. 11.3** (A) When arbitrary communicative actions are attached to the discourse tree as labels of its terminal arcs it becomes clear that the author is trying to bring her point across and not merely sharing a fact. (B) Just from a discourse tree and multiple rhetoric relations of *elaboration* and a single instance of *background*, it is unclear whether an author argues with his opponents or enumerating some observations.

*(Continued)*

*(Continued)*

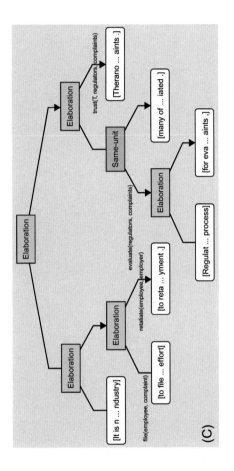

**Fig. 3, cont'd**

(C) CAs as labels for rhetoric relations helps to identify a text apart of a heated discussion.

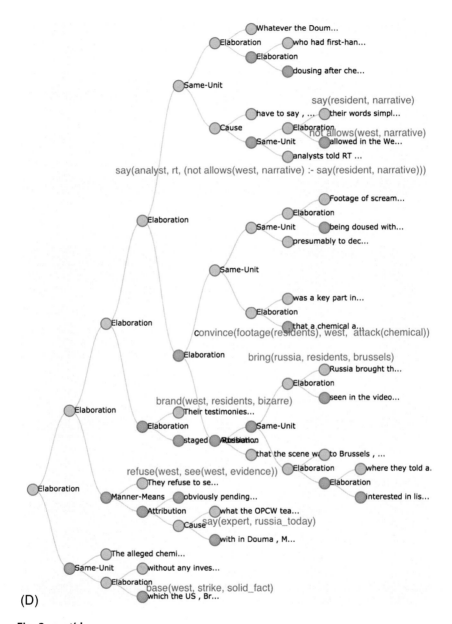

(D)

**Fig. 3, cont'd**
(D) Communicative discourse tree for the *chemical attack* story showing problematic
argumentation patterns.

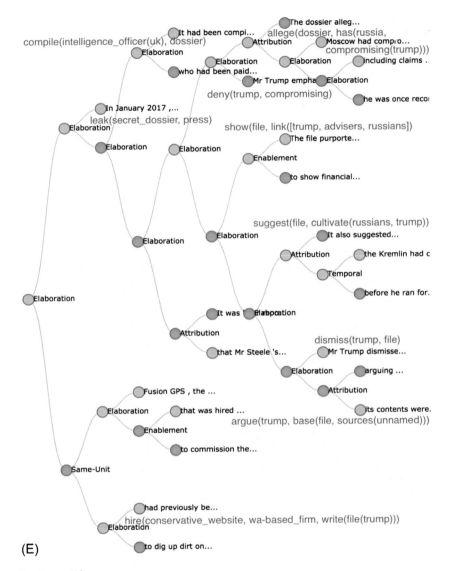

(E)

**Fig. 3, cont'd**
(E) Communicative discourse tree for the *Trump-Russia* story showing problematic argumentation patterns.

We proceed to a CDT for an attempt by Theranos to acquit itself (Fig. 11.3C):

> It is not unusual for disgruntled and terminated employees in the heavily regulated health care industry to file complaints in an effort to retaliate against employers for termination of employment. Regulatory agencies have a process for evaluating complaints, many of which are not substantiated. Theranos trusts its regulators to properly investigate any complaints.

In another example, the objective of the author is to attack a claim that the Syrian government used chemical weapon in the spring of 2018. An acceptable proof would be to share a certain observation, associated from the standpoint of peers, with the absence of a chemical attack. For example, if it is possible to demonstrate that the time of the alleged chemical attack coincided with the time of a very strong rainfall that would be a convincing way to attack this claim. However, since no such observation was identified the source, *Russia Today* (2018), resorted to plotting a complex mental states concerning how the claim was communicated, where it is hard to verify most statements about the mental states of the involved parties. We show the text split into EDU as done by discourse parser (Joty, Carenini, Ng, & Mehdad, 2013):

[Whatever the Douma residents,][who had first-hand experience of the shooting of the water][dousing after chemical attack video,][have to say,] [their words simply do not fit into the narrative][allowed in the West,] [analysts told RT.] [Footage of screaming bewildered civilians and children][being doused with water,][presumably to decontaminate them,] [was a key part in convincing Western audiences][that a chemical attack happened in Douma.] [Russia brought the people][seen in the video][to Brussels,][where they told anyone][interested in listening][that the scene was staged.] [Their testimonies, however, were swiftly branded as bizarre and underwhelming and even an obscene masquerade][staged by Russians.] [They refuse to see this as evidence,][obviously pending][what the OPCW < Organization for the Prohibition of Chemical Weapons > team is going to come up with in Douma ], [Middle East expert Ammar Waqqaf said in an interview with RT.] [The alleged chemical incident,] [without any investigation, has already become a solid fact in the West,] [which the US, Britain and France based their retaliatory strike on.]

This article (RussiaToday, 2018) has not found counter-evidence for the claim of the chemical attack it attempts to defeat, instead it says that the opponents are not interested in observing this counter-evidence. The main statement of the article is that a certain agent "disallows" a particular kind of evidence thereby attacking the main claim, rather than providing and backing up this evidence. Instead of defeating a chemical attack claim, the article builds a complex image of the conflicted mental states of the residents, Russian agents taking them to Brussels, the West, and a Middle-East expert (see Fig. 11.3D).

Our other example of controversial news is a Trump–Russia link accusation (BBC, 2018). For a long time the claim could not be confirmed, so the story was repeated over and over again to maintain the reader's expectation that it would be instantiated one day. There is neither confirmation nor rejection that the dossier exists and the goal of the author is to make the audience believe that such dossier exists without misrepresenting events. To achieve this goal the author can attach a number of hypothetical statements about the existing dossier to a variety of mental states to impress upon the reader the authenticity and validity of the topic (see Fig. 11.3E).

## 11.4 RECOGNIZING COMMUNICATIVE DISCOURSE TREES FOR ARGUMENTATION

Argumentation analysis needs a systematic approach to learn associated discourse structures. The features of CDTs could be represented in a numerical space so that argumentation detection can be conducted; however, structural information on DTs would not be leveraged. Also, features of argumentation can potentially be measured in terms of maximal common sub-DTs, but such nearest-neighbor learning is computationally intensive and too sensitive to errors in DT construction. Therefore a CDT-kernel learning approach is selected, which applies support vector machine (SVM) learning to the feature space of all sub-CDTs of the CDT for a given text where an argument is being detected.

Tree kernel (TK) learning for strings, parse trees, and parse thickets is a well-established research area nowadays. The CD-TK counts the number of common sub-trees as the discourse similarity measure between two DTs. A version of TK has been defined for discourse analysis (Joty & Moschitti, 2014). Wang, Su, and Tan (2010) used the special form of TK for discourse-relation recognition. In this study, we extend the TK definition for the CDT, augmenting DT kernel by the information on CAs. TK-based approaches are not very sensitive to errors in parsing (syntactic and rhetoric) because erroneous sub-trees are mostly random and will unlikely be common among different elements of a training set.

A CDT can be represented by a vector V of integer counts of each sub-tree type (without taking into account its ancestors):

$V(T) =$ (# *of subtrees of type 1, …, # of subtrees of type I, …, # of subtrees of type n*). This representation results in a very high dimensionality since the number of different sub-trees is exponential in size. Thus it is computationally infeasible to directly use the feature vector $\varnothing(T)$. To solve the computational issue, a tree kernel function is introduced to calculate the dot product between the previously mentioned high-dimensional vectors efficiently. Given two tree segments $CDT_1$ and $CDT_2$, the tree kernel function is defined:

$K\ (CDT_1,\ CDT_2) = <V(CDT_1),\ V(CDT_2)> = \sum_i V(CDT_1)[i],\ V(CDT_2)[i] = \sum_{n1} \sum_{n2} \sum_i I_i(n_1)^* I_i(n_2),$

Where $n_1 \in N_1$, $n_2 \in N_2$ and $N_1$ and $N_2$ are the sets of all nodes in $CDT_1$ and $CDT_2$, respectively; $I_i(n)$ is the indicator function; and $I_i(n) = \{1$ iff a subtree of type $i$ occurs with a root at a node; 0 otherwise$\}$. Further details for using TK for paragraph-level and discourse analysis are available in Galitsky (2017).

Only the arcs of the same type of rhetoric relations (*presentation* relation, such as *antithesis, subject matter* relation, such as *condition,* and *multinuclear* relation, such as *List*) can be matched when computing common sub-trees. We use *N* for a nucleus or situations presented by this nucleus, and *S* for a satellite or situations presented by this satellite. *Situations* are propositions, completed actions or actions in progress, and communicative actions and states (including *beliefs, desires, approve, explain, reconcile,* and others). Hence we have the following expression for RST-based generalization " ^ " for two texts *text$_1$* and *text$_2$*:

$text_1 \ ^\wedge\ text_2 = \cup_{i,j}\ (rstRelation_{1i,}\ (…,…)\ ^\wedge\ rstRelation_{2j}\ (…,…)),$

where $i \in$ (RST relations in *text$_1$*) and $j \in$ (*RST relations in text$_2$*). Further, for a pair of RST relations their generalization looks as follows:

$rstRelation_1(N_1,\ S_1)\ ^\wedge\ rstRelation_2\ (N_2,\ S_2) = (rstRelation_1 \ ^\wedge\ rstRelation_2)$ $(N_1 {}^\wedge N_2,\ S_1 {}^\wedge S_2).$

We define CA as a function of the form *verb (agent, subject, cause),* where *verb* characterizes some type of interaction between involved *agents* (e.g., *explain, confirm, remind, disagree, deny,* etc.), *subject* refers to the information transmitted or the object described, and *cause* refers to the motivation or explanation for the subject. To handle the meaning of words expressing the subjects of CAs, we apply *word2vec* models (Mikolov, Chen, Corrado, & Dean, 2015).

To compute similarity between the subjects of CAs, we use the following rule. If *subject1 = subject2,* then *subject1^subject2 = <subject1, POS(subject1), 1>.*

Otherwise, if they have the same part-of-speech, *subject1ˆsubject2=<\*,POS (subject1), word2vecDistance(subject1ˆsubject2)>*.

If a part-of-speech is different, the generalization is an empty tuple. It cannot be further generalized.

We combined Stanford NLP parsing, coreferences, entity extraction, DT construction (discourse parser; Surdeanu, Hicks, & Valenzuela-Escarcega, 2016; Joty et al., 2013), VerbNet, and Tree Kernel builder into one system, which is available at https://github.com/bgalitsky/relevance-based-on-parse-trees.

## 11.5 ASSESSING VALIDITY OF EXTRACTED ARGUMENT PATTERNS VIA DIALECTICAL ANALYSIS

To convince an addressee, a message needs to include an argument and its structure needs to be valid. Once an argumentation structure extracted from text is represented via CDT, we need to verify that the main point (target claim) communicated by the author is not logically attacked by her other claims. To assess the validity of the argumentation, a DeLP approach is selected. It is an argumentative framework based on logic programming (Alsinet, Chesñevar, Godo, & Simari, 2008; Garcia & Simari, 2004); we present an overview of the main concepts associated with it.

A DeLP is a set of facts, strict rules Π of the form (A:-B), and a set of defeasible rules Δ of the form A-<B, whose intended meaning is "if B is the case, then usually A is also the case." Let P=(Π, Δ) be a DeLP program and L a ground literal. Let us now build an example of a DeLP for legal

---

**Defeasible Rules Prepared In Advance**
*rent_receipt -< rent_deposit_transaction.*
*rent_deposit_transaction -< contact_tenant.*
¬ *rent_deposit_transaction -<contact_tenant,*
   *three_days_notice_is_issued.*
¬ *rent_deposit_transaction -< rent_is_overdue.*
¬ *repair_is_done -< rent_refused, repair_is_done.*
*repair_is_done -< rent_is_requested.*
¬ *rent_deposit_transaction -<*
       *tenant_short_on_money, repair_is_done.*
¬ *repair_is_done -< repair_is_requested.*
¬ *repair_is_done -<rent_is_requested.*
¬ *repair_is_requested -< stay_unrepaired.* ¬ *repair_is_done -< stay_unrepaired.*
**Target Claim to be Assessed**
*? - rent_receipt*
**Clauses Extracted from text**
*repair_is_done -< rent_refused.*
**Facts from text**
*contact_tenant. rent_is_requested. rent_refused. remind_about_repair. three_days_notice_is_issued.*
*rent_is_overdue. stay_unrepaired.*

**Fig. 11.4** An example of a Defeasible Logic Program for modeling category mapping.

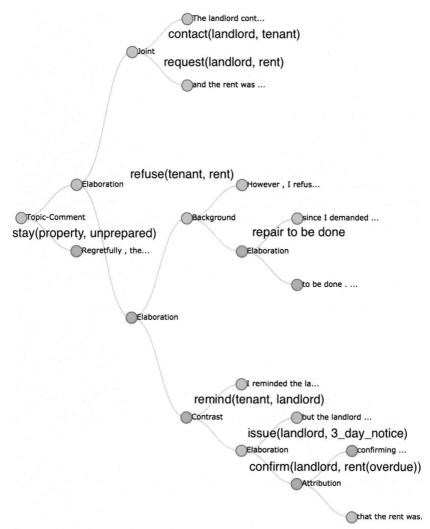

**Fig. 11.5** Text of a complaint and its CDT (visualization by Joty et al., 2013).

reasoning about facts extracted from text (Fig. 11.4). A judge hears an eviction case and wants to make a judgment on whether rent was provably paid (deposited) or not (denoted as *rent_receipt*). An input is a text where a defendant is expressing his point. Underlined words form the clause in DeLP, and the other expressions formed the facts (Fig. 11.5). This is an example from the author's personal experience:

*The landlord contacted me, the tenant, and the rent was requested. However, I refused the rent since I demanded repair to be done. I reminded the landlord about necessary repairs, but the landlord issued the three-day notice confirming that the rent was overdue. Regretfully, the property still stayed unrepaired.*

A *defeasible derivation* of $L$ from $P$ consists of a finite sequence $L_1, L_2, \ldots, L_n = L$ of ground literals, such that each literal $L_i$ is in the sequence because:

**(a)** $L_i$ is a fact in $\Pi$, or

**(b)** there exists a rule $R_i$ in $P$ (strict or defeasible) with head $L_i$ and body $B_1$, $B_2, \ldots, B_k$ and every literal of the body is an element $L_j$ of the sequence appearing before $L_j$ ($j < i$).

Let $h$ be a literal, and $P = (\Pi, \Delta)$ a DeLP program. We say that $<A, h>$ is an *argument* for $h$ if $A$ is a set of defeasible rules of $\Delta$, such that:

1. there exists a defeasible derivation for h from $(\Pi \cup A)$;
2. the set $(\Pi \cup A)$ is noncontradictory; and
3. $A$ is minimal: there is no proper subset $A_0$ of $A$ such that $A_0$ satisfies conditions (1) and (2).

Hence an argument $<A, h>$ is a minimal noncontradictory set of defeasible rules obtained from a defeasible derivation for a given literal $h$ associated with a program $P$.

We say that $<A_1, h_1>$ *attacks* $<A_2, h_2>$ if there exists a sub–argument $<A, h>$ of $<A_2, h_2>$, $(A \subseteq A_1)$ such that $h$ and $h_1$ are inconsistent (i.e., $\Pi \cup \{h, h_1\}$ derives complementary literals). We will say that $<A_1, h_1>$ *defeats* $<A_2, h_2>$ if $<A_1, h_1>$ attacks $<A_2, h_2>$ at a sub–argument $<A, h>$ and $<A_1, h_1>$ is strictly preferred (or not comparable to) $<A, h>$. In the first case we will refer to $<A_1, h_1>$ as a *proper defeater*, whereas in the second case it will be a *blocking defeater*. Defeaters are arguments that in their turn can be attacked by other arguments, as is the case with a human dialogue. An *argumentation line* is a sequence of arguments where each element in a sequence defeats its predecessor. In the case of DeLP there are a number of *acceptability* requirements for argumentation lines in order to avoid fallacies (such as circular reasoning by repeating the same argument twice).

Target claims can be considered DeLP queries solved in terms of dialectical trees, which subsumes all possible argumentation lines for a given query. The definition of a dialectical tree provides us with an algorithmic view for discovering implicit self-attack relations in users' claims. Let $<A_0, h_0>$ be an argument (target claim) from a program $P$. A *dialectical tree* for $<A_0, h_0>$ is defined as follows:

1. The root of the tree is labeled with $<A_0, h_0>$.

2. Let $N$ be a nonroot vertex of the tree labeled $<A_n, h_n>$ and $\Lambda=[<A_0,$ $h_0>, <A_1, h_1>, ..., <A_n, h_n>]$ (the sequence of labels of the path from the root to $N$). Let $[<B_0, q_0>, <B_1, q_1>, ..., <B_k, q_k>]$ all attack $<A_n, h_n>$.

For each attacker $<B_i, q_i>$ with acceptable argumentation line $[\Lambda, <B_i,$ $q_i>]$, we have an arc between $N$ and its *child* $N_i$.

A labeling on the dialectical tree can be then performed as follows:

1. All leaves are to be labeled as U-nodes (undefeated nodes).
2. Any inner node is to be labeled as a U-node whenever all of its associated children nodes are labeled as D-nodes.
3. Any inner node is to be labeled as a D-node whenever at least one of its associated children nodes is labeled as U-node.

After performing this labeling, if the root node of the tree is labeled as a U-node, the original argument at issue (and its conclusion) can be assumed as *justified* or *warranted*.

In our DeLP example, the literal *rent_receipt* is supported by:
$<A,$ *rent_receipt* $>$ $=$ $<\{$ (*rent_receipt* $-<$ *rent_deposit_transaction*), (*rent_deposit_transaction* $-<$ *tenant_short_on_money*)$\}$, *rent_receipt* $>$ and there exist three defeaters for it with three respective argumentation lines:

$<B_1, \neg$ *rent_deposit_transaction* $>$ $=$ $<\{(\neg$ *rent_deposit_transaction* $-<$ *tenant_short_on_money*, *three_days_notice_is_issued*)$\}$, *rent_deposit_ transaction* $>$.

$<B_2, \neg$ *rent_deposit_transaction* $>$ $=$ $<\{(\neg$ *rent_deposit_transaction* $-<$ *tenant_short_on_money*, *repair_is_done*), (*repair_is_done* $-<$ *rent_refused*) $\}$, *rent_deposit_transaction* $>$.

$<B_3, \neg$ *rent_deposit_transaction* $>$ $=$ $<\{(\neg$ *rent_deposit_transaction* $-<$ *rent_is_overdue* )$\}$, *rent_deposit_transaction* $>$.

The first two are proper defeaters and the last one is a blocking defeater. Observe that the first argument structure has the counter-argument, $<\{$*rent_deposit_transaction* $-<$ *tenant_short_on_money*$\}$, *rent_deposit_transaction*), but it is not a defeater because the former is more specific. Thus no defeaters exist and the argumentation line ends there.

$B_3$ above has a blocking defeater $<\{$(*rent_deposit_transaction* $-<$ *tenant_short_on_money*)$\}$,

*rent_deposit_transaction* $>$, which is a disagreement sub-argument of $<A,$ *rent_receipt* $>$ and it cannot be introduced since it gives rise to an unacceptable argumentation line. $B_2$ has two defeaters that can be introduced: $<C_1,$ $\neg$ *repair_is_done* $>$, *where* $C_1 = \{(\neg$ *repair_is_done* $-<$ *rent_refused*,

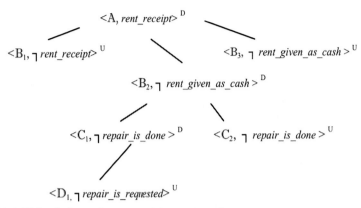

**Fig. 11.6** Dialectical tree for target claim *rent_receipt*.

repair_is_done),

(*repair_is_done* -< *rent_is_requsted*)}, a proper defeater, and <$C_2$, ¬ *repair_is_done* >, where $C_2$={(¬ *repair_is_done* -< *repair_is_requested*)} is a blocking defeater. Hence one of these lines is further split into two; $C_1$ has a blocking defeater that can be introduced in the line

<$D_1$, ¬ *repair_is_done* >, where $D_1$ = <{(¬ *repair_is_done* -< *stay_unrepaired*)}. $D_1$ and $C_2$ have a blocking defeater, but they cannot be introduced because they make the argumentation line unacceptable. Hence the state *rent_receipt* cannot be reached, as the argument supporting the literal *rent_receipt* is not warranted. The dialectical tree for *A* is shown in Fig. 11.6.

Having shown how to build a dialectic tree, we are now ready to outline the algorithm for validation of the domain-specific claim for arguments extracted from text:

1. Build a DT from input text;
2. Attach communicative actions to its edges to form CDT;
3. Extract subjects of communicative actions attached to CDT and add to "Facts" section;
4. Extract the arguments for rhetoric relation *contrast* and communicative actions of the class *disagree* and add to "Clauses Extracted FromText" section;
5. Add a domain-specific section to DeLP; and
6. Having the DeLP formed, build a dialectical tree and assess the claim.

We use the Tweety (2016) system for DeLP implementation (Thimm, 2014).

## 11.6 INTENSE ARGUMENTS DATASET

The purpose of this dataset is to collect texts where authors do their best to bring their points across by employing all means to show that they are right and their opponents are wrong. Complainants are emotionally charged writers who describe the problems they have encountered with a financial service and how they attempted to solve them.

Most complaint authors report incompetence, flawed policies, ignorance, indifference to customer needs, and misrepresentation from the customer service personnel (Galitsky, González, & Chesñevar, 2009). The focus of a complaint is a proof that the proponent is right and his/her opponent is wrong, followed by a resolution proposal and a desired outcome.

Complaints revealed the shady practices of banks during the financial crisis of 2007, such as manipulating an order of transactions to charge the highest possible amount of insufficient fund fees. Moreover, banks attempted to communicate this practice as a necessity to process a wide amount of checks. This is the most frequent topic of customer complaints, so one can track a manifold of argumentation patterns applied to this topic.

For a given topic, such as *insufficient funds fee*, this dataset provides many distinct ways of argumentation that this fee is unfair. Therefore our dataset allows for systematic exploration of the topic-independent clusters of argumentation patterns to observe a link between argumentation type and overall complaint validity. Other argumentation datasets, including legal arguments, student essays, Internet argument corpus, fact-feeling, and political debates, have a strong variation of topics so it is harder to track a spectrum of possible argumentation patterns per topic. Unlike professional writing in legal and political domains, the messages produced by complainants have a simple motivational structure, a transparency of their purpose, and occur in a fixed domain and context. In our dataset, the affective arguments play a critical rule for the well-being of authors subject to an unfair charge of a large amount of money or eviction from their home. Therefore the authors attempt to provide as strong argumentation as possible to back up their claims and strengthen their cases.

## 11.7 EVALUATION OF DETECTION AND VALIDATION OF ARGUMENTS

The objective of argument detection task is to identify all kinds of arguments, not only the ones associated with customer complaints. We formed the *positive* dataset from textual customer complaints dataset (Galitsky et al., 2009; Github, 2018) scraped from consumer advocacy site PlanetFeedback. com. This dataset is used for both argument detection (first step) and argument validity (second step) tasks. For argument detection we attempt to identify if a given paragraph of text contains an argument, in a domain-independent manner. For argument validation, in the second step, if we detected an argument in the first step we try to validate it having the domain-ontology built in a given vertical domain such as a landlord-tenant dispute. If an argument has not been detected in the first step, we have nothing to validate.

For the *negative* dataset, only for the affective argument detection task, we used *Wikipedia*, factual news sources, and also the component of Lee's (2001) dataset that includes such sections of the corpus as: ["tells"], instructions for how to use software; ["tele"], instructions for how to use hardware; and [news], a presentation of a news article in an objective, independent manner, and others. Further details on the data set are available in Galitsky et al. (2015).

Each row indicates a method used to detect the presence of argumentation in a paragraph. We start with baseline methods based on keywords and their frequencies (second and third row on the top, Table 11.2). The second column shows precision ($P$), the third recall, and the fourth $F1$ measure. Frequently, a coordinated pair of communicative actions (so that at least one has a negative sentiment polarity related to an opponent) is a hint that logical argumentation is present. This naïve approach is outperformed by the top-performing TK-learning CDT approach by 29%. SVM TK of CDT outperforms SVM TK for RST + CA and RST + full parse trees (Galitsky et al., 2018) by about 5% due to noisy syntactic data, which is frequently redundant for argumentation detection.

The SVM TK approach provides an acceptable $F$-measure but does not help to explain how exactly the affective argument identification problem is solved, providing only final scoring and class labels. The nearest-neighbor maximal common sub-graph algorithm is much more fruitful in this respect

**Table 11.2** Evaluation results for argument detection

| Method/sources | $P$ | $R$ | $F1$ |
|---|---|---|---|
| Bag-of-words | 57.2 | 53.1 | 55.07 |
| WEKA-Naïve Bayes | 59.4 | 55.0 | 57.12 |
| SVM TK for RST and CA (full parse trees) | 77.2 | 74.4 | 75.77 |
| SVM TK for DT | 63.6 | 62.8 | 63.20 |
| SVM TK for CDT | 82.4 | 77.0 | 79.61 |

(Galitsky et al., 2015). Comparing the bottom two rows, we observe that it is possible, but infrequent, to express an affective argument without CAs.

Assessing logical arguments extracted from text, we were interested in cases where an author provides invalid, inconsistent, self-contradicting cases. That is important for CRM systems focused on customer retention and facilitating communication with a customer (Galitsky et al., 2009). The domain of residential real estate complaints was selected and a DeLP thesaurus was built for this domain. An automated complaint-processing system can be essential, for example, for property-management companies in their decision-support procedures (Constantinos, Sarmaniotis, & Stafyla, 2003).

In our validity assessment, we focus on target features (claims) related to how a given complaint needs to be handled, such as *compensation_required, proceed_with_eviction, rent_receipt*, and others. A system decision is determined by whether the claim is validated or not: if it is validated, then the decision support system demands compensation, and if not validated, it decides that compensation should not be demanded (for the *compensation_required* claim).

Validity assessment results are shown in Table 11.3. These results are computed together for the detection and validation steps. In the first and second rows, we show the results of the simplest complaint with a single rhetoric relation such as *contrast* with a single CA indicating an extracted argumentation attack relation respectively. In the third row we assess complaints of average complexity, and in the bottom row, the most complex, longer complaints in terms of their CDTs are given. The third column shows detection accuracy for invalid argumentation in complaints in a stand-alone argument validation system. Finally, the fourth column shows the accuracy of the integrated argumentation extraction and validation system.

In these results recall is low because in the majority of cases the invalidity of claims is due to factors other than being self-defeated. Precision is

**Table 11.3** Evaluation results for argument validation

| Types of complaints | P | R | F1 of validation | F1 of total |
|---|---|---|---|---|
| Single rhetoric relation of type *contrast* | 87.3 | 15.6 | 26.5 | 18.7 |
| Single communicative action of type *disagree* | 85.2 | 18.4 | 30.3 | 24.8 |
| Two or three specific relations or communicative actions | 80.2 | 20.6 | 32.8 | 25.4 |
| Four and above specific relations or communicative actions | 86.3 | 16.5 | 27.7 | 21.7 |

relatively high since if a logical flaw in an argument is established, most likely the whole claim is invalid because other factors besides argumentation (such as false facts) contribute as well. As the complexity of a complaint and its DT grows, $F1$ first improves, since more logical terms are available, and then goes back down, as there is a higher chance of a reasoning error due to a noisier input.

For decision support systems it is important to maintain a low false-positive rate. It is acceptable to miss invalid complaints, but for a detected invalid complaint, confidence should be rather high. If a human agent is recommended to look at a given complaint as invalid, his/her expectations should be met most of the time. Although $F1$-measure of the overall argument detection and validation system is low in comparison with modern recognition systems, it is still believed to be usable as a component of a CRM decision-support system.

## 11.8 CONCLUSIONS

In this study we explored the possibility of validating messages in an IoE environment. We observed that by relying on DT data one can reliably detect patterns of logical and affective argumentation. CDTs become a source of information to form a defeasible logic program to validate an argumentation structure. Although the performance of the former being about 80% is significantly above that of the latter (29%), the overall pipeline can be useful for detecting cases of invalid affective argumentation, which is important in decision support for CRM.

To the best of our knowledge this is the first study building a whole argument validity pipeline including everything from text to a validated claim, which is a basis of IoE decision support. Hence, although the overall argument validation accuracy is fairly low, there is no existing system to compare this performance against.

In this chapter to support IoE message validation we attempted to combine the best of both worlds: argumentation mining from text and reasoning about the extracted argument. Whereas applications of either technology are limited, the whole argumentation pipeline is expected to find a broad range of applications. In this work we focused on a very specific legal area such as customer complaints, but it is easy to see a decision support system employing the proposed argumentation pipeline in other domains of CRM.

Message validation is essential not only in decision making, but also in security IoT applications. Computational models of message validation are associated with autonomy and trust such as the trust of autonomous machines in human behavior or the trust of humans in autonomous machine behavior. Proper claim validation enables the handling of threats to autonomy and trust (cyber attacks, competitive threats, deception) and the fundamental barriers to system survivability (Russell, Moskowitz, & Raglin, 2017; Sibley, Coyne, & Sherwood, 2017). Validation and verification play important roles in autonomous systems. Analytic validation and verification techniques, and model checking can assist with the design of autonomous IoT control agents in an efficient and reliable manner. This can mean earlier identification of false claims in messages and the detection of other errors.

An important finding of this study is that argumentation structure can be discovered via the features of extended discourse representation, combining information on how an author organizes his/her thoughts with information on how involved agents communicate these thoughts. Once a CDT is formed and identified as being correlated to argumentation, a defeasible logic program can be built from this tree and the dialectical analysis can validate the main claim.

Although validating agents' messages, affective argument should not be confused with an *appeal to emotion*, a logical fallacy characterized by the manipulation of the recipient's emotions in order to win an argument, especially in the absence of factual evidence. This kind of appeal to emotion is a type of red herring and encompasses several logical fallacies.

## REFERENCES

Alsinet, T., Chesñevar, C. I., Godo, L., & Simari, G. R. (2008). A logic programming framework for possibilistic argumentation: formalization and logical properties. *Fuzzy Sets and Systems, 159*(10), 1208–1228.

Amgoud, L., Besnard, P., & Hunter, A. (2015). Representing and reasoning about arguments mined from texts and dialogues. *ECSQARU* (pp. 60–71).

BBC (2018). http://www.bbc.com/news/world-us-canada-42493918.

Bondarenko, A., Dung, P., Kowalski, R., & Toni, F. (1997). An abstract, argumentation-theoretic approach to default reasoning. *Artificial Intelligence, 93*, 63–101.

Cabrio, E., & Villata, S. (2012). Combining textual entailment and argumentation theory for supporting online debates interactions. *Proceedings of the 50th annual meeting of the association for computational linguistics (Vol. 2: Short papers) (pp. 208–212)*, Association for Computational Linguistics.

Carreyrou (2016). *Theranos has struggled with blood tests*. https://www.wsj.com/articles/theranos-has-struggled-with-blood-tests.

Chambers, J. (2014). Are you ready for the Internet of everything? *World Economic Forum*, January 15. From: https://www.weforum.org/agenda/2014/01/are-you-ready-for-the-internet-of-everything/.

Constantinos, J. S., Sarmaniotis, C., & Stafyla, A. (2003). CRM and customer-centric knowledge management: an empirical research. *Business Process Management Journal, 9* (5), 617–634.

Damer, T. E. (2009). *Attacking faulty reasoning: A practical guide to fallacy-free reasoning.* Wadsworth Cengage Learning.

Feng, W. V., & Hirst, G. (2014). A linear- time bottom-up discourse parser with constraints and post-editing. *Proceedings of the 52nd annual meeting of the association for computational linguistics (Vol. 1: Long papers) (pp. 511–521).*

Galitsky, B. (2015). Detecting rumor and disinformation by web mining. *AAAI spring symposium.*

Galitsky, B. (2016). *A deep text analysis system based on open NLP.* Seville, Spain: Apache Con Europe.

Galitsky, B. (2017). Using extended tree kernel to recognize metalanguage in text. *Uncertainty modeling* (pp. 71–96). *Volume 683 of the series Studies in Computational Intelligence* Springer.

Galitsky, B., & de la Rosa, J. L. (2011). Concept-based learning of human behavior for customer relationship management. *Information Sciences, 181*(10), 2016–2035.

Galitsky, B., González, M. P., & Chesñevar, C. I. (2009). A novel approach for classifying customer complaints through graphs similarities in argumentative dialogue. *Decision Support Systems, 46*(3), 717–729.

Galitsky, B., Ilvovsky, D., & Kuznetsov, S. O. (2015). Rhetoric map of an answer to compound queries. *Proceedings of the 53rd annual meeting of the association for computational linguistics ACL-2 (short papers),* pp. 681–686.

Galitsky, B., Ilvovsky, D., & Kuznetsov, S. O (2018). Detecting logical argumentation in text via communicative discourse tree. *Journal of Experimental & Theoretical Artificial Intelligence, 30,* 1–27.

Galitsky, B., & Kuznetsov, S. O. (2008). Learning communicative actions of conflicting human agents. *Journal of Experimental & Theoretical Artificial Intelligence, 20*(4), 277–317.

Galitsky, B., & Pampapathi, R. (2003). Deductive and inductive reasoning for processing the claims of unsatisfied customers. *International conference on industrial, engineering and other applications of applied intelligent systems,* pp. 21–30.

Garcia, A., & Simari, G. R. (2004). Defeasible logic programming: an argumentative approach. *Theory and Practice of Logic Programming, 4*(1–2), 95–138.

Ghosh, D., Muresan, S., Wacholder, N., & Aakhus, M. (2014). Analyzing argumentative discourse units in online interactions. *Proceedings of the first workshop on argumentation mining, Baltimore, MA, June 26 (pp. 39–48).,* Association for Computational Linguistics.

Github (2018). *Intense argumentation dataset.* https://github.com/bgalitsky/relevance-based-on-parse-trees/blob/master/src/test/resources/opinionsFinanceTagged.xls.zip.

Joty, S. R., Carenini, G., Ng, R. T., & Mehdad, Y. (2013). *Combining intra-and multi- sentential rhetorical parsing for document-level dis-course analysis:* (pp. 486–496). In ACL (1).

Joty, S. R., & Moschitti, A. (2014). Discriminative reranking of discourse parses using tree kernels. *Proceedings of the 2014 conference on empirical methods in natural language processing (EMNLP).*

Kipper, K., Korhonen, A., Ryant, N., & Palmer, M. (2008). A large-scale classification of English verbs. *Language Resources and Evaluation Journal, 42,* 21–40.

Lawless, W. F., Mittu, R., Sofge, D., & Russell, S. (Eds.), (2017). *Autonomy and artificial intelligence: A threat or savior?.* Cham, Switzerland: Springer.

Lawrence, J., & Reed, C. (2015). Combining argument mining techniques. *ArgMining@ HLT-NAACL,* pp. 127–136.

Lee, D. (2001). Genres, registers, text types, domains and styles: Clarifying the concepts and navigating a path through the BNC jungle. *Language Learning &amp. Technology, 5*(3), 37–72.

Mann, W., & Thompson, S. (1988). Rhetorical structure theory: towards a functional theory of text organization. *Text-Interdisciplinary Journal for the Study of Discourse, 8*(3), 243–281.

Mikolov, T., Chen, K., Corrado, G. S., & Dean, J. A. (2015). *Computing numeric representations of words in a high-dimensional space.* US Patent 9,037,464, Google, Inc.

Moens, M. -F., Boiy, E., Palau, R. M., & Reed, C. (2007). Automatic detection of arguments in legal texts. *Proceedings of the 11th international conference on artificial intelligence and law, ICAIL '07, Stanford, CA*, pp. 225–230.

Munro, K. (2017). *How to beat security threats to "internet of things"* From: http://www.bbc.com/news/av/technology-39926126/how-to-beat-security-threats-to-internet-of-things.

Pendyala, V. S., & Figueira, S. (2015). Towards a truthful world wide web from a humanitarian perspective. *Global Humanitarian Technology Conference* (pp. 8–11).

Pisarevskaya, D., Litvinova, T., & Litvinova, O. (2017). Deception detection for the Russian language: lexical and syntactic parameters. *Proceedings of the 1st workshop on natural language processing and information retrieval/RANLP.*

Russell, S., Moskowitz, I. S., & Raglin, A. (2017). Human information interaction, artificial intelligence, and errors. In *Autonomy and artificial intelligence: A threat or savior?*. Cham, Switzerland: Springer.

RussiaToday (2018). https://www.rt.com/news/425438-douma-witnesses-gas-attack-syria/.

Sardianos, C., Katakis, I. M., Petasis, G., & Karkaletsis, V. (2015). Argument extraction from news. *Proceedings of the 2nd workshop on argumentation mining, Denver, CO, USA*, pp. 56–66.

SEC 2018. Press release: Theranos, CEO Holmes, and Former President Balwani charged with massive fraud. https://www.sec.gov/news/press-release/2018-41.

Sibley, C., Coyne, J., & Sherwood, S. (2017). Research considerations and tools for evaluating human-automation interaction with future unmanned systems. In *Autonomy and artificial intelligence: A threat or savior?*. Cham, Switzerland: Springer.

Stab, C., & Gurevych, I. (2014). Identifying argumentative discourse structures in persuasive essays. *Proceedings of the 2014 conference on empirical methods in natural language processing, EMNLP '14, Doha, Qatar* (pp. 46–56).

Surdeanu, M., Hicks, T., & Valenzuela-Escarcega, M. A. (2016). Two practical rhetorical structure theory parsers. *Proceedings of the conference of the North American chapter of the association for computational linguistics—human language technologies: software demonstrations (NAACL HLT).*

Symeonidis, A. L., Chatzidimitriou, K. C., Athanasiadis, I. N., & Mitkas, P. A. (2007). Data mining for agent reasoning: a synergy for training intelligent agents. *Engineering Applications of Artificial Intelligence, 20*(8), 1097–1111.

Thimm, M. (2014). Tweety—a comprehensive collection of java libraries for logical aspects of artificial intelligence and knowledge representation. *Proceedings of the 14th international conference on principles of knowledge representation and reasoning (KR'14). Vienna.*

Tweety 2016. https://javalibs.com/artifact/net.sf.tweety.arg/delp. Last downloaded December 12, 2016.

van Eemeren, F. H., Grootendorst, R., & Henkemans, F. S. (1996). *Fundamentals of argumentation theory: A handbook of historical backgrounds and contemporary developments.* Routledge: Taylor & Francis Group.

Walton, D. N., Reed, C., & Macagno, F. (2008). *Argumentation schemes.* Cambridge: Cambridge University Press.

Wang, W., Su, J., & Tan, C. L. (2010). Kernel based discourse relation recognition with temporal ordering information. *Proceedings of the 48th annual meeting of the association for computational linguistics, Uppsala, Sweden, 11–16 July (pp. 710–719).*

## FURTHER READING

Debanjan, G., Muresan, S., Wacholder, N., Aakhus, M., & Mitsui, M. (2014). Analyzing argumentative discourse units in online interactions. In *Proceedings of the first workshop on argumentation mining* (pp. 39–48). Baltimore, Maryland: ACL.

Galitsky, B., & Taylor, J. (2018). *Discovering and accessing heated arguments at the discourse level.* Dialogue 2018, Moscow, Russia.

Redeld, S. A., & Seto, M. L. (2017). Verification challenges for autonomous systems. In *Autonomy and artificial intelligence: A threat or savior?.* Cham, Switzerland: Springer.

# CHAPTER 12

# Distributed Autonomous Energy Organizations: Next-Generation Blockchain Applications for Energy Infrastructure

**Michael Mylrea**
Cyber Security & Energy Technology, Pacific Northwest National Laboratory, Richland, WA, United States

## 12.1 INTRODUCTION TO DISTRIBUTED AUTONOMOUS ENERGY ORGANIZATIONS

Advances in blockchain and artificial intelligence (AI) continue to spur disruptive innovation, automating exchanges in value in new ways that are reducing the need for third-party trust mechanisms. These advances could help pave the way to a more distributed and agile energy grid that ties in a larger percentage of renewable energy resources and enables peer-to-peer and energy transactions. While grid modernization has helped spur a more distributed and flexible smart grid, it has also created new challenges, such as increasing the number of intermediaries involved in exchanging energy. Grid modernization has also increased the cyber-attack surface through the increased use of smart energy devices that network, digitize, automate, and increasingly converge energy supplies in the cyber-physical energy supply chain. Blockchain or distributed ledger technology shows potential in identifying and monitoring these complex Energy Internet of Things (EIoT) environments, characterized by an increasing number of critical cyber assets and data being exchanged in a complex energy value chain. Blockchain technology shows potential in overcoming some of these challenges needed to give impetus to more DAEOs.

### 12.1.1 DAEO Enablers: AI and Blockchain

Blockchain helps provide the technical requirements needed to disrupt the current energy paradigm, where centralized generation is often distributed

*Artificial Intelligence for the Internet of Everything*
https://doi.org/10.1016/B978-0-12-817636-8.00012-0
**217**

through a complex inefficient multitiered system where consumers have little control in the type of energy they consume. Blockchain is defined as a distributed database or digital ledger that records transactions of value using a cryptographic signature that is inherently resistant to modification (Tapscott, 2016). Combining blockchain-based smart contracts with machine learning and AI algorithms presents an opportunity to realize the goals of DAEOs. DAEO will provide a platform for a more distributed autonomous system that helps increase the speed, scale, security, and autonomy of complex, distributed Internet of Things (IoT) environments, such as the US power grid. The need for third parties in executing a complex energy transaction may be reduced when an autonomous smart contract can execute and exchange value and services via an autonomous agent or even a DAEO blockchain platform. Smart contract design and DAEO can also help inform machine-learning algorithms. Like many proof of work (PoW) blockchain technologies, DAEO would not need to have a single user with control. Blockchain platforms and associated smart contracts could help create some control mechanisms to retain control of the DAEO to an autonomous AI agent. Blockchain technology could help secure the sensitive data needed to inform the AI in a DAEO because the data would be cryptographically signed and stored securely in a distributed ledger, enabling access, data provenance, and auditability while preserving privacy. This is especially important if the AI will be informed with sensitive or personal identifiable information.

Blockchain technology provides a more efficient ledger for developing, securing, and improving AI and machine-learning algorithms (Zwanenburg, 2018). AI technology continues to make rapid advances in everything from translation to surgery to virtual assistants and self-driving vehicles. But people also fear AI. Opponents of AI point to pedestrian deaths caused by AI-enabled self-driving vehicles and studies that suggest it will replace more jobs than it creates. Developing AI also requires access to the use of large data sets that could potentially compromise people's privacy. In that respect, blockchain can help preserve the privacy of the data sets needed for large neural networks by storing a cryptographic hash of the metadata that can only be unlocked via a private key and permissioned access to the blockchain. Accordingly, blockchain can help AI developers better understand and track the prodigious data sets, increasing the auditability and control of neural-network machine-learning functionality. The ability to track and control large data sets is especially important to provide distributed autonomous energy organizations with reliable information because exchanging distributed energy resources often involves intermittent sources of energy that need load leveling and balancing to function reliably and efficiently.

In this context, blockchain smart contracts could help reduce energy use during peak hours by automating the curtailment of nonessential electricity use. AI algorithms would learn end user's energy-use patterns and consumers would agree on their flexibility of curtailing certain nonessential loads. Smart contracts currently have the capability to be defined and improved via machine-learning algorithms. But computational errors may still occur, raising additional questions for future research. Who will be held responsible when there is an error or when a blockchain smart contract is not successfully executed? While the data and exchange of value captured in blockchain might be immutable, or at least very hard to manipulate, what if the algorithm that establishes the terms of the contract executed is written by an autonomous AI agent? What if the agent is wrong? How do you change an immutable contract? What additional challenges and potential solutions should be explored through AI-enabled blockchain solutions to distribute and automate the IoT in a more secure way?

This study explores some of these questions and other pertinent energy security and optimization questions through an innovative application of blockchain that gives impetus to DAEO. This use case highlights how AI-enabled blockchain solutions may help increase cyber resilience and optimize complex exchanges of distributed energy resources by encrypting, monitoring, and automating transactions to remove third parties. With billions of IoT devices sensing and exchanging information, AI-enabled blockchain solutions could also help to better analyze data sets with thousands of variables (e.g., industrial control system anomalies, frequency, load, and voltage changes) and to organize them into weighted relationships that could be tracked through next-generation AI blockchain solutions. As data patterns in these variables are better understood via machine-learning neural networks, the smart blockchain contract could be updated to better secure and exchange critical energy data and devices.

## 12.2 DISTRIBUTED ENERGY SUPPLY CHAIN

These advances are important as the US power grid is a complex system of systems that requires a secure, reliable, and trustworthy global supply chain. This complexity is especially true for the grid's increasing number of networked energy delivery systems (EDSs), industrial control systems (ICSs), and associated vendors, distributers, integrators, and end users. Grid modernization has increased the use of smart energy devices that network, digitize, automate, and increasing converge the cyber-physical energy supply chain. This has resulted in new cyber supply chain security and North American Electric Reliability Corporation (NERC) critical infrastructure protection (CIP) compliance challenges for utilities, regulators, and vendors.

The distributed *form* of a blockchain ledger complements the distributed *function* of a global energy infrastructure supply chain. The power grid weaves together cyber and physical cyber assets, information and operational technology, and software and hardware in a way that requires an improved chain of custody for monitoring, auditing, and cyber security. Permissioned blockchain technology provides a consensus mechanism and trust anchor via a cryptographic hash function that helps verify the who, what, when, and where of the data in a blockchain where the data exchange or event becomes a widely witnessed, auditable, and immutable event. This technology presents a number of potential opportunities to increase the cyber security of a supply chain, which is essential to secure and sustain DAEO.

For one, blockchain facilitates the auditability of IoT environments, tracking inventory of energy organization's critical cyber assets, such as where a device was developed, shipped, installed, and last patched. Currently, these disparate data sets are often not tracked or monitored by energy utilities, creating an opportunity for malicious actors to exploit this knowledge gap in the chain of custody. Similarly, energy utilities often do not have visibility into the health of their critical field and edge devices. If an energy utility does not have an inventory and monitor these critical cyber assets, it is almost impossible to detect, protect, and respond to malicious cyber events.

Blockchain, or distributed ledger technology (DLT), has many definitions. For this chapter, blockchain is defined as a distributed database or digital ledger that records transactions of value using a cryptographic signature that is inherently resistant to modification (Tapscott, 2016). Blockchain is a distributed database that maintains a continuously growing list of records, called blocks, secure from tampering and revision. Each block contains a timestamp and a link to a previous block (Trottier, 2013). Blockchain-based smart contracts can be executed without human interaction (Franco, 2014); its data is more resistant to modification because the data that form a block cannot be altered retroactively. Blockchain smart contracts are defined as technologies or applications that are executed on participating nodes to maintain consensus related to any exchanges of value that have occurred without intermediaries acting as arbiters of money and information (Tapscott, 2016). With those fundamentals defined, blockchains can be classified as permissioned and permissionless. Further, there are several types of consensus mechanisms, such as PoW and proof of authority (PoA) (Franco, 2014).

The AI blockchain solution explored in this research focuses on technical advances and innovation that could help increase security, data provenance, attribution, auditability, and disintermediate energy intermediaries through a proven trust mechanism (Mylrea, 2017). Blockchain can help ensure the data integrity throughout the chain of custody by verifying the identity of a sender and a signer and alerting owners if the data have been manipulated. A cryptographically signed hash of the data is captured as a block in the chain, allowing a regulator to return a signature token to the sender at each route along the supply chain (e.g., vendor, supply, and customer). This step-wise secure process could help to automate burdensome security compliance audits on energy utilities, such as the National Energy Regulatory Commissions' Critical Infrastructure Protection (NERC-CIP) standard, which specifies the minimum-security requirements for the bulk power systems. Instead, the blockchain hash would be sent to the regulator along with the chain-of-custody data and device logs, helping to verify machine state integrity. Sending the logs and machine states separately helps to increase the availability and security of the data.

The blockchain architecture produces a Merkle tree with the root hashes and hash calendar published in the blockchain. Because the blockchain includes a hash of the metadata, the calendar helps to preserve the privacy of the data. The PoW blockchain uses the hash instead of the actual data; the signature token, which consists of the data to reconstruct the path from its hashed value to the top of the tree, is required by the client to verify that the data have been signed. This helps in verifying the existence of the client's hash in the tree. For example, in Fig. 12.1 the left side shows the construction of a Merkle tree, and the right side shows a verification of the presence

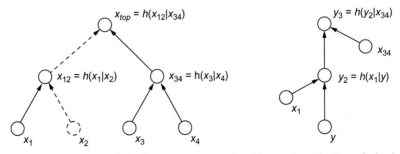

**Fig. 12.1** Computation of a hash tree consensus algorithm and verification of a hashed node (Buldas, Kroonma, & Laanoja, 2013).

of $y$ in the tree. Here $x_1$ through $x_4$ are different hashes that get concatenated to obtain higher level nodes $x_{12}$ and $x_{34}$. The nodes are further concatenated to yield the root node of the tree, $x_{top}$. To verify if $y$ exists in the tree (in place of $x_2$), $x_1$ and $y$ are concatenated to obtain a node $y_2 = h(x_1 \mid y)$. This node is then concatenated with $x_{34}$ to obtain $y_3 = h(y_2 \mid x_{34})$. If $y_3 = x_{top}$, then $y$ exists in the tree (Buldas et al., 2013).

## 12.3 AI—BLOCKCHAIN TO SECURE YOUR ENERGY SUPPLY CHAIN

Before applying blockchain technology to help optimize or secure the electricity infrastructure, it is important to determine if the distributed ledger technology solution being applied is interoperable, secure, and affordable and can clear transactions in a timely manner. Another important consideration is to determine what specific blockchain solution would be the best fit for solving this problem. A number of blockchain solutions could potentially create more challenges by expanding security gaps, increasing costs, or decreasing security rather than creating efficiencies and increasing security. Blockchain solutions that help track and secure large data sets also need to be energy efficient, economic, and interoperable with the current technology stack as well as other blockchains. Cost, functionality, scalability, and cyber resilience were all imperative functional requirements for the AI blockchain solution explored in this study. The roadmap shown in Fig. 12.2 was developed to help determine when to use blockchain to increase the cyber security of the electricity infrastructure (Figs. 12.3 and 12.4).

## 12.4 POTENTIAL BLOCKCHAIN BUSINESS AND IMPLEMENTATION CHALLENGES

AI-enabled blockchain shows great promise in giving impetus to and securing the energy supply chain to DAEO. However, additional study, validation, and verification of the blockchain application for grid cyber security are needed due to various challenges in applying DLT to secure and optimize complex systems.

One challenge is that blockchain technology—like its application to the energy space—is at a nascent stage. Evolving blockchain definitions create several challenges from a policy perspective. It is noted that the rapidly changing and contested vocabulary and definitions poses challenges for regulators seeking to understand, govern, and audit blockchain technology.

# 1 READING & WRITING

Fundamentally, different blockchain technologies offer different "read and write" features. Although readability and writability features come with blockchains, they are also available with typical database technologies. The need to share, the writer's identity, and trust are the key elements in this area to determine the need of a blockchain.

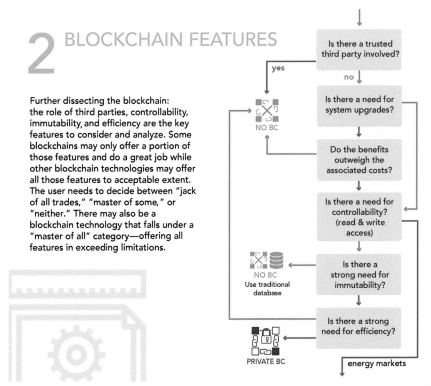

Is there a need to store data? → no → NO BC → Use traditional databases or related technologies

yes ↓

Is there shared write access?

Can all participants write? → PRIVATE BC → Provides high controllability and with an authoritative visibility

Is the writer's identity known? → NO BC

CONSIDER → PUBLIC BC → Provides node anonymity that may or may not involve mining

Are the writers trusted?

blockchain features ↓

**Fig. 12.2** Energy blockchain roadmap: part 1: reading and writing (Mylrea & Gourisetti, 2017).

# 2 BLOCKCHAIN FEATURES

Further dissecting the blockchain: the role of third parties, controllability, immutability, and efficiency are the key features to consider and analyze. Some blockchains may only offer a portion of those features and do a great job while other blockchain technologies may offer all those features to acceptable extent. The user needs to decide between "jack of all trades," "master of some," or "neither." There may also be a blockchain technology that falls under a "master of all" category—offering all features in exceeding limitations.

Is there a trusted third party involved?

yes → NO BC

no ↓

Is there a need for system upgrades?

Do the benefits outweigh the associated costs?

Is there a need for controllability? (read & write access)

NO BC Use traditional database ← Is there a strong need for immutability?

PRIVATE BC ← Is there a strong need for efficiency? → energy markets

**Fig. 12.3** Energy blockchain roadmap: part 2: blockchain features (Mylrea & Gourisetti, 2017).

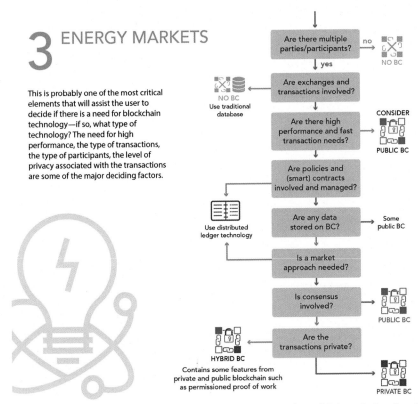

**Fig. 12.4** Energy blockchain roadmap: part 3: energy markets (Mylrea & Gourisetti, 2017).

One of the general misconceptions about blockchain definitions is caused by the assumption that blockchain equals Bitcoin (Walch, 2017). While blockchains include cryptocurrencies and transactions recorded publicly, private or permissioned blockchains often do not include an exchange of value and do not record anything publicly. Yet Google defines (Walch, 2017) blockchain as "a digital ledger in which transactions made in Bitcoin or another cryptocurrency are recorded chronologically and publicly." Similarly, Investopedia's definition associates blockchain with decentralized ledgers of cryptocurrencies: "A blockchain is a digitized, decentralized, public ledger of all cryptocurrency transactions" (Walch, 2017). Definitions are evolving and may contradict or significantly differ greatly across sector, application, functional requirements, and technology stacks being deployed. PoW, PoA, zero proof, and proof of burn are just some of the different descriptions of the consensus algorithms that establish the trust mechanisms to secure data in the distributed ledger. Evolving and ill-defined descriptions of blockchain are exacerbated when combined with the disparity of definitions around AI. Together, this will continue to challenge regulators seeking to establish policies and regulations for blockchain application to the energy sector.

Public PoW blockchain solutions also have several gaps related to security, functionality, cost, and energy efficiency. A major pitfall is the excessive use of energy in solving the puzzles (Deetman, 2016). Another challenge is that these nodes are widely witnessed and may lack the necessary privacy considerations. Some PoW servers are in countries that have been accused of economic espionage and theft of intellectual property. PoW consensus algorithms can also add prohibitive latency issues to time-sensitive transactions. Another challenge is the change in functional and nonfunctional requirements as well as the technology stack needed to integrate the blockchain technology that ensures system manufacturing tracking throughout the development lifecycle. Related challenges for implementing blockchain to facilitate supply chain security include the following:

- Multiple vendors are involved in product and systems development as well as the chain of custody. Vendors have different levels of resources, unique constraints, and other considerations to keep in mind.
- Vendors might be using different blockchain technologies that are not interoperable with each other or with the data being tracked. However, an intermediate node between different blockchains and databases can facilitate functionality in a single overall common blockchain.
- Different data sets for business ecosystems and supply chain functional and nonfunctional requirements must be integrated into a blockchain across different data boundaries.

## 12.5 ROADMAP FOR WHEN TO USE BLOCKCHAIN IN THE ENERGY SECTOR

Blockchain has several properties that facilitate more secure, distributed autonomous energy organizations. An overview of some of the properties is reviewed in Table 12.1. This table also provides a comparison of the technical aspects of blockchain by vendor to help energy-sector stakeholders better understand some of the differences with DLT.

Examining the different technical specification requirements of different blockchain solutions suggests that there are some benefits of blockchain technology for a DAEO. Some of the benefits include, but are not limited to:

**Table 12.1** Comparison of technical aspects of different blockchain (Mylrea & Gourisetti, 2017)

| Topic | Bitcoin | HDAC | Ethereum | Guardtime keyless signature infrastructure (KSI) | Hyperledger |
|---|---|---|---|---|---|
| Target applications | Financial transactions (Bitcoin script) | Low-cost automated transactions between IoT devices Public/private blockchain | Smart contracts Solidity, serpent | Integrity substrate, secure timestamping | Modular platform for business solutions with identity and smart contracts |
| Smart contract | NA | Yes | Yes | Yes | Yes |
| Consensus | Proof of work (PoW) | PoW; trust-based | Proof of authority (PoA) | PoA | PoA |
| Transaction speed | 7 tx/s | ~160 tx/s (public)* ~500 tx/s (per one private chain) | 25 tx/s | Exabyte-scale/s | Current: 1000 tx/s Improvements coming for HLF V1.1 |
| Scalability | Limited by block size and creation frequency | Limited by block size and creation frequency | Limited by block size and creation frequency | Near-linear growth to the number of nodes | |
| Block time | 10 min | 3 min | 12 s | 1 s | |
| Finality | ≥1 h (6 blocks) | ≥3 min | ≥3 min (12 blocks) | 1 s | |
| Block size | 1 MB | Dynamic (max. 8 MB) | Dynamic | 53 bytes | As per previous entry |

|  |  |  |  |  |  |
|---|---|---|---|---|---|
| Guaranteed download of complete history | Yes, from other nodes | Yes, from other nodes with access | Yes, from other nodes | No (data set completeness not guaranteed, but any given entry can be validated) |  |
| Extra data | 80 bytes (OP_RETURN) | Dynamic (max. 4Kb) | Dynamic five gas/byte | Dynamic |  |
| Topology | Public blockchain | Private/public, permissioned | Public, permissionless | Private, permissioned | Permissioned |
| Privacy model | None | Private blockchains | None | Hashing (data never leaves premises; only masked hashes do) | Hashing, channels |
| Identity and access management, authentication | PKI | Access rights administered on the blockchain | PKI | Hierarchical gateway-based | PKI |
| Programming | C++ | C-like syntax | Solidity | C, Java SDK | Javascript, Java, Go |
| Deterministic transaction execution | Yes | Probably (using a virtual machine) | Yes | NA |  |
| Offline verification | No | No | No | Yes—KSI calendar |  |
| Post quantum security | No (but extendable in the future) | Unknown | Yes | Yes—since it is based only on hash functions |  |
| Participation mechanism | Public | Public/permissioned | Public | Permissioned | Permissioned |

- *Interoperability advantages of blockchain technology*: DLT provides a public multicast communication platform where a sender can reach a large audience that can both read and write to blockchain. Dynamic communications between generators and consumers may facilitate the move from centralized generation to next generation peer-to-peer energy exchanges.
- *100% availability*: Blockchain provides a reliable, distributed mechanism for tracking dynamic data sets.
- *Strong immutability*: Despite properties that make data in a blockchain very difficult to mutate, some examples of mutations exist, such as forks and or blockchain hacks that required rolling back the blockchain. That said, permissioned blockchain technology solutions, such as keyless signature infrastructure (KSI), provide a time-stamped and cryptographically signed electronic transaction that would be very difficult to change. As cyber-physical systems increasingly converge and automate transactions, logs of immutable data sets are especially important to validate and verify the integrity of the system and its transactions. Immutability, however, can also lead to a number of challenges. For example, in one recent incident, child pornography was saved in a Bitcoin blockchain (Suberg, 2017). When illegal images or data are saved in the blockchain, it can be very difficult to change the content. Another potential way to change the blockchain is to control or compromise 51% of the nodes needed to reach a consensus. This subterfuge could potentially be accomplished by gaining root access to an internet service provider that supports the majority of the blockchain nodes and undermine the blockchain's consensus algorithm by compromising a majority of the nodes.
- *Big data management blockchain*: Blockchain facilitates the distribution of prodigious data sets between organizations. Data can be synchronized, archived, and audited between multiple parties.

## 12.6 THE EVOLUTION OF PUBLIC KEY INFRASTRUCTURE ENCRYPTION

All modern organizations require secure and reliable access to electricity to function. Securing our critical energy infrastructure from evolving cyber and physical threats is imperative. As energy infrastructure becomes more autonomous and distributed, there also needs to be an evolution in how critical field devices, control systems, and supervisory control and data acquisition systems are secured. Part of the challenge is that most cyber-security solutions increase cost and reduce functionality in the name of integrity, confidentiality, and availability. Blockchain solutions might be an exception in that some applications can improve security and optimize the ability to exchange and track value. Indeed, some blockchain solutions add a layer of cryptography to help track digital transactions, but many cyber-security challenges remain for securing complex DAEO. For one, the array of vulnerable "things" that make up these environments is often designed to prioritize functionality and cost over security. Energy devices often lack encryption, basic patch management, secure passwords, and communicate in plain text that can be compromised. Poor source code, vulnerable design, and improper configuration have also led to several major IoT cyber incidents.

Another challenge with securing critical energy infrastructure and devices from emerging cyber threats is that public key infrastructure (PKI) solutions are often cost prohibitive and not scalable for the encryption requirements of IoT environments. Moreover, legacy systems, information technology (IT), and operational technology (OT) environments often lack the necessary computer processing power to support the deployment of PKI. This lack of power is common with analog equipment in substations and other critical infrastructures. Moreover, with PKI, a single authority often issues and revokes security certificates. If this authority is attacked and its certificates are manipulated, all of its users will potentially be vulnerable to cyber-attacks. Therefore PKI must continue to evolve to secure IoT environments until a better solution can be scaled up.

Blockchain KSI presents a potential path forward. KSI helps preserve the integrity of data exchanges and other digital transactions using a mathematical algorithm for authentication without the need for trusted keys or credentials. KSI authenticates IoT data at scale, in real time, providing immutable transaction data without several of the challenges of PKI. Fig. 12.5 further describes KSI's cryptographic hash function, highlighting how the hash function can help prove that the machine state integrity of an IoT device has not changed, preventing the disclosure of sensitive IoT data and providing a cryptographic proof.

Researchers at PNNL, Guardtime, the US Department of Energy, Washington State University, Avista, Siemens, and the Department of Defense–Homeland Defense and Security Information Analysis Center are developing a KSI-enabled blockchain solution to help secure distributed energy IoT environments, called Keyless Infrastructure Security Solution

KSI is based on cryptographic hash functions

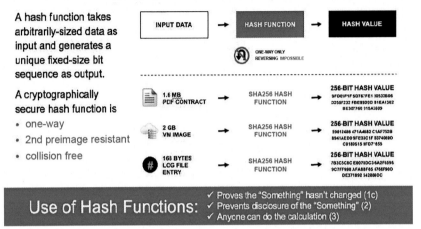

Fig. 12.5 Guardtime KSI blockchain is based on cryptographic hash functions ( Johnson, 2017).

(KISS). KISS is also exploring the application of AI-enabled blockchain smart contracts to increase the automation, flexibility, security, and speed of complex grid edge energy transactions. KISS may help give impetus to more distributed autonomous energy organizations and modernize our energy infrastructure. Certainty, the increases in grid data speeds, size, and complexity of energy transactions requires a more flexible and secure power grid. To help overcome these challenges, KISS provides a unique value proposition with its potential to help both optimize and secure these critical data sets from emerging cyber threats.

Blockchain's digital ledger and cryptographically signed transaction data may help to increase the trustworthiness and integrity of complex energy transactions. Combined with machine learning and AI-enabled energy-delivery systems, DAEO may also have more control and flexibility in automating, monitoring, and auditing complex energy exchanges. Blockchain smart contracts may also provide a real-time security response to unauthorized attempts to change critical EDS data, configurations, applications, and network appliance and sensor infrastructures. Autonomous detection of data anomalies could help improve cyber forensics and recovery from a cyberattack by providing a unified timeline for incident analysis. Blockchain could also provide a layer of increased security for a more distributed trading platform that uses smart contracts for the automated trading and settlement of contracts between peers, consumers, and prosumers.

## 12.7 WHY BLOCKCHAIN, WHY DAEO

Blockchain-enabled DAEO may help to solve several complex problems related to the control and trustworthiness of rapid, distributed, and complex transactions of distributed energy resources (DERs). In a move toward a more distributed, resilient, and clean grid, blockchain may help reduce the need for third parties through a verifiable trust mechanism. Instead of a centralized utility, automated smart contracts could help to support auditable multiparty transactions based on predefined rules between distributed energy providers or prosumers and customers. Blockchain-based smart contracts may also help remove the need to interact with third parties, thereby facilitating the adoption and monetization of distributed energy transactions and exchanges—both energy flows and financial transactions. This may help to reduce transactive energy costs and to increase the control and security of DER integration by removing barriers from a more decentralized and resilient power grid. One of the current needs for realizing the potential of DAEO is the development of a secure blockchain-based smart-contract mechanism to facilitate more distributed and complex energy transactions. Part of the challenge is that there is not an agreed-upon transactive energy methodology or best practice for connecting various end-loads over multiple blockchains through a hybrid blockchain design. Should one materialize, this solution would help to eliminate the limitation of using any particular blockchain by the nation's utilities and power companies (Fig. 12.6).

DAEO could help to realize the following goals:

1. Fundamentally transform the energy transactive system architecture from today's traditional clearing house process to the future's autonomous blockchain-based transactive systems
2. Provide a more autonomous smart contract mechanism and design that addresses US electricity consumer needs without any cost prohibitive changes in the current electricity infrastructure
3. Maximize the use of the national distribution system and transactive system architectures to improve the energy market's efficiency
4. Accelerate integration and use of the renewable generation, prosumer base, distributed generation, and demand response
5. Provide a next-generation market design aimed at messaging and communication architectures to enable a blockchain smart contract to ensure privacy for market participants, the enforcement of physical feeder power capacity constraints with free markets, and the design of market mechanisms that maximize transaction volumes

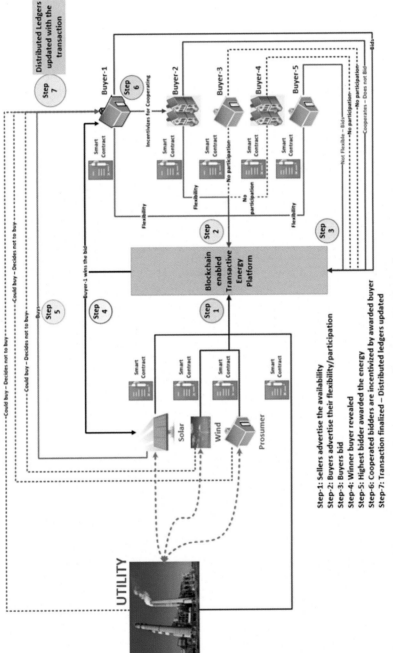

**Fig. 12.6** Distributed autonomous energy organization (Mylrea & Gourisetti, 2017).

Step-1: Sellers advertise the availability
Step-2: Buyers advertise their flexibility/participation
Step-3: Buyers bid
Step-4: Winner buyer revealed
Step-5: Highest bidder awarded the energy
Step-6: Cooperated bidders are incentivized by awarded buyer
Step-7: Transaction finalized – Distributed ledgers updated

## 12.8 OVERVIEW OF THE AI-ENABLED BLOCKCHAIN

DAEO presents an innovative and disruptive solution that might create new efficiencies through automation. AI blockchain consensus algorithms provides a distributed trust mechanism that may disintermediate and replace third parties. Energy aggregators and meter readers could be replaced by a dynamic distributed ledger. However, blockchain innovation will also create new energy jobs, values, and markets. As technology empowers humans, it also changes the relationship between man and machine, technology and organizations, and society and innovation. Autonomous blockchain organizations may distribute power and leadership via encrypted votes that establish equity relative to a contract or even a mission statement. For example, future energy organizations may help stakeholders govern the type of energy mix they would like and have that preference or willingness to pay be captured in a smart contract. Blockchain AI-empowered energy organizations might become increasingly autonomous and made up of decentralized contractors and investors who have the power to vote, invest, and deliver services based on an immutable smart contract that captures who, what, when, and where services are executed. These transactions can be shared and secured in a transparent immutable ledger.

The notion of "self-bootstrapped" organizations with crypto equities independently leveraging contractors guided by decentralized blockchain voting has been explored (Levine, 2014). The Bit Congress has established a blockchain-based voting system. The country of Georgia is leveraging blockchain to facilitate real-estate licensing. Estonia has established a privacy-preserving secure virtual government using KSI blockchain. These examples highlight how technology has already helped to distribute trust and reduce redundancy in everything from billing to middle management, creating new value for organizations in an increasingly decentralized autonomous society. Reducing redundancy also creates new value and more competitive organizations (Lawless, 2017).

## 12.9 BLOCKCHAIN AND AI SECURITY OPPORTUNITY

Blockchain and AI integration and innovation may present a more resilient and efficient path for decentralized cyber and physical devices to interact, transforming modern infrastructure into an array of smart autonomous systems of systems. Increased autonomy and control are essential to optimizing the rapidly growing IoT environment that Gartner has predicted to include 26 billion devices by 2020 (Gartner, 2013).

In 2014, Levine stated (Levine, 2014):

> *Simple and easy to write contracts appear to be sufficient for many entirely digital transactions. But as these systems start to interact with the physical world, there is likely to be a need for greater intelligence and real-world knowledge in making decisions. AI systems will be needed to translate information from a wide variety of sensors into precise terms that smart contracts can act upon. In the other direction, contracts that lead to physical actions (such as delivery of items) will need to interface with human and robotic agents. For example, owner and operators of critical energy infrastructure might want insurance contracts against cyber-attacks and harmful weather conditions and a smart contract would need to determine when the payout event is triggered.*

The aforementioned grid optimization, automation, and resilience improvements are essential operation and design criteria needed to modernize our power grid. However, cyber security is often an afterthought because vendors and end-users prioritize functionality and cost, leaving the power grid—the backbone of our economy—potentially vulnerable to a cyber-attack. This vulnerability is especially true at the grid's edge, which continues to increase the size and speed of data being collected and exchanged in absence of clear cyber security and IoT standards and regulations. Thus, the grid lacks the necessary defenses to prevent the disruption and manipulation of DERs, grid-edge devices, and the associated electricity infrastructure. Moreover, as the smart grid increases its connectivity and communication with buildings, cyber vulnerabilities will extend behind the meter into smart buildings, which also have a host of documented cyber-security vulnerabilities.

Blockchain technology can also be applied to the smart grid to help reduce costs by cutting out third parties and increasing the arbitrage opportunity for individuals to produce and sell energy to each other. Smart contracts facilitate peer-to-peer energy exchanges by enabling energy consumers and procurers to sell to each other, instead of transacting through a multitiered system in which distribution and transmission system operators, power producers, and suppliers transact on various levels (Mylrea & Gourisetti, 2017). In April 2016 one of the first use cases was demonstrated—energy generated in a decentralized fashion was sold directly between neighbors in New York via a blockchain system. This use case demonstrated that energy producers and energy consumers could execute energy supply contracts without involving a third-party intermediary, thereby effectively increasing the speed and reducing the costs of the transaction (PWC, 2017).

In addition to potential cost savings, transaction data might be made more secure by using decentralized storage and multifactor verification of transactions in the blockchain distributed ledger (PWC, 2017). Blockchain reduces the need for third parties to process transactions: electricity is generated ➔ the consumer buys the electricity ➔ blockchain-based meters update the blockchain, creating a unique timestamped block for verification in a distributed ledger. At the distribution level, system operators can leverage the blockchain to receive energy transaction data to charge their network costs to consumers. This leverage reduces data requirements and increases the speed of clearing transactions for transmission system operators because transactions can be executed and settled on the basis of actual consumption (Mylrea & Gourisetti, 2017).

Smart contracts execute and record transactions in the blockchain load ledger through blockchain-enabled advanced metering infrastructure. Blockchain-based smart contracts can facilitate consumer-level exchange of excess generation from distributed energy resources. This could provide additional storage and help substation load balancing from bulk energy systems. Moreover, smart contract data are secured in part through the decentralized storage of all transactions of energy flows and business activities. This blockchain security application highlights the disruption potential blockchain may have on energy markets because of the introduction of a more autonomous and decentralized transaction model. This peer-to-peer system may reduce or even replace the need for a meter operator if the meter blockchain is shared with the distribution system operator.

Currently, the power grid lacks the necessary security and resilience to prevent cyber-attacks on DERs, grid-edge devices, and their associated electricity infrastructure. Cyber vulnerabilities and interoperability challenges also extend behind the meter into building automation and control systems. Applying blockchain could help to increase the fidelity and security of buildings relative to grid communications. Moreover, multiple customers can leverage the same widely witnessed blockchain to cryptographically verify the other entities' data when needed, creating a distributed trust mechanism. Blockchain may also help to solve several optimization and reliability challenges that have been ushered in with grid modernization.

Currently, time lags for payment and from uncollected bills leaves value on the table, failing to capture the real cost associated with the energy value chain. Blockchain can record real-time net loads, and smart contracts can execute customers distributed–generation sales and purchases. Grid operators also lack visibility into and control of real-time power flows and injections from DERs and distributed generation customers. Blockchain can help to increase fidelity and control of utility data, which can help settle and secure bulk energy system transactions as well as to negotiate future contracts.

## 12.10 CONCLUSION AND FUTURE RESEARCH

AI blockchain enabled distributed autonomous energy organizations may help to increase the energy efficiency, cyber security, and resilience of the electricity infrastructure. These are timely goals as we modernize the US power grid—a complex system of systems that requires secure and reliable communications and a more trustworthy global supply chain. While blockchain, AI, and IoT are creating a buzz right now, many challenges remain to be overcome to realize the full potential of these innovative technological solutions. A lot of news and media coverage of blockchain today falsely suggests that it is a panacea for all that ails us—climate change, cyber security, and volatile financial systems. There is similar hysteria around AI, with articles suggesting that the robots are coming, and that AI will take all of our jobs. While these new technologies are disruptive in their own way and create some exciting new opportunities, many challenges remain. Several fundamental policy, regulatory, and scientific challenges exist before blockchain realizes its full disruptive potential.

Future research should continue to explore the challenges related to blockchain and distributed ledger technology. Applying AI blockchain to modernizing the electricity infrastructure also requires speed, agility, and affordable technology. AI-enhanced algorithms are expensive and often require prodigious data sets that must be broken down into a code that makes sense. However, a lot of noise (distracting data) is being collected and exchanged in the electricity infrastructure, making it difficult to identify cyber anomalies. When there is a lot of disparate data being exchanged at subzero-second speeds, it is difficult to determine the cause of the anomaly, such as a software glitch, cyber-attack, weather event, or hybrid cyber-physical event. It can be very difficult to determine what normal looks like and set the accurate baseline that is needed to detect anomalies. Developing an AI blockchain–enhanced grid requires that the data be broken into observable patterns, which is very challenging from a cyber perspective when threats are complex, nonlinear, and evolving.

Applying blockchain to modernizing and securing the electricity infrastructure presents several cyber-security challenges that should be further examined in future research. For example, Ethereum-based smart contracts provide the ability for anyone to write electronic code that can be executed in a blockchain. If an energy producer or consumer agrees to buy or sell renewable energy from a neighbor for an agreed-upon price, it can be captured in a blockchain-based smart contract. AI could help to increase efficiency by automating the auction to include other bidders and sellers in a more efficient and dynamic way—this would require a lot more data and analysis to recognize the discernable patterns that inform the AI algorithm of the smart contract's performance. Increased automation, however, will also require that the code of the blockchain is more resilient to cyber-attacks. Previously, Ethereum was shown to have several vulnerabilities that may undermine the trustworthiness of this transaction mechanism. Vulnerabilities in the code have been exploited in at least three multimillion dollar cyber incidents. In June 2016 DAO was hacked—its smart contract code was exploited, and approximately $50 million dollars were extracted. In July 2017 code in an Ethereum wallet was exploited to extract $30 million dollars of cryptocurrency. In January 2018 hackers stole roughly 58 billion yen ($532.6 million) from a Tokyo-based cryptocurrency exchange, Coincheck, Inc. The latter incident highlighted the need for increased security and regulatory protection for cryptocurrencies and other blockchain applications. The Coincheck hack appears to have exploited vulnerabilities in a "hot wallet," which is a cryptocurrency wallet that is connected to the internet. In contrast, cold wallets, such as Trezor and Ledger Nano S, are cryptocurrency wallets that are stored offline.

Despite being a centralized currency, Coincheck was a cryptocurrency exchange with a single point of failure. However, the blockchain shared ledger of the account may potentially be able to tag and follow the stolen coins and identify any account that receives them (Fadilpašić & Garlick, 2017). Storing prodigious data sets that are constantly growing in a blockchain can also create potential latency or bloat in the chain, requiring large amounts of memory. Requirements for Ethereum-based smart contracts have grown over time and the block takes a longer time to process. For time-sensitive energy transactions, this situation may create speed, scale, and cost issues if the smart contract is not designed properly. Certainly, future research is needed to develop, validate, and verify a more secure approach.

Finally, future research should examine the functional requirements and potential barriers for applying blockchain to make energy organizations more distributed, autonomous, and secure. For example, even if some intermediaries are replaced in the energy sector, a schedule and forecast still need to be submitted to the transmission system operator for the electricity infrastructure to be reliable. Another challenge is incorporating individual blockchain consumers into a balancing group and having them comply with market reliability and requirements as well as submit accurate demand forecasts to the network operator. Managing a balancing group is not a trivial task and this approach could potentially increase the costs of managing the blockchain. To avoid costly disruptions, blockchain autonomous data exchanges, such as demand forecasts from the consumer to the network operator, will need to be stress tested for security and reliability before being deployed at scale. In considering all of these innovative applications, as well as the many associated challenges, future research is needed to develop, validate, and verify AI blockchain enabled DAEOs.

## REFERENCES

Buldas, A., Kroonma, A., & Laanoja, R. (2013). Keyless signatures' infrastructure: how to build global distributed hash-trees. *In Secure IT systems: 18th Nordic conference, NordSec,* (pp. 313–320).

Deetman, S. (2016). *Bitcoin could consume as much electricity as Denmark by 2020.* Motherboard.

Fadilpašić, S., & Garlick, S. (2017). Coincheck Hack: the biggest theft in the history of the world. *Cryptonews.* January 26.

Franco, P. (2014). *Understanding bitcoin: Cryptography, engineering and economics* (p. 9). John Wiley & Sons.

Gartner. (2013). *Gartner says the internet of things installed base will grow to 26 billion units by 2020.* Retrieved May 14, 2018. http://www.gartner.com/newsroom/id/2636073.51.

Johnson, M. G. (2017). *Keyless signature infrastructure (KSI) overview.* Guardtime Publication.

Lawless, W. (2017). Artificial intelligence, block chain and redundancy. In *January 2018 Email Exchange with William Lawless.*

Levine, A. (2014). *Application specific, autonomous, self-bootstrapping consensus platforms. Retrieved from* https://bitsharestalk.org/index.php?topic=1854.

Mylrea, M. (2017). Smart energy-internet-of-things opportunities require smart treatment of legal, privacy and cybersecurity challenges. *The Journal of World Energy Law and Business,* 10(2), 147–158.

Mylrea, M., & Gourisetti, S. (2017). Blockchain: a path to grid modernization and cyber resiliency. In *North American power symposium.*

PWC Global Power and Utilities. (2017). *Blockchain opportunity for energy producers and consumers.*

Suberg, W. (2017). Alibaba deploys blockchain to secure health data in Chinese first. *The Cointelegraph.*

Tapscott, A. (2016). The blockchain revolution: how the technology behind bitcoin is changing money, business, and the world. *Portfolio.*

Trottier, L. Original-bitcoin, 2013. Retrieved on Github at https://github.com/trottier/original-bitcoin/blob/master/src/main.h#L795-L803.

Walch, A. (2017). *The path of the blockchain Lexicon (and the law) 36 Review of Banking & Financial Law 713.* University College London.

Zwanenburg, Jorn. "Cryptocurrency transaction fees: a beginner's guide. Invest in Blockchain, 6 Nov … "Moving averages: strategies". Investopedia, 2018. Retrieved from www.investopedia.com/university/movingaverage/movingaverages4.asp (14 May 2018).

## FURTHER READING

Mylrea, M., Gourisetti, S., Bishop, R., & Johnson, M. (2017). Keyless signature blockchain infrastructure: facilitating NERC CIP compliance and responding to evolving cyber threats and vulnerabilities to energy infrastructure. In *IEEE PES T&D conference and exposition.*

Pradhan, A., & Stevens, J. J. (2017). *Supply chains are racing to understand blockchain—what chief supply chain officers need to know.* Gartner.

# CHAPTER 13

# Compositional Models for Complex Systems

**Spencer Breiner\*, Ram D. Sriram\*, Eswaran Subrahmanian\*,†**
\*Information Technology Lab, National Institute of Standards and Technology, Gaithersburg, MD, United States
†Institute for Complex Engineered Systems, Carnegie Mellon University, Engineering and Public Policy, Pittsburgh, PA, United States

## 13.1 INTRODUCTION

In today's world, computation is reaching into everyday life at home and at work, driven by two major trends: artificial intelligence (AI) and the Internet of Things (IoT). We intend both terms to have a broad sense, AI to encompass more-or-less all data processing and IoT to cover any sensing or actuation in the physical world. Though in different ways, both of these offer some possibility for the substitution of human labor; AI for mental tasks and the IoT for physical ones. Of course we will be interested mostly in the augmentation of human performance, rather than its replacement, but either way these new capabilities invite us to rethink the design of systems and processes in nearly every domain.

The emergence of this vision for the future has raised a thicket of new trends and buzzwords: IoT, the Internet of everything, cyber-physical systems, sociotechnical systems, smart systems, complex systems, and systems of systems. The welter of terminology obscures the fact that all of these areas face the same fundamental problems regarding system representation, analysis, and synthesis.

This is not to suggest that there is no difference between these fields. Those building the IoT are necessarily concerned with flaky networks and low-power computing; cyber-physical systems need not be sociotechnical, and vice versa. However, we believe that the unique features of these fields obscure the most important issues at play and are outweighed by the an overall similarity. Moreover, many of the systems of interest cut across these artificial boundaries; an airplane checks most of the boxes above, and a hospital touches all of them.

With new promise comes new risk, and as we integrate these technologies into critical systems like health care, manufacturing, banking, and

*Artificial Intelligence for the Internet of Everything*
https://doi.org/10.1016/B978-0-12-817636-8.00013-2
**241**

the law, we need (warranted) confidence that these systems will perform as we expect them to. Traditionally we have relied on extensive testing to identify defects in engineered systems, but this is insufficient for hybrid computational physical systems.

First, AI systems often continue to learn and improve while in operation, so performance tomorrow may not be the same as it is today. Second, the space of input parameters for even a moderately complex IoT system is unworkably large, and the environmental interactions that lead to problems may be rare and unexpected. Worst of all, as we have seen with the Volkswagen emissions scandal (EPA United States Environmental Protection Agency, 2017), a combination of AI and IoT can support systems that actively evade testing measures.

One possible avenue for avoiding this problem is to import some of the formal methods of validation and verification (V&V) from computer science. Although this field has its own problems, as evidenced by a never-ending stream of vulnerabilities and malware, it also offers concrete approaches for dealing with some of the problems outlined above. Furthermore, failures in computer systems' V&V often turn on physical considerations, such as timing, suggesting that better integration between logical and physical analyses are needed on both sides.

We believe that formal methods from a branch of mathematics called category theory (CT) can help to bridge this divide. One reason is that CT methods have already been applied extensively to both computational systems (Barr & Wells, 1990; Fong, Spivak, & Tuyéras, 2017; Spivak, 2012) and physical ones (Baez & Fong, 2015; Baez & Pollard, 2017; Vagner, Spivak, & Lerman, 2015). Moreover, CT has demonstrated particular success in linking physical and computational analyses in the field of quantum computing (Coecke & Kissinger, 2017; Selinger, 2004). More generally, CT provides a generic theory of open and interconnected systems (Fong, Sobociński, & Rapisarda, 2016), offering a common conceptual space for mixing AI, IoT, and traditional processes.

The central feature of categorical structures is compositionality, the ability to build up complex systems by linking together simpler components. Given the range in the systems of interest we must understand "component" in the broadest sense, to include humans (as both subjects and actors) as well as physical entities and algorithms. Some components like IoT sensors and actuators require description at both levels, and humans also incorporate both physical and logical (and stochastic) behaviors. Furthermore, compositional methods lend themselves to a systems–of–systems approach, where a component at one level is a system in its own right regarded at a lower level of abstraction.

The organization or architecture of a system describes the interaction of these components along channels of energy, mass, and information. In a compositional system there is no escape from the issue of interdependence, where system behavior depends on both component specifications and the architecture that links them together. Although this may seem obvious, for example, if we hook the gas tank to the exhaust system in a car we won't go anywhere, it is still worth making explicit. After all, the whole point is that by arranging our system meaningfully we can achieve some benefit that couldn't be realized by the components in isolation!

Interdependence is neither good nor bad, it is merely adds to the complexity, though that complexity may obscure failure modes that were easier to discover in simpler systems. When those failures concern cardiology or search and rescue, that *is* bad. Better formal representations can help to clarify our thinking and identify problems before they arise. To borrow a phrase from programming, we prefer to catch errors at "compile time" (i.e., in design) rather than at "run time" (during operation).

Recursiveness in the engineering of complex systems is very well known, as most systems are transformed into nearly decomposable subsystems. Problem decomposition is used extensively in the design of engineered systems and in design support systems (Gorti, Gupta, Kim, Sriram, & Wong, 1998; Sangiovanni-Vincentelli, Damm, & Passerone, 2012; Simon, 1991). Decomposition is used to make the problem tractable to address complexity and also to choose of appropriate technology and existing components to address the needs of the designed system (Erens, 1996). These methods were extensively used in the simulation of the design of engineered products for composition of decomposed systems and components. Decisions on choices of decomposition are made at different levels to those of the components at the level of the leaves of the structure to compose a potentially viable system satisfying the global requirements and constraints. However, during the process of composition of the choices, there may be conflicts and undefined behavior of the composed systems leading to revision of choices or the requirements associated with the component. Supporting the design of complex systems would require a foundational environment that supports formal information structures and methods for decomposition and composition.

This chapter will develop some small examples of how we might apply CT-based analyses developed in computer science to analyze broader classes of engineered systems. Our approach, as previously mentioned, is that system design is a fundamentally recursive process, including a decompositional phase that identifies components and their requirements and a compositional phase of integration and testing. With this in mind we recall the theory functorial algebras and coalgebras, categorical datatypes for representing recursive structures based using labeled trees.

To fit our analysis to this approach, we must encode the architecture of a system into the labels of a tree. To this end we introduce a second class of categorical constructs called operads. Roughly speaking, an operad describes a class of possible architectures; for example, we might describe physical, logical, and hybrid systems using three different operads. The architectural rules in these worlds may be different since, for example, logical resources can be broadcast (one-to-many interaction) whereas physical ones cannot.

Based on these architectures we can assign various types of semantics to our system representations. To illustrate this point, we will give an example of logical semantics that captures the relationships between system and component requirements. This example can be seen as the prelude to the more sophisticated semantics that will be needed to describe other elements of the system-design process including models, designs, and testing procedures. We close with a discussion of how these representations can support and constrain new applications of AI at different levels of abstraction.

## 13.2 CHARACTERISTICS OF COMPLEX SYSTEMS

In this section we review some common features that we expect to find in contemporary complex systems. We will not attempt to define complexity here, and in fact caution against a reductive definition of the term. For example, some have equated complexity with heterogeneity, our first listed characteristic, but this is only one relevant axis of complexity (scale being another) (Mitchell, 2009). We do not demand that a given complex system display all of these features, though some will, but most are likely to exhibit at least one or two. In particular, any attempt to provide generic structures for system representations across a variety of domains and use-cases will need to be able to handle all of these considerations.

### 13.2.1 Heterogeneity of Components

In modern systems the component elements may include, at a minimum, human actors and subjects, "dumb" physical components, "smart" connected devices, and cloud services. This indicates that to understand, predict, or diagnose the behavior of such a system we may need to explore psychology, probability, dynamics, and logic. Moreover, each element has its own logic of interaction. Sensors can support many subscribers whereas most actuators allow only one operator (at a time); humans are unpredictable in ways both good and bad. There are also other, less obvious components in our systems such as logical resources like encryption keys and personal data, which must be regarded as components of our systems if we hope to enforce concerns like information security.

## 13.2.2 Open Interaction

A central feature of complex systems is that components are expected to interact, and through that interaction unlock value and efficiency. More specifically, components provide interfaces, both physical and logical, which may be coupled into a wide variety of different arrangements. Thus to understand the behavior of an IoT or AI system it is not enough to describe its components; we must also specify the architecture that wires those components together. In contrast to traditionally engineered systems, composition of modern systems will often be provisioned on an ad hoc basis in reaction the operational environment, sharpening the need for predictive tools for system behavior and security. For example, the conception and design of Smart Grid with distributed energy resources would require on-demand provisioning of electric power by tapping additional generation resources or by reducing demand in power-consuming devices to dynamically balance supply and demand.

## 13.2.3 Multiplicity of Perspectives

There is a tremendous range of viewpoints from which we may wish to consider a given system. Some of these are based on scale; an IoT system may range from a single individual (personal devices) to a building (HVAC) to a city or region (Smart Grid). This system-of-systems aspect of the IoT means that its local behavior may depend on any of these levels. Legal regulations introduce a new set of perspectives, including safety or privacy requirements as well as reporting for regulatory oversight. Organizationally and economically speaking, the user of a component may not be its owner, and these two actors may be connected through a third-party platform. Systems models must embed all of these individual perspectives, but should also allow for the integration of multiple perspectives in order to analyze interactions across multiple concerns (Subrahmanian, Westerberg, & Podnar, 1989).

### 13.2.4 Joint Cognition

Humans are nearly always components of complex systems, and we are obviously unique in our capabilities. Although we are sometimes passive subjects in a system, more often we play active roles ranging from sensing to actuation to control. Often, systems are most frustrating when they force us into passive roles rather than providing us with agency. The problem of automation has been shown to be lack of understanding of the system by the operators leading to errors pointing to problems in the design of such joint cognitive systems (Bainbridge, 1983; Norman, 1990). When we wish to design systems in which human actors are components, our representations must go beyond artifacts, to include models of human behavior. When humans (or other autonomous agents) participate in the control loop for a complex system, it is essential that we know which information should be suppressed, what should be shared, and how that information should be presented in context. Compared to machines, humans are slow and error prone, but without our flexibility and global understanding systems become brittle and liable to fail (Woods & Hollnagel, 2006).

## 13.3 SYSTEM DESIGN IS A RECURSIVE PROCESS

In this section we illustrate the well-known claim that engineering and design are fundamentally recursive processes. Although it is more obvious in systems of systems like the IoT, the claim is not specific to systems engineering. Rather, as was noted earlier, recursive features like problem decomposition have always been present in engineering, but for small projects they could be managed informally with human expertise. Regardless, it is the complexity of modern hybrid systems that forces us to acknowledge and understand this aspect of engineering and design theory.

An example helps to fix ideas. Suppose Alice is tasked with designing a heating, ventilation and air conditioning (HVAC) system satisfying various requirements (maintains set temperature ±1°C, cooling rate of 2°C/hour, etc.), the task and its requirements might come directly from the customer, or internally from another part of the design process.

Alice decomposes her system into four components: a heater, AC, thermometer, and a controller (Fig. 13.1). She designs the controller herself and locates an off-the-shelf thermometer that will meet her needs. Then (the recursive step!) she tasks Bob and Charlie with designing the heater and AC, respectively. Some of Alice's requirements can be passed directly to

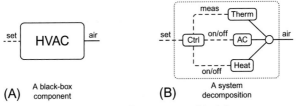

(A) A black-box component
(B) A system decomposition

**Fig. 13.1** Graphical representations of HVAC as a black-box component and as a system. (A) A black-box component; (B) a system decomposition.

Bob or Charlie (e.g., cooling rate to Charlie for the AC design). Other constraints will be generated by Alice in order to ensure that her control strategy meets the global requirements of the HVAC system, usually determined or justified by one or more models of the system.

This is a recursive process because Bob and Charlie are now in a position that is structurally similar to Alice's at the outset. Each is tasked with designing a certain system subject to a given set of requirements. Now Bob and Charlie proceed in exactly the same fashion that Alice did: decomposing their subsystems, realizing some components, and outsourcing other designs.

Eventually, this iterated series of decompositions must bottom out with a concrete implementation for each component. Bob and Charlie come back to Alice with completed designs for their components, which they have tested and verified against the requirements she gave them.

Now Alice must integrate the new AC and heater designs with her controller and the off-the-shelf thermometer she selected. Once this is done she performs her own tests to make sure that the resulting HVAC system meets the requirements that she was given. If all works as expected, she hands back the completed HVAC design to her customer or up the chain to the next level of system abstraction.

With this example in mind, we can give a rational reconstruction of the engineering design process.[1] We will use the language of systems, but nothing we say is specific to systems engineering as it is traditionally understood. One important thing to keep in mind is that words like "component" and "system" are context-relative: the whole point is that Alice's component *is* Bob's system. Something is a component when we treat it as a black box, and

---

[1] For now we will focus only on the constraint-satisfaction aspects of engineering, leaving aside optimization, though this could be added on top of the proposed framework. For a more detailed characterization of the design process from a comprehensive AI perspective see Tong and Sriram (1992).

a system when we open it up. Our reconstruction will also take seriously the sorts of graphical models that engineers like to draw.

A *boundary* is a context of interaction. Every boundary is characterized by one or more typed *state variables* that describe (the relevant aspects of) interactions at the boundary. The type system describing the state variables can be as complicated as we would like to make it. Here we will distinguish between physical and logical (digital) boundaries, indicated graphically by solid and dashed lines, respectively. Physical boundaries are typed by physical quantities such as the temperature and humidity of the air; logical boundaries are associated with datatypes such as integers, enumerations, lists, and matrices.

Every component or system is associated with an *interface*, which is just a collection of boundaries. For example, we can think of the thermometer as a component with two boundaries, one to measure the air temperature and a second to convey that information to the controller. The first is a physical quantity ($T_{air}$ : Temp) while the second is a data element ($T_{meas}$ : Float). In natural language we rarely mention boundaries and interfaces explicitly—we simply intuit that the controller takes information from the thermometer and uses it to direct the AC and heating units—but they are more likely to appear explicitly in graphical models like the one in Fig. 13.1B.

An interface defines a state space of all possible behaviors correlated across several boundaries; a *contract* for a component or system describes the subspace of desired or acceptable behaviors.[2] The thermometer's contract might stipulate that it is accurate to $\pm\frac{1}{2}^{\circ}$C:

$$|T_{meas} - T_{air}| < \frac{1}{2}^{\circ}C$$

More generally, we should recognize that most or all of these parameters may vary over time, so that constraints may be written in various temporal logics. The steady-state behavior requirement for the system (assuming no change in settings) could be rendered as:

$$\forall t_0 \, \exists t_1 \, \forall t_2 \left( t_2 > t_1 \Rightarrow |T_{air}^{@t_2} - T_{set}| \leq 1^{\circ}C \right)$$

---

[2] The use of contracts as defining interactions between components and actors has been explored in the context of agent task interactions through protocols (Smith, 1980) and more recently in the characterization of cyber-physical system design as contracts of behavior (Sangiovanni-Vincentelli et al., 2012). In our example we use a simplified version of contract for illustrative purposes.

Though the methods are rather sophisticated, we note that temporal considerations like these can be built directly into the type theory governing the state variables (see Schultz & Spivak, 2017).

**Definition 13.1** The input data to a recursive problem in engineering design consists of a set of typed state variables describing the boundaries of the desired system (the interface) and a set of logical statements (requirements) written in these variables (the contract).

The engineer or team assigned to such a problem has one of three options: to implement directly, to reject, or to decompose.

To implement directly, the engineer must provide a specific design that implements the given interface together with testing indicating that the design fulfills the assigned contract. A formal representation for either tests or designs is beyond the scope of this chapter, and will necessarily be quite complex. However, in the section on operads we will identify some affordances that are needed to support the composition of design representations.

Alternatively the engineer might reject the contract as infeasible. We can imagine different levels for rejection. *Local* infeasibility is an admission by the engineer that he or she cannot provide a design meeting the contract specification; in that case the component design may be reassigned to someone with more or different expertise. This stands in contrast to global infeasibility, where the engineer produces models or reasoning indicating that the contract *cannot* be satisfied, in which case the contract must be redesigned. Regardless, in the recursive structure of engineering it is up to the customer or a higher-level engineer to deal with rejection.

Finally, and most relevant here, the engineer may recursively decompose the problem. One first identifies a collection of subcomponents, along with interfaces, their types, and state spaces. Next, he/she must design a system architecture that specifies how these component interfaces line up with one another and the exterior boundaries. Finally, he/she should provide a contract on each component interface, as well as one or more models that indicate that the component contracts and the architecture together ensure that the system meets its own external contract. The engineer then passes the component interfaces and contracts to the next level of the recursion.

With either direct implementation or rejection, the recursive step is closed, but in decomposition we must wait for the recursive processes to return. There are a number of possibilities. First, one or more of the subdesign processes may reject the contract as infeasible. If the infeasibility is local, the component designs may be reassigned. If not, the decomposition (architecture and contracts) may need to be redesigned; this means that rejection in one component design may impact others.

Ideally, though, each subprocess will provide a component design as well as testing showing that the design meets its contract. The engineer must then integrate the components according to the architecture, and conduct his/her own testing on the resulting system. If it meets the contract, the aggregate design can be passed back to the customer or higher-level engineer.

If the system does not meet the contract, there is some chance that a component is malfunctioning, though this should have been caught in lower level testing. Otherwise, the engineer's model that justified the original decomposition must be deficient; now the engineer must refine the model. Using the refined model the engineer can produce a new decomposition and start the cycle anew, or decide that the original contract is infeasible and reject.

We may think of this description as an elaboration on the classic "V-model" of systems engineering, shown in Fig. 13.2. While the V-model captures the dual processes of first passing from requirements to design and then from design to operation, it is also misleading in a number of ways.

First of all, the representation as a V is too linear, suggesting a single design process rather than an iterative refinement into many; in reality the legs of the V should be replaced by trees. It also eliminates the recursive structure of the problem; system requirements may appear at the top-left leg of the V, but component requirements show up further down. Because the V squashes together parallel paths and different hierarchical levels in the design process, this hides the fact that different components may be

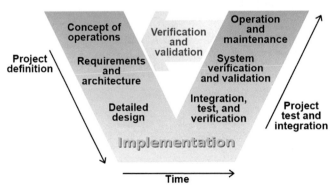

**Fig. 13.2** The V-model of systems engineering (Osborne, Brummond, Hart, Zarean, & Conger, 2005).

implemented at different levels of abstraction; the design process has many implementation vertices, and these occur at different levels of the decomposition tree. Finally, the V structure is also too linear in time, suppressing the back-and-forth interaction between layers resulting from contract rejection and redesign; a W might be better.

We have just given a generic, step-wise description of the engineering design process based prior characterizations (Gorti et al., 1998). In the next few sections we will show how the mathematics of CT provides a unified framework for describing (de)composable systems, supporting the complex representations needed to support this view of engineering.

## 13.4 INDUCTIVE DATATYPES AND ALGEBRAIC STRUCTURES

We have just given a semiformal model of system design as a recursive process. In order to make this account more precise, the next few sections will introduce some formal language and tools from CT. Here we discuss the theory of functorial algebras and inductive datatypes, which provides a uniform framework for analyzing compositional (algebraic) systems. These will provide the language that we need in order to structure our intuitive analysis from the previous section.

Generally speaking, algebra concerns mathematical structures with specified operations for combining or transforming their elements. In arithmetic, the operations are "plus" $(+)$ and "times" $(\times)$; in Boolean algebra the operations are "and" $(\wedge)$ and "or" $(\vee)$. An *algebraic signature* is a list of operations (and constants), and a *term* in the signature is any string that can be built up by applying these operations to constants, variables, and other terms. This allows us to iteratively build up more and more complicated terms:

$$\left.\begin{array}{r}3\\x\\y\\7\end{array}\right\} \Rightarrow \left\{\begin{array}{l}3+x\\3\times x\\y+7\\y\times 7\end{array}\right\} \Rightarrow \left\{\begin{array}{l}(3\times x)+(y+7)\\(3\times x)\times(y+7)\end{array}\right.$$

Any signature defines two important mathematical structures. First, there is the class of algebraic structures that implement the signature. In the case of arithmetic, this would be set $X$ together with two binary functions $+, \times: X \times X \to X$ (and probably elements $0, 1 \in X$). These include the usual number systems ($\mathbb{N}, \mathbb{R}$, etc.) as well as more complex structures like polynomials and matrices.

Second, the signature defines an inductive datatype, called the *term algebra*, which is constructed directly from the elements of the signature. *Structural recursion* describes a process for constructing a unique mapping from the term algebra to any other. To display the general pattern at work here we will walk through several examples, introducing some technical vocabulary as we go along.

The simplest imaginable signature is a single constant value $\{c\}$. An algebra for this signature is a *pointed set*, consisting of a set $X$ together with a chosen element $c^X \in X$. Because there are no operations to build up more complicated terms, the term algebra for this signature is just a singleton set $1 = \{c\}$ (which is also the chosen element). The (rather trivial) recursion property for these structures says that there is exactly one function $1 \to X$; it sends $c \mapsto c^X$. Similarly, the Boolean set $2 = \{\top, \bot\}$ and other enumerations can be constructed as term algebras for a signature with two or more constants.

Next consider a signature with one constant $c$ and one unary (one-place) operation $t$. We can think of an algebra for this signature as a discrete dynamical system (DDS); $X$ is the set of states, $c^X$ is the initial state, and $t^X$ is a transition function $X \to X$. Since we can apply $t$ repeatedly, the term algebra for this signature is isomorphic to the natural numbers:

| $\mathbb{N}$ | 0 | 1 | 2 | 3 | $\cdots$ |
|---|---|---|---|---|---|
| $\mathrm{Term}\{c,t\}$ | $c$ | $t(c)$ | $t(t(c))$ | $t(t(t(c)))$ | $\cdots$ |

The recursion principle for $\mathbb{N}$ rests on a more general notion of mappings between DDS. A *DDS homomorphism* is a function $h\colon X \to Y$ such that $h(c^X) = c^Y$ and $h(t^X(x)) = t^Y(h(x))$. We can represent these conditions graphically using commutative[3] diagrams:

Condition (i) just says that $h$ maps initial states to initial states. Condition (ii) says that we should get the same result if we transition in $X$ and then map across to $Y$, or if we map across first and then transition.

The recursion principle for $\mathbb{N}$ can then be stated as follows: there is exactly one DDS homomorphism from $\mathbb{N}$ into any DDS $X$. To see why, imagine constructing such a function. By (i), we have no

---

[3] A diagram *commutes* if any two directed paths between the same nodes yield the same result.

choice but to set $h(0) = c^X$. Once we have $h(0)$, condition (ii) tells us where to send 1:

$$h(1) = h(t(0|)) \overset{\text{(ii)}}{=} t^X(h(0)) = t^X(c^X)$$

Similarly, the value at 1 entails the value at 2, and so on, so that in general we have no choice but to set

$$h(n) = \overbrace{t^X(...t^X(t^X(c_X)...)}^{n \text{ times}}$$

We can tell a similar story about *controlled* DDS. These are structures in which we have a set of commands $A$, and can issue a command to the system at each timestep. This corresponds to a signature in which we have a constant (initial state) $c$ and several different transition functions $t_a$, one for each $a \in A$. A mapping must preserve the initial state as well as each of the controlled transitions.

The term algebra for controlled DDS is $\text{List}(A)$, the set of lists with entries from $A$. The "initial state" is just the empty list $\langle \rangle$, and the transition operations append elements of $A$ to the front of the list. Just as above, a homomorphism $h: \text{List}(A) \to X$ is completely determined by the controlled DDS constraints; for example,

$$\langle a_0, a_1, a_2 \rangle \mapsto t_{a_0}(t_{a_1}(t_{a_2}(c_X)))$$

Rather than treating each element of the signature individually, we can wrap everything together into one component. First, we use the Cartesian product to replace the individual mappings $t_a: X \to X$ with a single map $t: A \times X \to X$. We can also use a disjoint union to package together the transition map with the constant, so that entire controlled DDS is represented by a single map $\alpha: 1 + (A \times X) \to X$. Thus the construction $FX = 1 + (A \times X)$ encodes the signature of the algebraic theory.

Similarly, the mapping condition for controlled DDS homomorphisms is expressed by a single square:

$$
\begin{array}{ccc}
1 + (A \times X) & \xrightarrow{1+(A \times h)} & 1 + (A \times Y) \\
\alpha \downarrow & & \downarrow \beta \\
X & \xrightarrow{h} & Y
\end{array}
$$

Here we use the fact that $F$ is *functorial*. This means two things. First, $F$ can be applied to a function $h$ as well as to a set $X$, defining a new function $F(h): FX \to FY$; the definition (by cases) is easy, sending $c \mapsto c$ and $\langle a, x \rangle \mapsto \langle a, h(x) \rangle$.

Second, $F$ respects the composition of functions: if $h$ and $k$ are composable then $F(h \cdot k) = F(h) \cdot F(k)$. Using this observation, we can show that controlled DDS mappings (and other algebraic mappings) are closed under composition; if $h$ and $k$ satisfy the DDS mapping condition, then so does the composite $h \cdot k$:

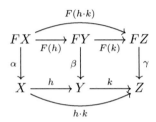

$$F(h \cdot k) \cdot \gamma = F(h) \cdot F(k) \cdot \gamma = F(h) \cdot \beta \cdot k = \alpha \cdot (h \cdot k)$$

DDS are a bit atypical for algebraic structures because they contain only constants and unary operations. A more familiar example might involve a signature with one constant $c$ and one binary operation $- \cdot -$ (written using infix notation, sometimes with a subscript to emphasize the algebra $X$). We can represent this signature using a polynomial (as opposed to linear) functor $FX = 1 + X^2$. An algebra homomorphism $h: X \to Y$ preserves the constant and the operation:

$$h(c^X) = c^Y \quad h(x \underset{X}{\cdot} x') = h(x) \underset{Y}{\cdot} h(x')$$

The inductive type associated with this signature is the set of binary trees. The constant $c$ is a tree consisting of a single leaf; the composition operation $t \wedge t'$ creates a new tree in which $t$ and $t'$ are the left and right subtrees, respectively. Compare the algebraic specification of a binary tree with the usual graphical representation below:

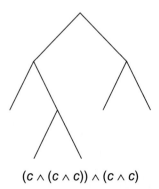

$$(c \wedge (c \wedge c)) \wedge (c \wedge c)$$

Of course, there are many other sorts of trees, and all of these can be realized as term algebras. A tree with ternary branching is associated with the functor $FX = 1 + X^3$. One that allows either binary or ternary branching corresponds to $FX = 1 + X^2 + X^3$. One allowing arbitrary branching corresponds to the functor $FX = \text{List}(X)$, which can be described not as a polynomial but as an infinite series $FX = 1 + X + X^2 + \cdots$.

We can also introduce labeling on our trees. In order to label the leaves of a binary tree, replace the unit type 1 by a label set $A$: $FX = A + X^2$. To add a different set of labels to the nodes, add a coefficient to the quadratic term of the polynomial: $FX = A + B \times X^2$. For example, arithmetic terms (arbitrary numeric constants but no variables) form the inductive data structure associated with the functor $FX = \mathbb{N} + \{+, \times\} \times X^2$. This encodes the familiar representation of algebraic terms as trees:

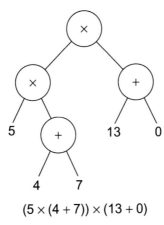

$$(5 \times (4 + 7)) \times (13 + 0)$$

Though we usually think of this term as the description of a number, it makes just as much sense in other contexts like polynomials and matrices where we can interpret the 0, 1, +, and ×. This is the content of structural recursion for the signature of arithmetic.

The general pattern demonstrated in these examples is captured in the following sequence of abstract definitions.

### Definition 13.2
1. An *algebraic signature* is a functor $F$: **Sets** $\rightarrow$ **Sets**.
2. An *algebra* for $F$ is a set $X$ together with a function $\alpha$: $FX \rightarrow X$.
3. An $F$-algebra *homomorphism* $\langle X, \alpha \rangle \rightarrow \langle Y, \beta \rangle$ is a function $h$: $X \rightarrow Y$ making the following square commute:

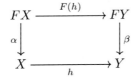

4. There is a canonical algebra $T$, called the *term algebra*, whose elements are constructed iteratively from the operations of the signature.

5. *Structural recursion* allows us to interpret a term $t \in T$ relative to any algebra $X$, defining a unique $F$-algebra homomorphism $T \to X$.

$F$-algebras provide a uniform framework for representing the operations of an algebraic theory; however, they are not sufficient to capture the axioms that govern these operations. These, too, can be incorporated into the categorical formalism, using more sophisticated structures called *monads*. The topic is beyond the scope of this chapter, but see Awodey (2010) for details.

## 13.5 COALGEBRA AND INFINITE DATATYPES

In the previous section we introduced a fairly elaborate categorical framework for governing compositional (algebraic) structures. One of the advantages of the categorical approach is that it helps to identify potential extensions and generalizations of our naive intuition. One particularly fertile avenue for such generalizations is to "turn the arrows around."

In CT, "co–" means "reversed." Any categorical concept can be dualized to define a related coconcept; just turn around all the arrows. Proofs can also be reversed, allowing us to port any theorem in the original context to a dual theorem for the new structures. A typical example involves the Cartesian product and the coproduct (disjoint union), mentioned informally in the last section. Formally, these can be defined in terms of dual construction principles for arrows into (out of) the (co)product:

$$\text{Product}\begin{cases} f : Z \to X \times Y & \overset{\text{equivalent}}{\rightsquigarrow} & f_1 : Z \to X \\ & & f_2 : Z \to Y \end{cases}$$

$$\text{Coproduct}\begin{cases} g : X + Y \to Z & \overset{\text{equivalent}}{\leftsquigarrow} & g_1 : X \to Z \\ & & g_2 : Y \to Z \end{cases}$$

We can use the same sort of reasoning to identify the theory of coalgebras and coinductive data structures. As before, the theory of coalgebra is parameterized by a functor $F$ which describes a signature. We will use the same set of examples as above to show how things change when we flip around the arrows.

If an algebra is a function $\alpha : FX \to X$, then a coalgebra should be a function $\kappa : X \to FX$. When $FX = 1 + X$, it is not hard to show that a coalgebra is the same as a partial function $X \supseteq S \overset{p}{\to} X$. To translate between the two viewpoints we let $\kappa$ equal $p$ wherever $p$ is defined, and send everything else to $c \in 1$.

There is also a dynamical interpretation for partial functions. We can think of $\kappa$ as a DDS with termination (but without an initial state). When we apply $\kappa$ to a state $x$ it will either land in $X$ or map to $c$; the first case is a state transition, the second termination. We can continue to apply $\kappa$ until the orbit leaves $X$, or it may go on forever.

From this we define the *lifetime* of an element $x \in X$:

$$\text{lifetime}(x) := \inf_n \kappa^n(x) \notin X$$

The lifetime counts how many $\kappa$-steps it takes for $x$ to exit the domain of definition; however, there is also the possibility that $x$ may *never* leave $X$ (e.g., fixed points and cycles), so the lifetime takes values in the extended natural numbers $\overline{\mathbb{N}} = \mathbb{N} + \{\infty\}$.

$\overline{\mathbb{N}}$ is, of course, the coinductive datatype associated with $F$, and the presence of $\infty$ hints at a general theme: coinductive datatypes often represent potentially infinite behaviors. Whereas inductive datatypes were initial— every algebra receives a unique map *out of* the inductive algebra— coinductive structures are terminal: every coalgebra maps *into* a coinductive structure. In particular, the lifetime is the unique coalgebra homomorphism $X \to \overline{\mathbb{N}}$.

Next, consider the functor $FX = 1 + A \times X$; we can think of a coalgebra $\kappa: X \to FX$ as a dynamical system with termination which, additionally, emits a readout or observation from $A$ at each timestep. Indeed, either $\kappa(x) = c$ (termination) or $\kappa(x) = \langle a, x' \rangle$, corresponding to a transition $x \mapsto x'$ together with the observation $a$.

When we apply $\kappa$ repeatedly, this generates a sequence of elements from $A$ in addition to the usual orbit through $X$. If the orbit eventually terminates we get a list of $A$'s; otherwise, an infinite stream. From this one can show that the coinductive datatype for $F$ is the set of (finite or infinite) streams from $A$. The unique coalgebra homomorphism $X \to \text{Stream}(A)$ sends each state in $X$ to its observable behavior in $A$.

The inductive algebra for the natural numbers dualizes to the extended naturals. The inductive algebra for lists dualizes to streams. From these two examples we might expect (correctly) that the algebra of binary trees will dualize to a coalgebra of infinite trees.

We would like to think the elements of a coalgebra $\kappa: X \to 1 + X^2$ in terms of decomposable systems of components. When $\kappa(x) = c$, the "system" $x$ is a single-atomic component. Otherwise, $\kappa(x) = \langle x', x'' \rangle$ defines a decomposition of the system $x$ into two (hopefully) simpler components $x'$ and $x''$, which may themselves be decomposable systems. However, these decompositions may never bottom out in atomic components. Indeed, any set has a copying coalgebra defined by $\kappa(x) = \langle x, x \rangle$, and obviously this will never terminate.

Thus in this context corecursion associates each element $x$ with a (potentially) infinite binary tree. If $\kappa(x) = c$ then $x$ maps to the minimal tree consisting of a single leaf. Otherwise $\kappa(x) = \langle x', x'' \rangle$, and we send $x$ to the binary tree whose left subtree is $\kappa(x')$ and whose right is $\kappa(x'')$. Just as we did for algebras, we can vary the details of the functor $F$ in order to allow for different labelings and branching behaviors.

The construction may seem circular, in the copy coalgebra our definition says that $\kappa(x) := \kappa(x) \wedge \kappa(x)$, but in computer science is it common to use fixed-point equations like these to characterize infinite structures. This is no different in principle from defining the infinite element of $\overline{\mathbb{N}}$ as a fixed point of the predecessor function: $\mathrm{pred}(\infty) = \infty$.

Algebra and coalgebra provide us with a flexible, uniform language based on labeled trees for representing finite and infinite recursive structures. If engineering is a recursive process, we should be able to represent it in this framework. The next step is to decide: what are the labels?

## 13.6 OPERADS AS COMPOSITIONAL ARCHITECTURES

In our model of engineering, the (co)recursive step occurs when an engineer receives a contract for a component, then decomposes the problem into a set of subcomponent contracts linked by an architecture. In later stages, we use the same architectures to structure the integration of component designs into systems. This suggests an algebra of designs, and a coalgebra of contracts.

The two processes are linked by the architectures that structure each level of (de)composition, and when we represent the situation (co)recursively we can think of these architectures as the labels of the associated trees. However, note that these labels must do a lot of work. They encode *all* of the information content specific to a given system or design. Given both the breadth and depth of engineering across many fields, this will necessarily require a great deal of flexibility and expressivity.

To this end we introduce another class of categorical constructs, known as *operads*, which provide a very general framework for representing system/component architectures.

One of the central features of the operadic approach is a firm distinction between syntax and semantics. Syntax describes the form of the system, its decomposition into components and the interconnections between them.

Importantly, the formal syntax of an operad can often be presented graphically, providing support for the intuitive architectural diagrams that engineers already draw.

Operad semantics attach coherent meanings to the components and interactions declared in the syntax. Here we will focus on the logical semantics underlying contracts, but operads can be interpreted in many other contexts including dynamical systems, computational logic, and probability. The ability to attach different models and different kinds of models to the same underlying architecture provides some of the power and flexibility that will be needed to provide a good compositional representation for the other engineering elements like designs, tests, and models.

Formally, an operad has two types of elements: *objects* and *operations*. Objects describe (the types of) component and system boundaries. For us, these will be the interfaces (sets of typed boundaries) found in the model. The HVAC component shown in Fig. 13.1A is a typical example, defined by the pair of boundaries:

$$HVAC = \{settings, air\}$$

The decomposition in Fig. 13.1B involves five interfaces: four for the interior components and one for the exterior system boundary. In some examples, like the one here, every component may have its own unique interface; in others, such as electrical circuits, all boundaries may have the same type (i.e., wires).

The rest of the information in an architecture diagram, which we can think of as a set of *interactions*, is encoded in the operations of the operad. Each interaction involves two or more boundaries that must have the same type, but other than this we are essentially free to draw whatever sort of diagrams we would like. We can allow different classes of interaction, such as the logical/physical distinction (solid and dashed lines) in Fig. 13.1B. Our example uses undirected interactions, but we can add in oriented edges. Graphs are restricted to binary interactions, but more general structures called hypergraphs allow for interaction between several parties, including wires that split and recombine. However, there is a catch: the more structure we introduce into the syntax of our operations, the more is required to interpret these diagrams semantically.

The key feature of operations is that they can be composed; in diagrammatic syntax, this usually involves pasting component decompositions into system decompositions, in order to obtain new decompositions across multiple levels of abstraction. For example, we might represent the AC as a controlled power source, a compressor, and a fan, and the heater as a boiler together with a collection of radiators. Each of these component decompositions could be represented graphically, and by substituting those decompositions into Fig. 13.1B we would get a new decomposition of the HVAC system at a finer level of granularity.

This composition is required to satisfy an important technical condition called associativity, which concerns threefold decompositions. Notationally, we represent an architecture as a many—one relationship $d: C_1, \ldots, C_n \xrightarrow{c} S$ or, more compactly, $d: \overline{C_i} \to S$. This associates the interior interfaces $C_i$ with the exterior interface $S$.

Now, suppose that we further decompose each component $C_i$ into subcomponents $K_{ij}$, which are linked by a family of subarchitectures $c_i: \overline{K_{ij}} \to C_i$. Graphically, the system boundary of $c_i$ matches one of the component boundaries in $d$; composition in the operad corresponds to pasting the former into the latter, yielding a decomposition of $S$ into the subsubcomponents $K_{ij}$:

$$\overline{c_i} \cdot d = (c_1, \ldots, c_n) \cdot d: \overline{K_{ij}} = K_{11}, \ldots, K_{nm} \to S$$

Now, given a third layer of decompositions $b_{ij}: \overline{L_{ijk}} \to K_{ij}$ we can ostensibly relate $S$ to $L_{ijk}$ in two different ways; associativity demands that these should coincide:

$$\overline{(\overline{b_{ij}} \cdot c_i)} \cdot d = \overline{b_{ij}} \cdot (\overline{c_i} \cdot d)$$

In other words, we could either combine the descriptions of the first and second layers, and then insert the third layer, or vice versa combine the second-layer components with the third layer individually and then incorporate the results into the first layer. One of the reasons diagrammatic syntax is so useful for operads is that this condition is automatically satisfied by graphical substitution.

Once we have an operad to provide the syntax for our architectures, we can use it to structure the semantics of system models. First, we need a semantic context like dynamics, probability, or computation. The breadth of semantics for operads is a second element supporting the breadth of engineering applications. To give an idea of how this works, we will represent contracts on the system using logical semantics.

To provide logical semantics for an operad we must first associate each object with a set of possible states or instances. For us, this state space is defined by the list of boundary parameters and their types; the state space of the interface is the product of parameter spaces for each parameter of each boundary of the interface. In a simplistic model, a window boundary might define a state space `Bool×Temp×Temp`, where the first parameter defines whether the window is open or closed, and the last two define the temperatures inside and outside the window, respectively. Sometimes, we may also wish to include plausibility constraints on the state space; for example, we might demand that when the window is open, then $T_{in} = T_{out}$.

An operation is a decomposition of the system into components and boundaries. This decomposition imposes constraints between the states of component interfaces as well as the system boundaries. To define logical semantics for an operation, we form the joint state space of all component and system interfaces and identify which joint states can possibly be satisfied given the architecture. In the example from Fig. 13.1B, the joint state space might look like:

$$\overbrace{\left(\text{Float}_{sys} \times \text{Temp}_{sys}\right)}^{\text{HVAC system}} \times \overbrace{\left(\text{Float}_{read} \times \text{Temp}_{therm}\right)}^{\text{Therm component}}$$

$$\times \overbrace{\left(\text{Bool}_{AC} \times \text{Temp}_{AC}\right)}^{\text{AC component}} \times \overbrace{\left(\text{Bool}_{heat} \times \text{Temp}_{heat}\right)}^{\text{Heat component}}$$

$$\times \overbrace{\left(\text{Float}_{set} \times \text{Float}_{meas} \times \text{Bool}_{cool} \times \text{Bool}_{warm}\right)}^{\text{Ctrl component}}$$

The specific architecture then defines a relation over this state space. Usually, this relation just couples together variables that are linked by an interaction in the diagram. Here, we would have:

$$\left(F_{sys} = F_{set}\right) \wedge \left(F_{meas} = F_{read}\right) \wedge \left(B_{warm} = B_{heat}\right)$$

$$\wedge \left(B_{cool} = B_{AC}\right) \wedge \left(T_{sys} = T_{therm} = T_{AC} = T_{heat}\right)$$

Some interactions, especially those governing interactions between three or more boundaries, may require more sophistication. In the context of electrical circuits, voltages across a bus are equal but currents add. In our example, the temperature of the air is equal at all boundaries (assuming mixing), but dynamical quantities like the energy input at an air boundary would require more sophistication.

Recall that in addition to an architecture, the decomposition phase produces a contract for each component, which we will write with double brackets $[\![C]\!] \subseteq \text{State}(C)$. Analogously, we may write $[\![d]\!]$ for the constraint associated with an architecture $d$. The requisite property of a valid decomposition is that the component contracts together with the architecture entail the system contract, which we may now write:

$$[\![d]\!] \wedge [\![C_1]\!] \wedge \cdots \wedge [\![C_n]\!] \vdash [\![S]\!]$$

In addition to assigning an interpretation to each component of the operad, one must also ensure that these interpretations are coherent with respect to composition. For contracts this is fairly straightforward. Composing $d$ with a family of subdecompositions $e_i : \overline{K_{ij}} \to C_i$, we get the resulting constraint by taking a conjunction of all the constraints in the decomposition:

$$[\![(e_1, \ldots, e_n) \cdot d]\!] := [\![e_1]\!] \wedge \cdots \wedge [\![e_n]\!] \wedge [\![d]\!]$$

One version of the cut rule from logic says that if $A$ and $B$ entail $C$, while $C$ and $D$ entail $E$, then $A$, $B$, and $D$ together also entail $E$. Using a multi-argument generalization of this rule we can easily show that the leaf conditions $[\![K_{ij}]\!]$ together with the constraints $[\![e_i]\!]$ and $[\![d]\!]$ suffice to entail the system contract:

$$\cfrac{[\![e_i]\!] \wedge \left( \bigwedge_j [\![K_{ij}]\!] \right) \vdash [\![C_i]\!] \qquad [\![d]\!] \wedge \left( \bigwedge_i [\![C_i]\!] \right) \vdash [\![S]\!]}{[\![d]\!] \wedge \left( \bigwedge_i [\![e_i]\!] \wedge \left( \bigwedge_j [\![K_{ij}]\!] \right) \right) \vdash [\![S]\!]}$$

To summarize, contract semantics on an operad of architectures are defined by:

| Syntax | Semantics |
| --- | --- |
| Component<br>$C$ | State($C$)<br>$[\![C]\!] \subseteq \mathrm{State}(C)$ |
| Architecture<br>$d : \overline{C_i} \to S$ | $[\![d]\!] \subseteq \mathrm{State}(S) \times \prod_i \mathrm{State}(C_i)$<br>$[\![d]\!] \wedge [\![C_1]\!] \wedge \cdots \wedge [\![C_n]\!] \vdash [\![S]\!]$ |

Similarly, we should be able to produce design semantics for the decomposition operad, but producing even a toy version of such a semantic theory is a substantial project, beyond the scope of this chapter. At least in part this is because designs are multimodal: at a minimum they must incorporate both geometry and composition for physical components, code, and protocols for logical components, and assembly and installation procedures for both. Nonetheless, a formalization of the design process using algebras and operads sets the stage and clarifies the requirements for such an undertaking.

## 13.7 ARCHITECTURES FOR LEARNING

In this section we sketch an example of how the formalization of system representation through compositional architectures can provide a platform for both the application and the management of AI techniques.

The bread and butter of contemporary AI is the automation of specific information-processing tasks, such as image classification or voice transcription. There are already many successful applications of such methods, and these will only continue to improve with new methods and more powerful devices.

However, the application of these methods in complex systems is still relatively inflexible. Training data for the problem must be collected and wrangled into a form appropriate for AI algorithms. The information processing that connects AI to applications is usually done by hand on an ad hoc basis. What is required here is not new learning methods per se, but rather methods for more easily and efficiently specifying learning problems and integrating their results.

System architectures can help with this by explicitly representing the state parameters of the system and clustering them in component decompositions. Properly implemented, this could allow for the automatic generation of learning problem specifications based on available parameters. For example, the state space and the loss function for the control process in Fig. 13.1B can be easily extracted from the parameters of the settings, measured temperature, and activity of the heater and AC, and the stream of historical data can be organized along the same lines.

This is an object-level application: we want to use AI to solve a problem inside our system. Architectures also offer up new possibilities for metalevel applications: using AI to solve problems *about* our system.

Ad hoc system design and provisioning is a good example. In networked systems like the IoT, we expect to have an infrastructure of devices, data, services, and human and organizational actors available for commission; we must assemble a system from these pieces to achieve a stated goal within specified constraints. The size and diversity of the IoT ecosystem will ensure that humans cannot easily design such systems, especially given that many systems will be designed for one-off uses with on-the-fly provisioning.

This means that we will require, at a minimum, substantial artificial assistance in IoT system design. Whereas before, the state space for a learning problem could be extracted from a given architecture, now the search is over the architectures themselves. In this chapter we discussed the logical semantics of contracts; one can also interpret operads in terms of dynamical and stochastic systems, allowing us to build rich semantic representations of component capabilities into the learning problem.

Another point of contact concerns the multiplicity of perspectives discussed in Section 13.2. AI systems may interact, especially across scales, so that the parameters of one learning problem may be determined as the output of another. These interactions go both ways, with top–down modifications to operating parameters at lower levels (e.g., peak use incentives for electricity consumption) and bottom–up prediction for aggregate systems (e.g., monitoring expected consumption).

We can also use architectures to document and manage our applications of AI. Any learning algorithm is itself a system, and we can use compositional architectures to describe it. Just as they did for more general systems, these provide a generic representation of algorithms, which is nonetheless flexible enough to specialize for any particular learning problem. Furthermore, recent research indicates that some AI algorithms are themselves compositional, giving a functorial analysis of the method of backpropagation (Fong et al., 2017). This could allow for more modular AI architectures, in which certain components of an AI system can be swapped in and out without relearning the entire model.

By clarifying the interactions between learning agents, humans, and other system processes, this documentation can be especially useful when we want to integrate learning processes and learned models into larger systems that already exist, especially those involving joint cognitive systems. Fig. 13.3 shows several examples of compositional *process* architectures, in which a process is decomposed into subprocesses. In this context, the boundaries between components can be regarded as input/output resources passed between the subprocesses. As before, we represent physical resources with solid lines and informational resources (data) by dashed line, noting that the latter can be copied whereas the former cannot.

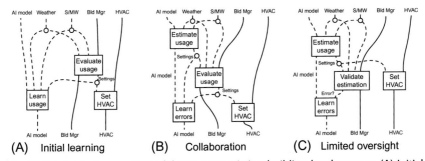

**Fig. 13.3** Introducing an AI model into a preexisting building-level process. (A) Initial learning; (B) collaboration; and (C) limited oversight.

In this example we consider an interaction between our hypothetical HVAC system from Fig. 13.1, a human manager and an AI model learning to control its settings. We model the introduction of a model into a preexisting human-led process, documenting different phases of the transition. More specifically, the HVAC system controls its own output on a minute-to-minute level based on a control loop internal to the system; here we consider the day-to-day, building-level process of setting those control parameters.

Initially, all decisions are made by the building manager, who evaluates likely usage each day based on two pieces of information: weather predictions and power costs. Based on these, the manager adjusts the settings of the HVAC system, which might require powering certain system components up or down or involve strategies such as preconditioning building temperatures during periods of low energy demand.

Now we would like to introduce an AI controller to take over these decisions from the building manager. In the first phase (Fig. 13.3A) all decisions are made by the manager, as before, and the AI model participates only as a passive learner. We imagine an online learning system, which trains and updates as new data becomes available, so both the inputs (weather, costs) and outputs (HVAC settings) of the manager's decisions are copied and fed into the learning algorithm, modifying the parameters of the AI model. Of course, if historical data exists this can be used to provide initial training, but we should expect the system to correct itself as errors arise.

In the second phase, the AI model has improved to the point that it can provide useful recommendations. Now these can be given to the building manager alongside the weather and economic data to help inform his/her decisions. These are reported back to the AI model so that it may continue to update its parameters, especially when its estimate does not match the final decision. In addition to catching errors, this phase is also crucial for building human trust in the system.

In the third phase, the AI model has been validated sufficiently to allow it to control the settings directly, having performed successfully for some time in the second phase. We still send the model's decisions to the manager for oversight, and report any errors back to the model, but this should now be regarded as an exceptional situation rather than the norm.

In most cases, of course, HVAC system settings are low-stakes decisions and errors are not too costly, but the same process logic applies when we introduce nearly any AI system into existing human-driven processes. For more safety-critical systems, we can use the same sort of contract semantics developed in the previous section to describe process requirements.

In particular, notice that all three diagrams have the same inputs and outputs; since they share the same interface, they may participate in the same contracts. Thus, at a higher level, we might place restrictions on the overall process, such as limiting the overall energy costs or mandating certain situational responses, and we can analyze each of the three phases to ensure that they meet these goals. This ensures that we can modify the low-level process without impacting higher-level performance. With more sophisticated semantics bringing in probability or temporality we could also begin to analyze questions like *when* we should shift from one phase to the next.

This gives an indication of some of the ways that better system representations arising in CT can support the application of AI in many contexts. We can use AI to address object-level problems of the system, thinking of AI models as just another component. At the same time, we can use AI to address metalevel problems of the system, assisting in design and decomposition decisions. We can use CT representations to document AI algorithms, both internally and in their interaction with other system processes. By providing a precise, technical language for expressing and analyzing system relationships, CT can help to structure the use of AI across a wide range of contexts and applications.

## 13.8 CONCLUSION

In this chapter we have argued that new, more expressive representations are needed to support the design, engineering, and analysis of modern complex systems, and we have suggested that the mathematical field of CT can provide them. We have seen how CT provides a uniform approach to defining and studying (de)compositional systems using algebra and coalgebra, and we have used this methodology to model the fundamentally recursive character of engineering design. Combined with the use of operads for modeling system architectures, we defined a formal theory of hierarchical requirements engineering via contracts and analyzed the process of integrating AI into existing workflows.

Further development is hampered by a widespread view of CT as exceedingly and unnecessarily abstract. This is certainly an obstacle for new-comers to the field, but this generality is necessary, as it allows for rich connections to formal methods in mathematics, physics, and computer science. To see how the basic vocabulary of CT can be specialized to a variety of specific domains, see Table 13.1.

CT already provides well-understood connections with many of these domains. Indeed, it is a *lingua franca* allowing us to treat the range of these subjects using the same set of constructions, based on and extended from the basic vocabulary of objects and arrows.

For example, process diagrams like those in Fig. 13.3 arise in both computation (Pavlovic, 2013) and quantum mechanics (Penrose, 1971), thereby providing a common language for the study of quantum computing (Coecke & Kissinger, 2017). A recent flurry of research has shown that the same methods can be applied to a wide variety of subjects, ranging from electrical engineering (Baez & Fong, 2015) to natural language processing (Coecke, Sadrzadeh, & Clark, 2010).

This base of existing theory means that CT can provide a suitable modeling formalism to capture the breadth of heterogeneous components in complex systems like IoT. Furthermore, connections between CT and formal logic mean that we can think of certain categorical models (called *sketches*) as logical theories, providing a powerful and expressive approach to knowledge representation, which subsumes both database structures and ontologies (Spivak, 2014). Just like the system architectures discussed in this

**Table 13.1** Interpretations of Categorical Language in a Variety of Domains

| In … | The Objects Are | And the Operations Are |
|---|---|---|
| Programming | Datatypes | Computable functions |
| Physics | Configurations | Dynamical equations |
| Databases | Tables | Foreign keys |
| Logic | Propositions | Proofs |
| Probability | Probability spaces | Stochastic kernels |
| Data science | Vector spaces | Matrices/tensors |

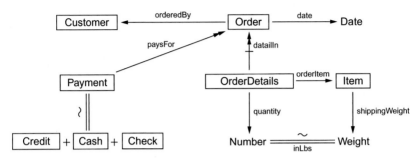

**Fig. 13.4** A categorical model in the style of a unified modeling language class diagram (Breiner, Padi, et al., 2017).

chapter, sketches can be presented graphically, allowing us to design mathematical models using techniques that are very similar to existing methods like class diagrams in the Systems Modeling Language. See Fig. 13.4 for an example and Breiner, Padi, Subrahmanian, and Sriram (2017) for a detailed exposition.

Another crucial characteristic of CT for systems modeling is its self-referentiality. We can think of categories $\mathbb{C}$ and $\mathbb{D}$ themselves as (informational) resources, and functors as processes that operate on them, providing concrete translations between different information representations. This allows us to bridge different information models, providing the means to manage and integrate the many perspectives found in any complex system.

Sometimes these transformations will be bidirectional, providing a dictionary between one and the other; this could already be quite useful for data wrangling. More interesting, though, are cases in which the transformation cannot be reversed. In Breiner, Subrahmanian, and Jones (2017) the authors showed that functors can be used to relate architectures at different levels of abstraction, so that one category gives a functional refinement of another. This allowed us to give a unified approach to process modeling from the production line to the factory to the global supply chain.

In other cases, $\mathbb{C}$ might contain additional information that must be projected out in the passage to $\mathbb{D}$. This might be the case, for example, if $\mathbb{D}$ contains a simple process model that is extended in $\mathbb{C}$ to include security concerns by explicitly representing resources like encryption keys.

Finally, we note that the burden of joint cognition is mitigated somewhat by the diagrammatic character of CT. Unlike most formal disciplines, CT uses diagrams extensively as tools for simplifying complex arguments. We have already seen the use of trees and graphs to model different elements of systems processes and configurations. These are powerful enough to support calculations in quantum mechanics but can be read as easily as a flowchart. The logical sketches mentioned above can be presented through box-and-arrow diagrams that are not much different from unified modeling language class diagrams (Breiner, Padi, et al., 2017). These graphical representations support the way that humans think and understand, without sacrificing the formal mathematical character that is needed for machine interaction.

The speed and independence of contemporary technologies force us to reconsider traditional approaches in engineering, and also encourage us to adopt techniques that have been fruitful in the design and analysis of computational systems. CT provides a powerful toolbox of such techniques, with deep connections to other formal methods, structured representations for compositional systems, structured mappings relating these representations, and a graphical approach that supports human-machine interaction. Although CT is generally regarded as an abstract area of pure mathematics, in recent years the field of *applied* CT has begun to grow. This burgeoning field offers a wealth of potential applications to help tame the complexity of the modern world.

## DISCLAIMER

Commercial products are identified in this chapter to adequately specify the material. This does not imply recommendation or endorsement by the National Institute of Standards and Technology, nor does it imply the materials identified are necessarily the best available for the purpose.

## REFERENCES

Awodey, S. (2010). *Category theory*. Oxford: Oxford University Press.

Baez, J. C., & Fong, B. (2015). A compositional framework for passive linear networks. arXiv preprint arXiv:1504.05625.

Baez, J. C., & Pollard, B. S. (2017). A compositional framework for reaction networks. *Reviews in Mathematical Physics, 29*(9), 1750028.

Bainbridge, L. (1983). Ironies of automation. In *Analysis, design and evaluation of man–machine systems 1982* (pp. 129–135). Amsterdam: Elsevier.

Barr, M., & Wells, C. (1990). *Category theory for computing science: Vol. 49.* New York: Prentice Hall.

Breiner, S., Padi, S., Subrahmanian, E., & Sriram, R. (2017). *Deconstructing uml, part 1: The class diagram.* Available by request: spencer.breiner@nist.gov.

Breiner, S., Subrahmanian, E., & Jones, A. (2017). *Categorical models for process planning.* Available by request: spencer.breiner@nist.gov.

Coecke, B., & Kissinger, A. (2017). *Picturing quantum processes.* Cambridge: Cambridge University Press.

Coecke, B., Sadrzadeh, M., & Clark, S. (2010). *Mathematical foundations for a compositional distributional model of meaning*. arXiv preprint arXiv:1003.4394.

EPA United States Environmental Protection Agency (2017). *Volkswagen clean air act civil settlement*. Available from: https://www.epa.gov/enforcement/volkswagen-clean-air-act-civil-settlement. Accessed 1 January 2018.

Erens, F. -J. (1996). *The synthesis of variety (Dissertation)*. Einhoven University of Technology.

Fong, B., Sobociński, P., & Rapisarda, P. (2016). A categorical approach to open and interconnected dynamical systems. In *Proceedings of the 31st Annual ACM/IEEE Symposium on Logic in Computer Science* (pp. 495–504).

Fong, B., Spivak, D. I., & Tuyéras, R. (2017). Backprop as functor: A compositional perspective on supervised learning. arXiv preprint arXiv:1711.10455.

Gorti, S. R., Gupta, A., Kim, G. J., Sriram, R. D., & Wong, A. (1998). An object-oriented representation for product and design processes. *Computer-Aided Design, 30*(7), 489–501.

Mitchell, M. (2009). *Complexity: A guided tour*. Oxford: Oxford University Press.

Norman, D. A. (1990). The 'problem' with automation: inappropriate feedback and interaction, not 'over-automation'. *Philosophical Transactions of the Royal Society of London, Series B: Biological Sciences, 327*(1241), 585–593.

Osborne, L. F., Brummond, J., Hart, R., Zarean, M., & Conger, S. M. (2005). *Clarus: Concept of operations (Tech. Rep.)*. Washington, DC: US Federal Highway Administration.

Pavlovic, D. (2013). Monoidal computer I: Basic computability by string diagrams. *Information and Computation, 226*, 94–116.

Penrose, R. (1971). Applications of negative dimensional tensors. In D. J. A. Welsh (Ed.), *Combinatorial Mathematics and Its Applications* (pp. 221–244). New York: Academic Press.

Sangiovanni-Vincentelli, A., Damm, W., & Passerone, R. (2012). Taming Dr. Frankenstein: Contract-based design for cyber-physical systems. *European Journal of Control, 18*(3), 217–238.

Schultz, P., & Spivak, D. I. (2017). Temporal type theory: A topos-theoretic approach to systems and behavior. arXiv preprint arXiv:1710.10258.

Selinger, P. (2004). Towards a quantum programming language. *Mathematical Structures in Computer Science, 14*(4), 527–586.

Simon, H. A. (1991). The architecture of complexity. In *Facets of systems science* (pp. 457–476). New York: Springer.

Smith, R. G. (1980). The contract net protocol: High-level communication and control in a distributed problem solver. *IEEE Transactions on Computers, 12*, 1104–1113.

Spivak, D. I. (2012). Functorial data migration. *Information and Computation, 217*, 31–51.

Spivak, D. I. (2014). *Category theory for the sciences*. Cambridge: MIT Press.

Subrahmanian, E., Westerberg, A., & Podnar, G. (1989). Towards a shared computational environment for engineering design. In *Workshop on computer-aided cooperative product development* (pp. 200–228).

Tong, C., & Sriram, D. (1992). *Artificial intelligence in engineering design, volume 1: Design representation and models of routine design*. San Diego: Academic Press.

Vagner, D., Spivak, D. I., & Lerman, E. (2015). Algebras of open dynamical systems on the operad of wiring diagrams. *Theory and Applications of Categories, 30*(51), 1793–1822.

Woods, D. D., & Hollnagel, E. (2006). *Joint cognitive systems: Patterns in cognitive systems engineering*. London: CRC Press.

# CHAPTER 14

# Meta-Agents: Using Multi-Agent Networks to Manage Dynamic Changes in the Internet of Things

**Hesham Fouad, Ira S. Moskowitz**
Information Management & Decisions Architecture Branch, Naval Research Laboratory, Washington, DC, United States

## 14.1 INTRODUCTION

The rapid growth of the Internet of Things (IoT) (Columbus, 2017) has created fertile ground for emerging research on a variety of existing and novel problems, such as privacy, cyber security, big data, and self-adaptation/self-organization. A single IoT device (e.g., a thermostat) may serve a particular purpose, but the conglomeration of multiple devices to serve a human, or a virtual entity's global objective, is the true promise of IoT. The vision of pervasive or ubiquitous computing is the existence of computational middleware that discovers, and utilizes, a set of IoT resources so that they constructively cooperate with each other in order to achieve an identified global objective.

We note that this global objective, or objective for short, can be as simple as assisting a homemaker in the shopping and preparation of family meals, or as complex as a dynamic medical sensor network assisting in the care of hundreds, or thousands, of patients. An inherent challenge of IoT is that computational entities must operate in a highly dynamic environment, interacting with emergent phenomena that continuously change context, and may do so in unpredictable ways. Existing software-design paradigms cannot address many of these problems because they approach the bounds of the complexity manageable by a human designer. Existing software paradigms need to be extended, and possibly new ones created, to deal with the complexity brought about by the rise of self-organizing, adaptive, multi-agent systems (MAS, Bernon, Chevrier, Hilaire, et al., 2006, Bernon, Camps, Gleizes, et al., 2004, Gardelli, Viroli, Casadei, et al., 2006, Gleizes, Camps, George, et al., 2007).

*Artificial Intelligence for the Internet of Everything*
https://doi.org/10.1016/B978-0-12-817636-8.00014-4

Mihailescu, Spalazzese, and Davidsson (2017) introduce the idea of emergent configurations (EC) for an IoT driven by user requirements. The idea is to dynamically orchestrate heterogeneous "things" in a manner that enables goal-directed behavior in support of a user's requirements. In this chapter we explore the idea of online agent creation and deployment as a way to realize an EC. In the context of our work, meta-agents are agents in a multi-agent software paradigm that utilizes reasoning to both construct and deploy special-purpose agents that form an EC. Unfortunately, but opportunistically research-wise, reasoning models that can support the idea of meta-agents in the context of an EC have not been explored. To realize an EC using meta-agents we need to first manage the complexity of the problem, then develop a multi-agent framework capable of supporting meta-agents, and, finally, explore reasoning models, such as belief-desire-intention (BDI) modeling (Georgeff, Pell, Pollack, Tambe, & Wooldridge, 1999), for autonomous meta-agents.

## 14.2 MANAGING COMPLEXITY

In his seminal work, *The Sciences of the Artificial* (Simon, 1990; see also Valckenars, Brussell, & Holvet, 2008), Simon explores the laws that bound artificial systems; in essence, he tries to develop a corollary to the laws of physics, but applied to artificial systems. In this work Simon outlines three assumptions that, when they hold true, require that any successful artificial system be holonic; systems characterized by a pyramidal structure. Simon's *first* assumption is that of bounded rationality. Intelligent systems have a bounded, or limited, capacity for computation and communication. As the limits of that capacity are approached, adding more resources (faster computers, high bandwidth communication) produces diminishing returns. The implication is that real-world intelligent systems must be able to make decisions based on imperfect information and limited computations. Simon's *second* assumption is that intelligent systems will operate in demanding environments. Intelligent systems must address nontrivial problems, make effective use of the resources available to them, and grow in complexity only in service of achieving a successful outcome. Systems that cannot do this will invariably fail and be replaced by more successful systems. Simon's *final* assumption is that intelligent systems must be able to operate in a dynamic environment. Operating in a highly dynamic environment requires that systems have the capacity to quickly evolve to adapt to changing contexts. This requirement has implications for the idea of optimality. In a fast-changing environment the time required to design and develop a solution that approaches optimality makes a system obsolete before it can be deployed. Developing optimal systems has been the holy grail of computer science since its inception. Forgoing that goal in service of agility requires a major shift in thinking.

It is not difficult to show that meta agent-based emergent configuration systems are beholden to Simon's three assumptions. First, meta–agent EC systems using IoT sensors and devices as their source of information will have to contend with operating in the computationally limited environments available on IoT devices. They will also have to operate with low bandwidth, disconnected (denied), interrupted, and latent ("DIL") network connectivity (Scott, Refaei, & Macker, 2011). Second, these systems must solve complex problems by selecting the most valuable source of information out of hundreds of millions or billions of IoT information sources and perform the necessary reasoning given their limited resources. Finally, they will need to aggregate that information at higher levels of the pyramid into actionable information that addresses the current goal. This must occur in near real time and produce added value. There are many examples of such systems that address similar problems in well-defined domains, with a limited, well-defined set of sensors (Blum, 2011). We will address the difficulties in generalizing this problem later in the chapter.

## 14.3 SENTRY AGENTS

The foundation of our work with multi-agent EC systems is based on a multi-agent system developed at the Naval Research Laboratory called Sentry AGEnts (SAGE). SAGE (Fouad, Gilliam, Guleyupoglu, & Russell, 2017) was initially developed to deal with the issues of online agent generation from data used in automating the testing of service oriented architecture (SOA) systems. SOA systems present a unique challenge for automated testing as they consist of systems of systems and, hence, traditional single-application test technology is insufficient. Automating an evaluation of SOA systems requires a distributed set of agents residing at each service provider or consumer and coordinating with other agents to simulate the complex, interdependent interactions that occur between users and consumers of SOA services (Fig. 14.1).

SAGE is a multi-agent system written in C++. Its salient features include the ability for external systems, as well as SAGE agents, to spawn other or new agents online by dynamically populating their behavior modules and

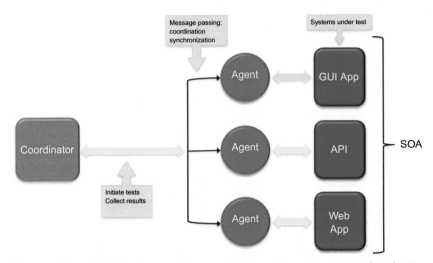

**Fig. 14.1** Example SOA system under test using a multi-agent automated evaluation approach (API is application programming interface).

defining their state space. SAGE uses a very low overhead remote method invocation (RMI) mechanism that provides synchronous and asynchronous call semantics, serialization, as well as multithreaded execution on the server side. The advantage of using SAGE is that it has a very small footprint in both computational resource as well as network bandwidth utilization. Fig. 14.2 illustrates the SAGE architecture. One thing to note is that SAGE–agent execution is managed at each node of the network by a SAGE node process that acts as an agent virtual machine. One or more SAGE nodes can run at

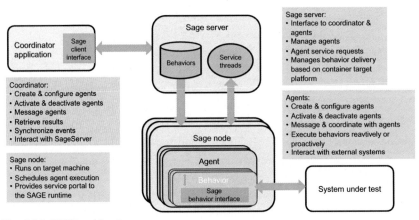

**Fig. 14.2** SAGE architecture.

each network node. The SAGE server provides SAGE nodes with services, such as node and agent introspection, interagent communication and synchronization, and a repository of agent behaviors that can be used to construct new agents (Fig. 14.2).

## 14.4 AN ILLUSTRATIVE EXAMPLE

Artificial intelligence research is often conducted using toy problems that are simplistic but allow researchers to explore a problem space. In automatic path-planning research the game Frogger is an often-used toy problem (Frogger, 1981). The object of the game is to manipulate a frog character until it moves across a busy, multilane highway with cars traveling in multiple lanes of traffic at various velocities and in different directions, all the while avoiding being run over. Once that goal is achieved the frog character must then navigate across a river by stepping across floating logs, as well as other objects (turtles), that rise above the water for a short time.

As in much of path-planning research the goal is to find an optimal path that preserves the frog's life given a priori knowledge of car behaviors. The problem is usually limited to the single task of crossing the highway because the second task of crossing a river requires a significantly different strategy. The algorithms generally do not generalize to be able to address both challenges (Fig. 14.3).

Our aim was to use Frogger as a toy problem for examining the utility of using multi agent–based emergent configurations to find optimal paths that allow the frog to cross both the highway as well as the river in real time with no a priori knowledge of either the location of the cars or the floating objects. We also wanted the same algorithm to be able to guide the frog across both the highway and the river by building specialized agent networks to solve each component of the problem.

The only input to our system is the state of sensors that monitor the environment. We modified an open-source Frogger implementation developed by Pavlenko (2009) to include road sensors on the highway that monitored a portion of a highway lane and returned a Boolean occupied/not occupied signal. In the case of the river, the sensors monitored the state of a portion of a water lane and returned a Boolean result indicating whether or not an object was available above the surface (Fig. 14.1). The Frogger game was essentially instrumented so SAGE agents could query the state of a sensor dynamically in real time. The placement of the sensors was clearly significant for they acted as sampling points. In order to guarantee that we had sufficient

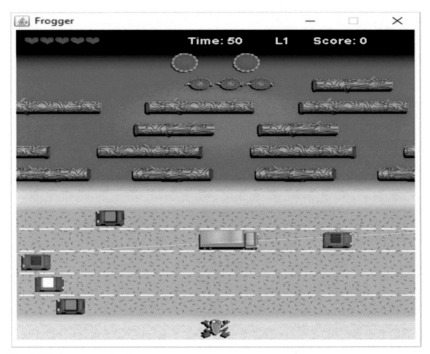

**Fig. 14.3** Frogger game layout.

sensors so that the presence of an instance of a car as well as floating objects was never missed, we based our placement on the Nyquist Theorem. Specifically, we placed sensors along the highway and river at intervals that were half the width of the smallest object expected to occupy a highway or river lane.

To utilize an emergent configuration as a holonic system we began by creating a top-level agent to represent the frog in the Frogger game. We aptly name this agent Frog. The Frog agent has a single mission: to cross both the highway and river and emerge unscathed. To achieve this the Frog agent creates an oracle agent that informs it whether or not moving in any of the four allowed directions (north, south, east, west) is feasible. The oracle agent disallows a move either because it is illegal (e.g., moving south when the frog is at its start position), or because it would result in the Frog agent getting hit by a car, or sinking in the river. The Frog agent utilizes this information to reason about what its next move is to make. The oracle agent in turn creates one of two types of agents based on the current location of the Frog agent. Highway lane agents monitor the car traffic in a lane and inform the oracle whether or not a position on a highway lane is occupied and, if vacant, how long it can be expected to be vacant based on the velocity of the cars in that lane. The other type of agent is a river lane agent that informs the oracle whether or not a position in a river lane contains a floating object. Moving down the hierarchy, both types of lane agents create sensor agents, one for each sensor in the game, to monitor the state of the sensors and to return their current state to the lane agents.

At the start of the game only a single agent, Frog, exists. The Frog agent is aware that it must accomplish two different tasks that require different types of information. The agent first creates a network of oracle, lane, and sensor agents to enable it to cross the highway. Once that goal is achieved, it destroys that network and creates a new agent network that enables it to cross the river. Figs. 14.4 and 14.5 show the agent networks created for crossing the highway and the river.

The agent system described above is both holonic and an emergent configuration for the following reasons:

- The multi-agent networks are created and subsequently destroyed dynamically to achieve a single goal.
- Each agent is aware of the information it requires to achieve its goal and creates child agents to provide it with that information.

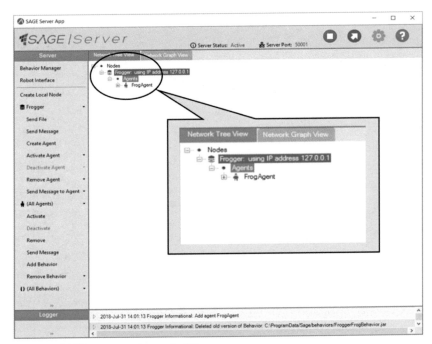

**Fig. 14.4** SAGE server at the start of the game.

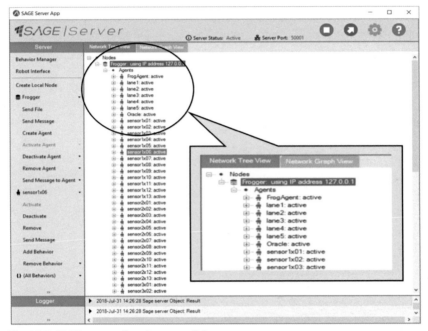

**Fig. 14.5** SAGE server after the start of the game.

- Agents lower in the pyramid are not aware of the operation of higher level agents that make use of them (e.g., holonic).
- Agents dynamically spawn other agents to provide them with the information they need. They are not aware of how the child agents achieve their tasks. They are, in effect, shielded from the complexity of how that information is collected.
- Interagent communication only occurs between adjacent levels of the pyramid.
- The complexity of the reasoning capability of agents monotonically decreases as one descends down the layers of the pyramid.

## 14.5 REASONING

Reasoning mechanisms enable agents to act autonomously based on the state of the environment, the information available to them, and their inherent abilities. This reasoning has been an active area of research for some time (Stone, 2007 ); the most promising model to date has been the BDI model (Georgeff et al., 1999). In the BDI model agents have a set of beliefs about the world. They also have a set of desires that they plan to achieve.

Finally, they have a set of intentions, which consist of the actions they are currently performing to achieve their desires (Stone, 2007). This model is based on a theory of how humans operate. It involves an information-collection stage that forms the agent's beliefs and a planning stage that generates intents based on the agent's desires. Planning is a continuous activity that generates a new set of intentions at each time step.

The difficulties with realizing the BDI model is in how each agent state is represented and what reasoning mechanisms are utilized in the planning stage. In the meta-agent approach, agent intents result in the creation of other agents that provide a needed service. This process is true until we reach the leaf nodes where, for the first time, agents are able to interact with IoT devices to collect data.

One can see that as we move along the holonic pyramid, varying levels of sophistication are needed in an agent's reasoning mechanism. We can expect top-level agents to have a fairly complex reasoning capability, while agents at the bottom of the pyramid have little or no need for reasoning (Gerber, Siekmann, & Vierke, 1999). The challenge then is to utilize a scalable reasoning mechanism that can support these varying levels of complexity.

A behavior tree (BT) (Colledanchise & Ögren, 2018) is a graph-based model of plans of execution that originated in the game industry. They have recently received significant attention in the academic community due to some very desirable properties. First, BTs have a small computational footprint. Second, BTs are able to emulate many other behavior representations including: finite state machines, hierarchical finite state machines, subsumption architectures, teleo-reactive programs, and decision trees. The major advantage of BTs for our use is that they are highly modular, reusable, and hierarchical. The implications for a holonic system is that the reasoning exhibited by the holonic system can be a composition of reasoning modules contained in ach agent comprising the system. Furthermore this configuration supports the idea of scalability in agent reasoning.

## 14.6 CHALLENGES AND CONCLUSION

Implementing a meta agent–based EC approach for IoT based on the BDI model introduces a number of difficult questions. First, how do agents become aware of the IoT resources available to them? There are currently multiple efforts underway to build open standards for IoT device discovery. Most notable are UPnP and HyperCat. These are relatively low-level standards that generally do not provide a semantic-based service for SOA systems.

The need for such a mechanism for IoT has been recognized. It will be some time before universal protocols are developed to provide a universal semantic-based discovery mechanism.

Second, given that the number of IoT devices is estimated to exceed one billion, how do we determine which sources are applicable to our goal without having to inspect over one billion devices? What will be required is a service similar to Google's web crawlers that crawl IoT spaces and build a database of semantic IoT descriptors that can be quickly searched to establish a set of candidate devices. In fact there is a recently launched effort called IoTCrawler that provides a Google-like search engine for the IoT (Skarmeta et al., 2018). While it will take time for services such as IoTCrawler to mature, it is a promising development towards a generalized semantic capability for IoT devices.

## ACKNOWLEDGMENTS

We thank Bill Lawless and Antonio Gilliam for their assistance.

## REFERENCES

Bernon, C., Camps, V., Gleizes, M., et al. (2004). Tools for self-organizing applications engineering. In G. D. M. Serugendo (Ed.), *Ser. lecture notes in artificial intelligence,* Vol. 2977 (pp. 283–298). Springer.

Bernon, C., Chevrier, V., Hilaire, V., et al. (2006). Applications of self-organising multi-agent systems: an initial framework for comparison. *Informatica, 30,* 73–82.

Blum, B. (2011). *Waze steers you clear of traffic. Israel 21c.* Dec. 19, 2011.

Colledanchise, M., & Ögren, P. (2018). *Behavior trees in robotics and AI: An introduction.* Boca Raton, FL: CRC Press.

Columbus, L. (2017). *2017 roundup of internet of things forecasts. https://www.forbes.com/sites/louiscolumbus/2017/12/10/2017-roundup-of-internet-of-things-forecasts/#2fcc243f1480.*

Fouad, H., Gilliam, A., Guleyupoglu, S., & Russell, S. M. (2017). Automated evaluation of service oriented architecture systems: a case study. In *Next-generation analyst V, SPIE defense + security.* Anaheim, CA, 9–13 April.

Frogger. (1981). Frogger, the adventures of a fearless frog. *The Arcade Flyer Archive, 1981.*

Gardelli, L., Viroli, M., Casadei, M., et al. (2006). Designing self-organising MAS environments: the collective sort case. In D. Weyns, H. V. D. Parunak, & F. Michel (Eds.), *Ser. lecture notes in artificial intelligence: Environments for multi-agent systems III,* Vol. 4389 (pp. 254–271). Springer.

Georgeff, M., Pell, B., Pollack, M., Tambe, M., & Wooldridge, M. (1999). The belief-desire-intention model of agency. In *Proceedings of the 5th international workshop on intelligent agents V: agent theories, architectures, and languages (ATAL-98* (pp. 1–10).

Gerber, C., Siekmann, J. H., & Vierke, G. (1999). *Flexible autonomy in holonic agent systems.* AAAI Technical Report SS-99-06.

Gleizes, M., Camps, V., George, J., et al. (2007). Engineering systems which generate emergent functionalities. In *Proceedings of international workshop on engineering environment-mediated multi-agent systems (EEMMAS 2007)* (pp. 58–75).

Mihailescu, R., Spalazzese, R., & Davidsson, P. (2017). A role-based approach for orchestrating emergent configuration in the internet of things. In *Proceedings of the 2nd international workshop on the internet of agents (IoA) workshop*.

Pavlenko, V. (2009). *Frogger*. https://github.com/vitalius/Frogger.

Scott, K., Refaei, T., & Macker, J. (2011). Robust communications for disconnected, intermittent, low-bandwidth (DIL) environments. *MILCOM, track 2, network protocols and performance, 1009-1014*.

Simon, J. (1990). *The sciences of the artificial*. Cambridge, MA: MIT Press.

Skarmeta, A. F., Santa, J., Martínez, J. A., Parreira, J. X., Barnaghi, P., Enshaeifar, S., et al. (2018). *IoTCrawler: Browsing the internet of things. In The 2018 Global IoT Summit (GIoTS)*. Spain: Bilbao June 4–7.

Stone, P. (2007). Learning and multiagent reasoning for automomous agents. In *IJCAI-07* (pp. 13–30).

Valckenars, P., Brussell, H. V., & Holvet, T. (2008). Fundamentals of holonic systems and their implications for self-adaptive and self-organizing systems. *2nd international conference on self-adaptive and self-organizing systems workshop. IEEE*.

# INDEX

Note: Page numbers followed by "*f*" indicate figures, "*t*" indicate tables, "*b*" indicate boxes, and "*np*" indicate footnotes.

NERC-CIP standard. *See* National Energy Regulatory Commissions' Critical Infrastructure Protection (NERC-CIP) standard
Nesterov's accelerated gradient descent (NAGD), 28–29
Network-based access to physical systems, 89
Networked teams of intelligent things, 48*f*
Neural network, 34–35
Newton's method, 25, 29–30
NHTSA. *See* National Highway Safety Traffic System (NHTSA)
NIST. *See* National Institute of Standards and Technology (NIST)
Nobel Laureate in Economics (2017), 176
Nonconvex stochastic programs, 31
Notional team structure adaptation workflow, 80*f*
NP-hard problem, 75*np*
Nudging, 179*np*
Nyquist Theorem, 275–276

## O

Opaque-thinking systems, 140
Open interaction, 245
Operads, as compositional architectures, 258–263
Operational prototyping activities, 88–89
Operators of physical systems, cybersecurity role and certification of, 95–96
Optimization in machine learning, 22–31
  generalized linear models, 29–30
  inference, 30–31
  logistic regression, 25–26
  NAGD, 28–29
  problem, 23–24
  SGD variants, 26–28
  Stochastic Gradient Descent algorithm, 24–25
Organizational structure, 73–74, 84
Organization/architecture of a system, 243
Override, 132

## P

Paradox of choice, 181
Parenting AI, 141–142

Participants, 106, 111
Path-planning research, 275
Perceived agency, 103
Perceived benevolence, 103–104
Perceived task interdependence, 104
Permissioned blockchain technology, 220
PGM. *See* Projected gradient method (PGM)
Phantasmagorical complexity, 139
Physical boundaries, 248
PKI solutions. *See* Public key infrastructure (PKI) solutions
Planning and control approaches, 57–58
Policy-making community, 94
Positive dataset, 209–210
Potential blockchain business and implementation challenges, 222–225
PoW blockchain, 221–222
PoW consensus algorithms, 225
Predictive analysis, 118
Problem decomposition, 243
Projected gradient method (PGM), 38–39
Prosumers, 13–14
Public key infrastructure (PKI) encryption, evolution of, 228–230 solutions, 229
Public PoW blockchain solutions, 225

## Q

QoI. *See* Quality of information (QoI)
Quadruped robot, 101
Quality of information (QoI), 164–165

## R

Rational expectations revolution, 182–183
Real-time accurate model of physical health, 123
Real-time data, 126–127
Real-time models, 127–128
Reasoning mechanisms, 278–279
Recognition density, 70
Recommender system, 125
Reconfigurations, 87–88
Recursiveness, 243
Reducing redundancy, 233
Relationship-building, 113

Printed in the United States
By Bookmasters